Essentials of Mathematics 10

Essentials of Mathematics 10

Celia Baron

Rick Wunderlich

Leanne Zorn

British Columbia Ministry of Education
Victoria Canada

This textbook was developed for the British Columbia Ministry of Education by Pacific Educational Press, Faculty of Education, University of British Columbia, 6365 Biological Sciences Rd., Vancouver, Canada V6T 1Z4.

Canadian Cataloguing in Publication Data
Baron, Celia
    Essentials of mathematics 10

    "Developed for the British Columbia Ministry of Education by Pacific Educational Press, Faculty of Education, University of British Columbia"—t.p. verso.
        ISBN 0-7726-4675-9

        1. Mathematics.   2. Business mathematics.
I. Wunderlich, Rick. II. Zorn, Leanne. III. British Columbia. Ministry of Education.   IV. Title.

QA107.B37 2001   510   C2001-960304-5

Consulting: David Robitaille
Editing: Catherine Edwards
Photo Research: Debbie Gajdosik
Design: Warren Clark

Printed and bound in Canada

01 02 03 04 5 4 3 2 1

Acknowledgements
Funding for this student resource was provided by the British Columbia Ministry of Education; Manitoba Education, Training and Youth; the Yukon Department of Education; the Northwest Territories Department of Education; and the Nunavut Territory Department of Education. Original materials developed by Manitoba Education and Youth have been adapted for this publication.

This resource was made possible through the support and contributions of the following: Bruce McAskill, British Columbia Ministry of Education; Richard V. DeMerchant, British Columbia Ministry of Education; Wayne Watt, Manitoba Education and Youth; Carole Bilyk, Manitoba Education and Youth; Marcel Druwé, Manitoba Education and Youth; Lee Kubica, Yukon Department of Education; Steven Daniel, Northwest Territories Department of Education; Sue Ball, Nunavut Department of Education.

Contents

Chapter 3
Spreadsheets
Power Tools *145*

Chapter 4
Consumer Decisions
Shopping Wisely *195*

Chapter 5
Geometry Project
Designing in Three Dimensions 247

Chapter 6
Sampling and Probability
Publishing an E-Zine for Teens 335

How To Use This Book

Essentials of Mathematics 10 demonstrates how to use mathematics in everyday life. The skills that are taught are those that informed citizens need. The textbook has six chapters and each focusses on a particular topic. Topics include wages, salaries, and expenses; banking services; computer spreadsheets; making sound consumer decisions; creating a three-dimensional model of a structure using geometry and trigonometry skills; and using sampling and probability techniques to solve problems.

Chapter Introduction

Each chapter begins with an introduction that describes what the chapter will teach and lists the goals of that chapter. The introduction also starts you thinking about the chapter project.

Chapter Project

Each chapter contains a project related to the mathematical theme of the chapter. The project is ongoing and you will accumulate materials in your project file as you work through the chapter. At the end of the chapter, you will organize the materials in your file into a presentation.

Explorations

Chapters are divided into explorations. Each exploration is a lesson on a particular mathematical topic. First, a short introduction describes the topic and lists the goals of the lesson. Examples and solutions are provided that show you how to use the mathematical ideas to solve problems. Many explorations contain activities to complete in small groups or with the rest of your class. Explorations may also contain activities connected to the chapter project. Each exploration concludes with a notebook assignment that allows you to practise the skills you have learned.

Chapter Review

The chapter review helps you revisit the mathematical ideas and skills explored in the chapter and solve problems using these skills.

Project Presentation

The final step in the chapter project is to organize the materials you have researched or created into a presentation.

Case Study

Each chapter concludes with a case study that allows you to apply the mathematics of the chapter in a new context.

Other Features of the Text

Career Connection

Each Career Connection contains a profile of a fictitious individual. The description of the job, current wages, educational requirements, career goal, and keyword search are based on real possibilities. The keyword search invites you to do an internet search on the career and will provide links to colleges and other institutions that have specific career or educational information.

New Terms

Mathematical terms that may be new or unfamiliar are defined or explained in the new terms box.

Hints

Hints suggest ways to deal with the mathematics and provide useful reminders, abbreviations, conversion factors, and other techniques helpful in solving the problems.

Technology

This section shows how technology such as computers can be used to help solve problems or do research.

Mental Math

Mental math invites you to practise solving mathematical exercises in your head.

Problem Analysis

Each chapter contains a problem activity that allows you to use a variety of problem-solving strategies. Some activities were chosen to illustrate consumer applications of mathematics. Others challenge you to analyze mathematical thinking.

Games

Each chapter contains a challenging mathematical game. Some of these games have been played since ancient times and in different cultures around the world. You are required to play each game and to analyze it in order to increase your chances of winning.

Answer Key

The answer key at the back of the book lists the answers to each notebook assignment.

Chapter 1

Wages, Salaries, and Expenses

Looking Towards Independence

Think about the future when you will live on your own. What type of job would you like? How much money might you earn at that job? What are your expenses likely to be? What saving goals might you set? This chapter will help you find answers to these questions.

As you work through this chapter, you will investigate some career options that interest you. You will research how much money they pay and what education they require. You will learn how your pay will be calculated by your employer—or by yourself, if you become self-employed. You will use your research into rates of pay and expenses to develop a realistic budget.

You will explore the connection between the career you choose and the lifestyle you will be able to afford. The skills you learn will help you plan and reach your financial goals.

Chapter Goals

In this chapter, you will learn how to calculate hours worked, gross pay, payroll deductions, net pay, and changes in income. You will learn how to prepare a budget that balances income and expenses.

Chapter Project

The project for this chapter will be to research three future career possibilities. You will do in-depth research into the career option that interests you most. When you have completed the project, you will have the following information for your project file:

1. A list of three careers that interest you and the amount of income that each pays.
2. A description of the educational requirements for each career.
3. A list of job-related expenses for the career that interests you most, along with an estimate of your transportation and lunch costs.
4. A sample pay statement for the same career.
5. A wish list of what you would like to spend and what you are likely to earn.
6. A realistic budget, in which your expenses match your predicted income.

Career Connection

Name: Teresa Morgan

Job: pipefitter's assistant

Current wages: $18.00 an hour

Education: grade 12; ten-month piping trades course at Assiniboine Community College, Brandon, Manitoba

Career goal: journeyman pipefitter

Keyword search: Canada college pipefitter trades

New Terms

budget: an estimate of the amount of money to be spent on a specific project or over a given time frame.

income: money or other assets received.

Technology

To do a keyword search, type the string of search words on the search line of the search engine you use. Using a string of relevant search words limits the number of websites that will be displayed.

Exploration 1

Investigating Career Options

In this exploration, you will consider career options. Exploring an option does not mean that this option must be your final choice. It is wise to be flexible and consider a number of options.

In choosing a career, there are several factors to consider. Keep your interests and abilities in mind. Consider the level of education a career requires and the amount of income it is likely to pay. Think about the lifestyle you wish to have. You need to choose a career that pays enough money to support this lifestyle. You may be suited for a job at an existing company or you may wish to become self-employed.

The rate of pay is not the only financial measure to consider when choosing a career. Many companies offer benefits to their employees and these benefits have a financial value. A job that offers lower pay may have excellent benefits that mean it actually pays more than another job with more pay but fewer benefits. A company that offers dental and medical benefits may be a better choice than one that does not. Benefits can also have a positive impact on your lifestyle. For example, if you work at a ski hill, you might receive a free ski pass as part of your job.

Whatever career you choose, it is wise to consider how your choice will affect your income and the lifestyle you will be able to afford.

Example 1

Shawn is considering a career in the pulp and paper industry. He is also considering a career as a heavy equipment operator in the forestry industry. What information might help him make a choice between these two options?

Goals

In this exploration, you will consider career choices and the financial and lifestyle factors that may influence your career selection.

New Terms

benefits: money or allowances such as life insurance, clothing allowance, dental coverage, or extended health care.

Solution

Shawn could find out whether there are job openings in these industries. He could investigate the type of work he would be doing, the average income paid, how secure jobs in these industries are, and whether there is the possibility of learning new skills in each job. He could also research the working conditions, for example, whether shift work would be required or whether he would need to live in a remote logging camp. He could investigate the benefits commonly offered to employees in each occupation.

Project Activity

Work in a small group to brainstorm a list of possible careers until each member has three career ideas he or she is interested in investigating.

Record the three career possibilities that interest you most in your project file. Use sources such as your career or counselling centre to research the starting income paid in your region for each option. Design a "Help Wanted" ad for each career and add them to your file.

HELP WANTED

Journeyman pipefitter wanted for west coast pulp and paper mill. Must be willing to relocate to Vancouver Island. Current wage is $29.10 per hour, including excellent benefits. Fax your résumé to 250 123-4567.

Technology

Information on incomes and careers can be found by searching:

1. www.schoolfinder.com/careers

2. http://cx.bridges.com

3. www.bcopportunities.com

Career Connection

Name: Ben Wiebe

Job: self-employed bookkeeper

Current wages: charges $35.00 an hour, but pays his own office expenses

Education: grade 12; several bookkeeping courses from the University of Northern British Columbia in Prince George, B.C.

Career goal: accountant

Keyword search: Canada accounting courses

Notebook Assignment

1. Suppose you were job hunting and found a job advertised at a diamond mine in northern Canada. List 5 benefits that might be important to receive.

2. What is meant by the term "self-employed"? Suggest two benefits of self-employment.

3. Naomi is considering becoming either a carpenter or an electrician. What information might help her decide which would be the better choice?

This young woman is enrolled in an electrical trades course at Vancouver Community College.

Technology

There are several software packages for small business bookkeeping needs, such as MYOB and Simply Accounting.

Exploration 2

Beginning a Budget: Income and Expenses

A budget is a financial plan that balances your income and expenses. To create a budget, you need to know or estimate your income and your expenses. If they do not balance, your budget needs to be adjusted.

Income includes any money you expect to earn. Some jobs pay wages and others pay salaries. Wages are most often expressed as an hourly amount. A salary refers to an annual amount. For example, teachers are usually paid an annual salary, while service industry workers are usually paid an hourly wage. If you are preparing a monthly budget, you need to convert both wages and salaries to a monthly amount.

Your budget is based on your take-home pay. Take-home pay refers to the amount you receive after deductions are taken off. These will be considered in more detail later in this chapter.

Expenses include living expenses such as rent, telephone, clothing, food, and so on. There will likely be some expenses related to your job as well, such as transportation, lunches, and possibly special equipment or tools.

Class Discussion

As a class, list three careers that are common in your area. What job-related items might a person working in these careers need to buy? For example, an accountant might have to buy paper and computer disks, a logger might have to buy safety boots, and an artist needs to purchase art supplies.

Estimate the monthly work-related expenses for the careers on your list. Order the list from the most expensive to the least expensive career.

Goals

In this exploration, you will begin the budgeting process by estimating income and expenses.

New Terms

salary: a fixed regular payment, usually calculated on an annual basis and paid monthly.

take-home pay: often called net pay; refers to the money paid to an employee after deductions.

wage: payment made by an employer in exchange for work or services provided.

Career Connection

Name: John Tan

Job: Parks Canada worker

Current wages: $17.80 an hour

Education: grade 12 graduation

Career goal: park ranger

Keyword search: Parks Canada careers

Example 1

Sam estimates that her wages at a new job will be about $30.00 an hour, and that she will work a 40-hour week. Her take-home pay will be about 60% of her total income. List the monthly living expenses that Sam is likely to have. Include an amount for savings. Estimate the amount she should spend on each item, keeping her rate of pay in mind.

Solution

First, calculate Sam's weekly income:
$30.00/hour x 40 hours = $1200.00

Next, estimate her average monthly income:
$1200.00/week x 52 weeks ÷ 12 months = $5200.00/month

Then, estimate her take-home pay:
$5200.00 x 0.60 = $3120.00

Continued on the next page.

Hints

1. To convert hourly income to average monthly income, multiply the hourly rate by the number of hours worked in a week and then by 52 weeks. Divide the result by 12 to find the average monthly income.

2. To find 60% of total income, multiply by 0.60.

3. Financial advisors often recommend saving 10% of total income.

Mental Math

How many hours are there in a work week that consists of five 7.5 hour days?

Solution to example 1 continued

Make a list of Sam's likely living expenses and estimate the amount she will need to spend:

Rent:	$1000.00	Telephone:	$ 50.00
Utilities:	$ 180.00	Food:	$ 360.00
Clothing:	$ 125.00	Recreation:	$ 150.00
Personal Care:	$ 80.00	Books, Magazines:	$ 50.00
Cable TV:	$ 50.00	Transportation:	$ 555.00
Savings:	$ 520.00	**Total:**	**$ 3120.00**

Example 2

Matthew is a self-employed mechanic. He rents shop space for $450.00 a month. He has additional business expenses that average $100.00 a month. Matthew charges his customers $36.00 an hour. If he charges for an average of 32 hours a week, what will his monthly earnings be after his rent and business expenses are deducted?

Solution

First, find Matthew's average monthly income:
32 hours x $36.00/hour x 52 weeks ÷ 12 months = $4992.00

Next, find his total monthly expenses:
$450.00 + $100.00 = $550.00

Subtract his expenses from his monthly income to find his earnings:
$4992.00 – $550.00 = $4442.00

Mental Math

1. Find the total income for a 40-hour work week if the hourly wage is $7.50.

2. How much does a graphic artist make an hour if she receives $150.00 to design a poster and she completes the job in 2 hours?

Technology

Computer spreadsheets can be helpful when creating a budget. Personal finance software such as Quicken often includes budget templates.

Project Activity

a) Create a list of expenses that might be associated with the career option that interests you most. Consider expenses such as work clothes, safety equipment, travel expenses, tools, and equipment. If possible, find out whether any of the items, for example, safety equipment, are provided by the employer. Leave any items paid for by the employer off your list.

b) Consider the transportation costs related to one of your career choices. Assume that your job is near your home, and answer the following questions.

How will you get to work?

If you use public transportation, how much will it cost each month? If you travel by car, multiply the distance in kilometres by 40 cents a kilometre to estimate the actual cost of taking your car to work.

How long will it take to get to work? What time will you have to get up? What time will you leave for work?

c) You will need to take or buy lunch and snacks when you work. Select two restaurants where you might eat lunch. Choose a lunch and list the items and the cost at each place. Include taxes and tip and calculate the total you would spend at lunch in each place. How much money do you think is reasonable to spend on refreshment breaks?

Hints

1. $0.40/km is an estimate of the actual costs of owning a car. It covers costs of purchase or lease, maintenance, fuel, insurance, and taxes.

2. A good tip for a restaurant meal is 15% of the bill.

3. Taxes on restaurant meals vary by province or territory.

Notebook Assignment

1. Work in pairs to estimate your living expenses for a month using the categories below. If you prefer to share an apartment with a roommate, you may reduce rent and utilities because you will share these expenses.

    Rent   Telephone
    Utilities   Food
    Clothing   Recreation
    Personal Care   Magazines, Books, and CDs
    Savings   Other Expenses

2. Rudie earns a salary of $30,500 a year. If his take-home pay is 60% of his salary, what would he receive for a year's work? A month's work? Create a budget similar to the one in question 1 that would allow Rudie to save 10% of his take-home pay.

3. List five expenses you would have if you owned your own car, motorcycle, or truck. Can you think of ways to keep these costs to a minimum?

Extension

4. Mona-Jean is saving money for a college course that costs $1780.00. Her job pays $8.00 an hour and she works 30 hours a week. If her monthly expenses are about $700.00, how long will it take her to save enough to pay for the college course?

Exploration 3

Gross Pay

The total amount of money a person earns at his or her job is called gross pay. Gross pay is one factor you can consider when you select a career. To calculate gross pay, you multiply the hourly rate of pay by the number of hours worked. At many jobs, if you work extra hours or on statutory holidays, you earn a higher hourly rate. The word "overtime" can refer both to the extra time worked or the extra money earned. Self-employed people sometimes charge a higher rate for work done on weekends or holidays.

Example 1

Paul's regular rate of pay is $9.40 an hour and he works 25 hours a week. What is his gross pay?

Solution

Multiply the number of hours by the hourly rate to find Paul's gross pay:
25 hours x $9.40/hour = $235.00
Paul's gross pay is $235.00.

Example 2

Charles' regular hourly rate of pay is $6.75 an hour. Find his time and a half hourly rate. Then find his double time hourly rate. Round answers to the nearest cent.

Solution

His time and a half hourly rate is:
$6.75 x $1\frac{1}{2}$ or $6.75 x 1.5 = $10.13

His double time rate is:
$6.75 x 2 = $13.50

Goals

In this exploration, you will calculate gross pay using the number of hours worked and the hourly rate of pay.

New Terms

gross pay: the total amount of money earned; also called gross earnings.

overtime: 1. hours worked beyond the regular hours; **2.** payment for this time.

Example 3

Mary earns $7.70 an hour. She is paid time and a half for overtime hours. How much will she earn if she works four hours of overtime?

Solution

First, multiply Mary's hourly rate by 1.5 to find her overtime rate:
$7.70/hour x 1.5 = $11.55/hour

Then multiply her overtime rate by the number of overtime hours:
4 hours x $11.55/hour = $46.20

Example 4

Ilona's rate of pay at the Jelly Bean Factory is $7.05 an hour. What are her gross weekly wages if she works the following hours?

Monday	$4\frac{1}{4}$ h	Friday	3 h
Wednesday	$3\frac{3}{4}$ h	Saturday	$5\frac{1}{4}$ h

Solution

Ilona works these hours:
$4\frac{1}{4} + 3\frac{3}{4} + 3 + 5\frac{1}{4} = 16\frac{1}{4}$ **hours**

Her gross weekly pay is:
$16\frac{1}{4}$ **hours x $7.05/hour or 16.25 hours x $7.05/hour**
= $114.56 (rounded to the nearest cent)

Mental Math

1. A millwright earns $20.00 an hour, with time and a half paid for overtime hours and statutory holidays. What will he earn if he works an 8-hour statutory holiday?

2. Is a worker whose wage is $10.00 an hour earning overtime pay if she is paid $50.00 for five hours of work?

Hints

1. One way to calculate time and a half earnings is to add one half the regular pay rate to the regular pay. Another way is to multiply the regular pay by 1.5.

2. $1/4$ h = 0.25 h
$1/2$ h = 0.50 h
$3/4$ h = 0.75 h

Example 5

Jeanne works full-time in a clothing store. Her regular work week is 38 hours and she earns $8.50 an hour. If she works more than 38 hours a week, she earns time and a half for the extra hours. One week, she works the hours listed below. What will Jeanne's gross pay for that week be?

Monday	7
Tuesday	7
Wednesday	8
Thursday	8
Friday	8
Saturday	4

Solution

First, add Jeanne's hours to find her total hours:
7 + 7 + 8 + 8 + 8 + 4 = 42 hours

Then find her overtime hours:
42 hours – 38 hours = 4 hours

Next calculate the gross pay for her regular hours and her overtime hours.
38 hours x $8.50/hour = $323.00
4 hours x $8.50/hour x 1.5 = $51.00

Add these amounts to find Jeanne's total gross pay.
$323.00 + $51.00 = $374.00

Example 6

The manager of the fast-food restaurant where you work asked you to work a four-hour shift on Labour Day. Employees are paid double time for statutory holidays. You also work 20 hours this week. The regular rate of pay is $7.75 an hour. What is your gross pay?

Solution

First, calculate the regular pay for 20 hours:
20 hours x $7.75/hour = $155.00

Then calculate the overtime pay for the four-hour shift:
4 hours x $7.75/hour x 2 = $62.00

Add these amounts to find your gross pay:
$155.00 + $62.00 = $217.00

Notebook Assignment

1. Briefly define the following terms:

    a) regular time
    b) overtime
    c) wage
    d) time and a half
    e) gross pay
    f) double time

2. Calculate the gross earnings for the employees listed below.

EMPLOYEE	RATE/HOUR	HOURS	GROSS PAY
a) Okalik J.	$14.00	40	
b) Bond F.	$13.80	38	
c) Kaski N.	$8.25	37.5	
d) Abbott J.	$9.50	39.5	
e) Neufeld K.	$14.85	40	

3. Calculate the gross pay for the employees listed below. Their regular work week is 40 hours and they earn time and a half if they work more than 40 hours a week.

EMPLOYEE	M	T	W	TH	F		HOURLY WAGE
a) Chang M.	10	7	8	8.5	9		$7.65
b) Singh B.	10	8	7.5	8	8.75		$9.23
c) Martes R.	9	7	8.5	10	9		$7.95
d) O'Ray A.	8	8	6	8	7.75		$8.85
e) Vermet R.	8	10	9	8	8		$9.77

4. The employees listed below are paid time and a half if they work more than eight hours a day. They are paid time and a half on Saturdays and double time on Sundays. Find the gross pay for each employee.

EMPLOYEE	M	T	W	TH	F	S	SU	HOURLY WAGE
a) Adams R.	8	8	8	8	8	4		$11.86
b) Nakagowa B.	9	8	7.5	9	8			$12.30
c) Meyook C.	7	7	10	9	8	4		$12.82
d) Charlie D.	8	10	8	8	8	4		$11.07
e) Lavallée F.	8	8	8	9	10	6	4	$10.54
f) Greyeyes C.	10	9.5	8	7	8	4	4	$15.89

5. A baker works a regular 7.5-hour day and his hourly rate of pay is $13.50. He is paid time and a half if he works more than 7.5 hours a day, and time and a half for Saturdays. He earns double time if he works on Sundays and holidays. The baker's hours for last week are shown below. Find his gross pay.

Monday	7.5
Tuesday	7.5
Wednesday	8.5
Thursday	9
Friday	7.5
Saturday	3
Sunday	2.5

6. Complete the following chart.

Regular Time	Time and a Half	Double Time
$6.90		
$7.50		
		$13.00
$9.40		
	$9.00	

7. Find the gross weekly pay for each of the following employees if they are paid time and a half on Saturdays and double time on Sundays.

EMPLOYEE	M	T	W	TH	F	S	SU	HOURLY WAGE
a) Anderson		4		4	4			$6.80
b) Audette	3$^1/_2$			4$^3/_4$		5		$7.35
c) Cheung		3$^3/_4$		3$^3/_4$	5$^1/_2$			$7.90
d) Ennis	5$^1/_2$			4$^1/_4$	4	4$^1/_4$		$6.95
e) Taylor		4$^1/_2$			8	7$^1/_2$		$9.15

8. Sophie works the following hours at the Class Act Clothing Store: Monday $3^1/_2$, Tuesday $4^3/_4$, Thursday $3^3/_4$, and Saturday $5^1/_2$. If Sophie's hourly rate of pay is $6.95, find her gross weekly earnings.

9. Otto works at Zag's Gas Station. He works $3^1/_2$ hours each day Monday through Friday as well as $6^1/_4$ hours Sunday. If his hourly rate is $7.05, and he gets paid time and a half on Sundays, find his gross weekly pay.

10. Meeka works at UC Video. During the first week of winter break, she works 18 hours plus 6 hours on Boxing Day. During the second week, she works 16 hours plus $5^1/_2$ hours on New Year's Day. If her regular rate of pay is $6.80 an hour and she is paid double time for Boxing Day and New Year's Day, what is her gross pay for the two weeks?

11. A film crew carpenter works the following hours:

Monday	8
Tuesday	7.5
Wednesday	6.5
Thursday	12
Friday	8

    a) If the regular work day is 7.5 hours and the hourly rate of pay is $17.00, find the carpenter's gross pay if she is paid time and a half when she works more than 7.5 hours a day.

    b) Using the same rate of pay, find the gross pay if the carpenter is paid overtime only after she has worked a 40-hour week.

    c) Which method pays more money to the employee?

12. Marilee Smith installs and repairs telephone lines. She works a 40-hour week and her regular hourly rate is $22.58. She is paid double time for each hour she works on holidays and weekends. She is paid time and a half for all other overtime hours. One week Marilee works 53.5 hours from Monday through Friday, including eight hours on a Monday statutory holiday. Find her gross pay for the week.

13. A welder works a 40-hour week plus he receives time and a half for any overtime hours. If his rate is $20.35 and he works 55 hours one week, what is his gross pay?

Extension

14. Arnold gets time and a half on Saturdays and double time on statutory holidays. Is it better for Arnold to work two Saturdays or one statutory holiday? Explain your answer.

15. Ray Partridge earns $16.00 an hour driving a truck but he receives no extra benefits. Wayne Jong earns $15.00 dollars an hour and he also has a family dental plan, life insurance, and an eyeglasses purchase plan. Explain why it is hard to determine who is paid better.

Exploration 4

Keeping Track of Time

In this exploration, you will learn about keeping track of time. This skill is important in a variety of workplaces. In many workplaces, you will need to record the amount of time you spend on a particular project. This information is used by companies to bill their customers or to keep track of the costs of a certain job. Mechanics, lawyers, accountants, and plumbers often charge their customers for the amount of time they spend on a job. Keeping track of the total hours you spend at your job will help you estimate the amount of money you are owed.

Some companies use a 24-hour clock to record their employees' hours. A 24-hour clock begins at 00:00, which is midnight, and numbers each hour consecutively to 23:59, rather than dividing the day into two cycles of 12 hours (am/pm). If you use a 24-hour clock, 9:00 am is written 09:00, 1:00 pm is written 13:00, 2:00 pm is 14:00, and so on. You can convert hours above 12:00 on a 24-hour clock to hours on a 12-hour clock by subtracting 12:00. For example, if you subtract 12:00 from 13:00 hours, you get 1:00 pm.

Career Connection

Name: Edward Chen

Job: self-employed graphic artist

Current wages: on average, $2700.00 a month

Education: grade 12, diploma in graphic arts, Emily Carr College, Vancouver, B.C.

Keyword search: Canada graphic arts college

Goals

In this exploration, you will investigate ways to track the amount of time spent at your job and on projects or work orders. You will learn to use a 24-hour clock to find the number of hours worked.

Hint

In most workplaces, coffee breaks are paid and lunch breaks are not paid.

Class Discussion

Brainstorm reasons why it might be important for a self-employed person such as a mechanic or a graphic artist to keep track of time carefully. What ideas do you have for tracking time spent on a project? Why might a painter or sculptor have difficulty tracking his or her project time in the same way?

Why should students who work part-time keep track of the hours they worked and when they worked them? How could students use a calendar to keep a record of their hours?

Example 1

Convert 2 hours and 18 minutes into hours.

Solution

2 hours is already expressed in hours.

15 minutes is $\frac{15}{60}$ of an hour, which can be reduced to $\frac{1}{4}$.

So $\frac{18}{60}$ can be written 0.3.

$2\text{ h }18\text{ m} = 2\frac{3}{10}\text{ h or }2.3\text{ h}$

Mental Math

1. If you worked from 23:00 to 01:00, how many hours did you work?

2. If you worked from 01:00 to 23:00, how many hours did you work?

Hints

1. 2 hours, 9 minutes, 6 seconds can be abbreviated as 2 h 9 m 6 s.

2. 1 h = 60 m.

3. To convert minutes to hours, divide by 60.

4. In this chapter, the following abbreviations are used:

   hour h
   minute m

Example 2

Susan's workplace uses a 24-hour clock. She started work at 09:00 and finished at 17:00. How many hours was she at work?

Solution

Since Susan's workplace uses a 24-hour clock, she can calculate the time she spent at work by subtracting the time she started from the time she finished:

17:00 – 09:00 = 8 h
Susan was at work 8 hours.

Example 3

Fred started work at 08:30 and finished at 13:00. How long did he work?

Solution

From 08:30 to 12:30 is 4 h. From 12:30 to 13:00 is another half-hour.
Fred worked 4.5 h.

Example 4

One day, Stefan works from 11:38 am to 4:20 pm. How many hours and minutes did he work?

Solution

From 11:38 am to noon is 22 m. Noon to 4:00 pm is 4 h. From 4:00 pm to 4:20 pm is another 20 m. Add these to find Stefan's total:

22 m + 4 h + 20 m = 4 h 42 m

Expressed as a decimal, Stefan worked 4.7 h.
There are other strategies that may be used to solve this problem. For example, you could quickly calculate that 11:38 to 4:38 is 5 h, which is 18 m more than Stefan worked.
So you could subtract 18 m from 5 h (4 h 60 m) to arrive at 4 h 42 m.

Example 5

Jason is called in to the sawmill to fix an electric motor. He works from 22:58 Thursday to 01:48 on Friday. How many hours and minutes did he work on the motor?

Solution

One way Jason could calculate the time he worked is to divide it into two portions, one worked before midnight and one worked after. Since he started at 22:58 Thursday, he worked 1 h 2 m before midnight. He then worked an additional 1 h 48 m after midnight. To find his total, add the two amounts together.

1 h 2 m + 1 h 48 m = 2 h 50 m
Jason worked 2 h 50 m repairing the motor.

Technology

1. Personal digital assistants (PDAs) such as Palm Pilots or Handsprings can be used to keep track of time spent on jobs or projects.

2. Some software for desktop computers, such as Microsoft Outlook, includes personal organizer functions.

Notebook Assignment

1. Wendy works for 5 hours and 45 minutes. Express this time in hours to two decimal places.

2. Mary works for 34 hours and 155 minutes. Express this time in hours and minutes, where the number of minutes is less than 60.

3. Sung works for 22 hours and 85 minutes. Express this time in hours and minutes, where the number of minutes is less than 60.

4. Kay works for 27 hours and 127 minutes. Express this time in hours and minutes, where the number of minutes is less than 60.

5. Andrea works from 09:00 to 11:48 and 13:33 to 17:55. How many hours and minutes did she work today?

6. Tory worked Monday from 9:05 am to 11:43 am and 1:03 pm to 4:54 pm. On Tuesday, she worked from 9:03 am to 11:55 am and 1:07 pm to 4:49 pm. How many hours did she work? Give your answer to two decimal places.

7. Karen works mornings. One week she worked 9:05 am to 11:55 am; 9:00 am to 12:04 pm; 8:55 am to 11:51 am; 8:57 am to 11:54 am; 9:08 am to 10:58 am; and 9:01 am to 11:33 am. How many hours and minutes did she work that week?

8. Joe worked the following afternoon shifts: 1:03 pm to 4:47 pm; 12:55 pm to 5:01 pm; 1:06 pm to 4:57 pm; 1:02 pm to 4:58 pm; 12:58 pm to 4:51 pm; 12:56 pm to 5:03 pm; and 1:13 pm to 4:35 pm. How many hours and minutes did he work?

9. Marg worked Monday from 13:02 to 17:47, Tuesday from 14:24 to 17:54; Thursday from 09:53 to 14:14; and Friday 18:12 to 21:58. How many hours and minutes did she work?

10. Sunny worked from 11:00 am to 3:00 pm. How would you express this using the 24-hour clock?

11. Lwan worked an 8-hour shift that started at 22:00. What time did he finish? Assume a half-hour lunch break.

12. Suppose you were self-employed and charged your customers for the time you spent on their jobs. Describe a way you could keep track of time if you were working on several different jobs throughout the day. Where would you record the times? What is one thing that prevents a company from overcharging for time spent on a job?

Extension

13. Sean is considering two restaurant jobs. Each job requires 40 hours of work a week and pays the same hourly rate. The first job has a day shift from 07:00 to 16:00, with a one-hour unpaid lunch break. The second job has a split shift. The first part runs from 07:00 to 11:00; the second part runs from 17:00 to 21:00. What are the advantages and disadvantages of each job? Which would you prefer? Why?

Exploration 5

Time Cards

In this exploration you will learn to use and read time cards. Time cards are one way to keep track of the amount of time spent at work. Some companies do not adjust your pay if you are a few minutes late or early. Other employers use time cards to calculate their payrolls. They round the employees' time to the nearest quarter or half hour, and pay them accordingly. Employers may check time cards to see whether employees often arrive late or leave early. Employees who are often late or leave early may be dismissed by the employer.

Usually, overtime rates are not paid if you work a few minutes more than your regular shift. In most workplaces, overtime rates are only paid if the extra time is requested by the employer.

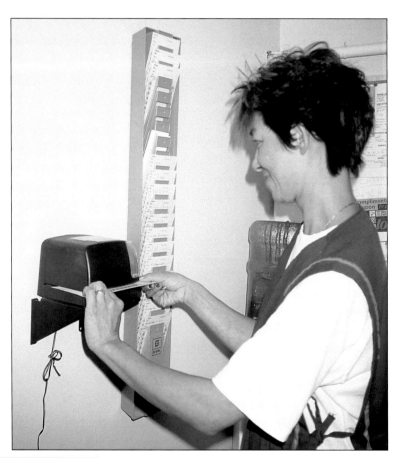

Goals

In this exploration, you will learn to read time cards and to calculate gross wages based on the time a person works.

Example 1

Examine the following time card and find out how many hours Pavel worked.

Time Card

Employee Number: **67891**

Name: **PAVEL NOTREMOV**

Signature *Pavel Notremov*

Week Ending: **28/06/02**

Date	Morning		Afternoon		Overtime		Hours		Total
	In	Out	In	Out	In	Out	Reg	OT	Hours
June 24	09:00	12:00					3		3
June 25			16:00	21:00			5		5
June 26	09:00	12:00					3		3
June 27			16:30	22:00			5.5		5.5
June 28	08:30	12:00					3.5		3.5
Total									_____

Solution

3 + 5 + 3 + 5.5 + 3.5 = 20 h
Pavel worked 20 hours.

Example 2

Examine the following time card and calculate how many hours Susan worked. Her employer rounds her weekly time to the nearest quarter hour.

Time Card

Employee Number: **67892**

Name: **SUSAN ADAMOVICH**   Signature   *Susan Adamovich*

Week Ending: **20/12/02**

Date	Morning		Afternoon		Overtime		Hours		Total
	In	Out	In	Out	In	Out	Reg	OT	Hours
Dec. 16	7:59	12:02	1:03	4:00					
Dec. 17	8:02	12:00	1:00	4:03					
Dec. 18	7:57	12:10	12:59	3:59					
Dec. 19	8:00	12:11	1:10	4:00					
Dec. 20	8:03	11:59	1:02	4:00					
Total									____

Solution

Susan worked the following hours:

Dec 16: 4 h 3 m in the morning; 2 h 57 m in the afternoon: a total of 7 h
Dec 17: 3 h 58 m in the morning; 3 h 3 m in the afternoon: a total of 7 h 1 m
Dec 18: 4 h 13 m in the morning; 3 h in the afternoon: a total of 7 h 13 m
Dec 19: 4 h 11 m in the morning; 2 h 50 m in the afternoon: a total of 7 h 1 m
Dec 20: 3 h 56 m in the morning; 2 h 58 m in the afternoon: a total of 6 h 54 m

Susan worked 35 h 9 m. Rounded to the nearest quarter hour, she worked 35.25 h. At $13.60 an hour, her gross earnings are $479.40.

Example 3

Gina Johnny's regular work day is 07:00–12:00 and 13:00–15:00. She earns $14.50 an hour. Her employer does not pay overtime unless it is authorized. For authorized overtime, Gina earns time and a half. How many hours is Gina paid for this week? What is her gross pay?

Time Card

Employee Number: **12345**

Name: **GINA JOHNNY**   Signature *Gina Johnny*

Week Ending: **11/01/02**

Date	Morning		Afternoon		Overtime		Hours		Total
	In	Out	In	Out	In	Out	Reg	OT	Hours
Jan. 7	07:00	12:00	13:02	15:02					
Jan. 8	06:58	11:59	12:58	15:00	15:00	17:30			
Jan. 9	06:59	12:02	13:01	15:00	15:00	18:00			
Jan. 10	07:01	12:11	13:01	15:04					
Jan. 11	07:00	12:03	13:04	14:59					
Total									_____

Solution

Gina's regular work week is 35 hours. This week she works 35 h 16 m but is only paid for 35 hours. She also works 5.5 h of overtime.

35 hours x $14.50/hour = $507.50
5.5 hours x $14.50/hour x 1.5 = $119.63
$119.63 + $507.50 = $627.13
Gina's gross pay is $627.13

Mental Math

How many hours did Kevin work if his time card shows that he started at 06:30 and finished at 12:45?

Technology

Some companies issue their employees cards with encoded magnetic strips to swipe through a time clock.

Notebook Assignment

1. Calculate the number of hours for which each of the following employees is paid. Their morning shift is from 8:00 to 12:00. The employees are penalized a quarter of an hour's pay for every quarter of an hour or part thereof that they arrive late or leave early.

Ameralik	7:58 – 12:00
Bancroft	8:01 – 12:00
Boulanger	8:14 – 12:00
Combhoaua	8:15 – 12:00
Gauthier	8:16 – 12:00
Krivan	8:00 – 12:02
McIvor	8:00 – 11:58
Orsi	8:00 – 11:32
Peart	8:00 – 10:50
Romanko	8:01 – 12:05

2. Calculate the number of hours for which each of the following employees is paid. Their afternoon shift is from 1:00 to 5:00. The employees are docked a quarter of an hour for every quarter of an hour or part thereof that they arrive late or leave early.

Heft	12:58 – 5:02
McKee	1:03 – 5:04
Sandahl	1:00 – 4:48
Singh	12:59 – 4:26
Teese	1:09 – 4:13
Worsley	1:35 – 3:56

3. Answer the questions about the following time card.

Time Card

Employee Number: **33343**

Name: **MAXINE TANCHAK**   Signature *Maxine Tanchak*

Week Ending: **JULY 17**

Day	Morning		Afternoon		Overtime		Hours		Total
	In	Out	In	Out	In	Out	Reg	OT	Hours
M	7:32	11:30	12:01	4:00					
T	7:30	11:25	12:02	4:00					
W	7:25	11:32	12:00	3:59					
TH	7:35	11:30	11:59	4:01					
F	7:30	11:31	11:58	4:03					
Total									

a) What time did Maxine begin work on Monday and Thursday?

b) What days did she leave for lunch at 11:30?

c) What time did she return from lunch on Tuesday and Friday?

d) How much time does this company allow for lunch?

4. Using this time card, answer the questions below.

Time Card

Employee Number: **54321**

Name: **SHEILA O'NEILL**

Signature *Sheila O'Neill*

Week Ending: **OCTOBER 27**

Day	Morning		Afternoon		Overtime		Hours		Total
	In	Out	In	Out	In	Out	Reg	OT	Hours
M	08:00	12:00	13:00	17:05					
T	08:01	11:59	12:59	16:59					
W	07:59	12:01	13:05	17:00	17:00	19:00			
TH	07:58	12:00	12:58	17:00					
F	07:59	11:55	13:01	17:02	17:30	18:30			
Total									——

a) On which day did Sheila work two hours of overtime?

b) If Sheila's regular starting time is 08:00, on which day(s) was she late?

c) If the lunch break ends at 13:00, on which day(s) did Sheila return late?

d) How much time is Sheila allowed for lunch?

e) On which days did she work overtime?

f) On which afternoons did she leave work early?

g) How long is Sheila's regular work day?

5. Use the time cards below to find out how many hours Jorge Escobar worked in a two-week period. Jorge starts work at 8:00 am, breaks for lunch at noon, returns at 1:00 pm, and leaves at 5:00 pm. Jorge is penalized a quarter of an hour's pay for every quarter of an hour or part thereof that he arrives late or leaves early.

WEEK 1

Time Card

Employee Number: **24681**

Name: **JORGE ESCOBAR**

Signature *Jorge Escobar*

Week Ending: **08/03/02**

Date	Morning		Afternoon		Overtime		Hours		Total
	In	Out	In	Out	In	Out	Reg	OT	Hours
M	8:25	12:01	1:12	5:02					
T	8:02	12:03	1:00	5:01					
W	8:15	12:00	1:02	5:00					
TH	8:07	11:59	12:58	5:08					
F	7:56	12:02	12:47	4:59					
Total									

WEEK 2

Time Card

Employee Number: **24681**

Name: **JORGE ESCOBAR**

Signature *Jorge Escobar*

Week Ending: **15/03/02**

Date	Morning		Afternoon		Overtime		Hours		Total
	In	Out	In	Out	In	Out	Reg	OT	Hours
M	7:59	11:56	1:02	5:04					
T	8:14	12:05	1:01	5:05					
W	8:00	12:01	12:59	5:01					
TH	8:00	12:00	12:58	5:00					
F	8:05	11:58	1:00	4:40					
Total									

6. Find the gross pay for each of the four employees whose time cards follow. To calculate gross pay, round the daily hours to the nearest quarter hour. Overtime during the week is paid on a daily time and a half basis and all Saturday work is double time. The regular day is 08:00 to 12:00 and 13:00 to 17:00.

EMPLOYEE 1

Time Card

Employee Number: **37**

Name: **L. LAM**

Week Ending: **JUNE 10**

Signature: *L. Lam*

Date	Morning		Afternoon		Overtime		Hours		Total
	In	Out	In	Out	In	Out	Reg	OT	Hours
M	08:00	12:00	12:59	17:00					
T	07:59	11:59	13:00	17:01					
W	08:01	12:01	13:05	17:02					
TH	08:02	12:02	13:00	16:59					
F	07:58	12:00	12:55	17:00					
S									
SU									
Total							____	____	____

	HOURS	RATE	AMOUNT
REGULAR		$15.25	
OVERTIME			

EMPLOYEE 2

Time Card

Employee Number: **16**

Name: **A. GILL**

Signature *A. Gill*

Week Ending: **JUNE 10**

Date	Morning		Afternoon		Overtime		Hours		Total
	In	Out	In	Out	In	Out	Reg	OT	Hours
M	07:59	12:01	12:59	17:01	17:30	19:30			
T	07:52	12:02	12:57	17:03					
W	07:48	12:00	12:58	17:06	17:15	19:30			
TH	07:57	12:03	13:02	15:48					
F	07:53	12:01	12:57	17:03	17:30	18:15			
S	08:00	12:03							
SU									
Total									

	HOURS	RATE	AMOUNT
REGULAR		$15.25	
OVERTIME			

EMPLOYEE 3

Time Card

Employee Number: **03**

Name: **C.V. FERNANDEZ**

Signature *C.V. Fernandez*

Week Ending: **JUNE 10**

Date	Morning		Afternoon		Overtime		Hours		Total
	In	Out	In	Out	In	Out	Reg	OT	Hours
M	07:58	12:00	12:54	17:01					
T	07:55	12:00	13:00	17:00	17:00	18:30			
W	07:59	12:00	13:00	16:15					
TH	08:00	12:01	12:58	17:02	17:30	19:15			
F	08:01	12:05	12:59	17:03					
S									
SU									
Total									

	HOURS	RATE	AMOUNT
REGULAR		$7.90	
OVERTIME			

EMPLOYEE 4

Time Card

Employee Number: **11**

Name:	**L. ZOE**	Signature	*L. Zoe*

Week Ending: **JUNE 10**

Date	Morning		Afternoon		Overtime		Hours		Total
	In	Out	In	Out	In	Out	Reg	OT	Hours
M	08:01	12:00	13:00	16:59					
T	08:00	12:01	13:00	17:01					
W	07:55	11:59	12:59	17:00	17:00	19:00			
TH	07:57	12:00	13:05	17:02					
F	07:56	12:05	13:00	17:03					
S	08:00	11:30							
SU									
Total							____	____	____

	HOURS	RATE	AMOUNT
REGULAR		$8.90	
OVERTIME			

7. Nunia's hours are from 8:00 am to 12:00 pm or 1:00 pm to 5:00 pm. Find her hours and her gross pay. Identify your assumptions.

Time Card

Employee Number: **5432**

Name: **NUNIA KALLUK**

Week Ending: **NOVEMBER 13**

Signature   *Nunia Kalluk*

Date	Morning		Afternoon		Overtime		Hours		Total
	In	Out	In	Out	In	Out	Reg	OT	Hours
M	8:00	12:01							
T	7:53	12:02							
W	7:58	11:43							
TH	8:09	12:01							
F			1:09	5:09					
S			1:03	5:01					
SU									
Total							——	——	——

	HOURS	RATE	AMOUNT	POSITION
REGULAR		$12.20		Ass't Manager
OVERTIME				

8. Ellen's shift is from 9:00 am to 12:00 pm and 1:00 pm to 5:00 pm.
   Calculate how many hours and minutes she worked and find her
   gross pay. Her employer rounds her weekly hours to the nearest half
   hour.

Time Card

Employee Number: **2864**

Name: **ELLEN ARDAK**   Signature   *Ellen Ardak*

Week Ending: **MAY 10**

Date	Morning		Afternoon		Overtime		Hours		Total
	In	Out	In	Out	In	Out	Reg	OT	Hours
M	9:00	12:00	1:00	5:01					
T	9:03	12:01							
W	9:00	12:03	1:00	4:57					
TH			1:09	5:06					
F	8:55	11:52	1:17	5:01					
S									
SU									
Total							___	___	___

	HOURS	RATE	AMOUNT	POSITION
REGULAR		$14.70		Ass't Supervisor
OVERTIME				

9. Ron has a part-time job. What is his gross pay if he is paid to the nearest quarter hour on a daily basis?

Time Card

Employee Number: **3586**

| | | Signature | Ron Tell |

Name: **RON TELL**

Week Ending: **SEPTEMBER 21**

Date	Morning		Afternoon		Overtime		Hours		Total
	In	Out	In	Out	In	Out	Reg	OT	Hours
M			4:32	8:31					
T			4:30	8:30					
W			4:38	8:32					
TH			4:29	8:31					
F			4:29	8:17					
S									
SU									
Total							___	___	___

	HOURS	RATE	AMOUNT	POSITION
REGULAR		$7.80		Stock Clerk
OVERTIME				

10. Mark works either in the morning or the afternoon. What is his gross pay? His employer rounds his daily hours to the nearest quarter hour.

Time Card

Employee Number: **1357**

Name: **MARK RAIN**

Week Ending: **APRIL 11**

Signature   *Mark Rain*

Date	Morning		Afternoon		Overtime		Hours		Total
	In	Out	In	Out	In	Out	Reg	OT	Hours
M	9:09	1:00							
T	9:09	1:02							
W			4:35	8:32					
TH			4:29	8:20					
F	9:08	1:01							
S									
SU									
Total							___	___	___

	HOURS	RATE	AMOUNT	POSITION
REGULAR		$9.75		Cashier
OVERTIME				

11. Sam Ross works from 9:00 am to 1:00 pm or from 4:30 pm to
8:30 pm. Find the number of hours and minutes he worked and
then find his gross pay. His employer pays him to the nearest half
hour on a weekly basis.

Time Card

Employee Number: **2468**

Name: **SAM ROSS**　　　　　　Signature　*Sam Ross*

Week Ending: **JANUARY 24**

Date	Morning		Afternoon		Overtime		Hours		Total
	In	Out	In	Out	In	Out	Reg	OT	Hours
M	9:00	1:00							
T			4:40	8:31					
W			4:30	8:30					
TH									
F									
S	9:05	1:00							
SU									
Total							____	____	____

	HOURS	RATE	AMOUNT	POSITION
REGULAR		$7.65		Bagger
OVERTIME				

12. Christa Maise normally works from 9:00 am to 1:00 pm or from 1:00 pm to 5:00 pm. This week she worked one additional shift from 2:00 pm to 6:00 pm. Find her gross pay. She is penalized one-quarter of an hour's pay for every quarter-hour or part thereof she arrives late or leaves early.

Time Card

Employee Number: **1778**

Name: **CHRISTA MAISE**

Signature　*Christa Maise*

Week Ending: **FEBRUARY 25**

Date	Morning		Afternoon		Overtime		Hours		Total
	In	Out	In	Out	In	Out	Reg	OT	Hours
M	9:00	1:00							
T			1:00	5:01					
W			1:03	5:00					
TH			1:09	5:03					
F	9:18	1:01	2:00	6:02					
S									
SU									
Total							——	——	——

	HOURS	RATE	AMOUNT	POSITION
REGULAR		$9.40		Cashier
OVERTIME				

Extension

13. Find out how businesses in your community require their employees to keep track of time worked.

14. Time cards often have to be signed by the employee. List reasons why an employee might have to sign a time card.

15. Some cards are filled out automatically by passing the card through a machine. Why might employers use a machine to record the times that their employees arrive and leave?

16. Why do the military services use a 24–hour clock?

Exploration 6

Payroll Deductions

Usually, you do not take home the total amount of gross pay that you earn. Sums of money are deducted from your gross pay for taxes and other purposes. These amounts are called deductions and your pay after deductions is called net pay or take-home pay.

The money deducted from your gross pay can benefit you, your community, or your country. Canada Pension Plan (CPP) deductions are used to pay citizens an income after they are sixty-five years old. Employment Insurance (EI) may provide an income replacement program should you lose your job. Income taxes (IT) are used for many government expenses, including building and maintaining roads, schools, and hospitals.

There are other payroll deductions that reduce your gross pay. You may have an amount deducted for union dues, health care, and benefits your company offers, such as a dental plan or a pension plan.

Some deductions are required by law, while others are voluntary. Some company pension plans are voluntary. Often, if you take part in the pension program, your employer will contribute a certain amount on your behalf. When you retire, you will be paid a pension from the fund.

Goals

In this exploration, you will find payroll deductions and calculate net pay.

Technology

Deduction tables can be ordered from the Canada Customs & Revenue Agency or downloaded from its website:
www.ccra-adrc.gc.ca.

Claim Codes

When an employee begins working at a job, they fill out a TD1 form that identifies whether they are able to claim certain deductions that reduce their taxable income, such as child care expenses or the expense of caring for an elderly or ill person. The amount of these deductions determines an employee's claim code and tells his or her employer how much income tax to deduct from their gross pay. The employer consults two claim code tables, one federal and one provincial/territorial. An example from British Columbia is shown below.

Federal Claim Codes

Total claim amount ($)	Claim Code
No claim amount	0
Minimum–7412.00	1
7412.01–9056.00	2
9056.01–10,700.00	3
10,700.01–12,344.00	4
12,344.01–13,988.00	5
13,988.01–15,632.00	6
15,632.01–17,276.00	7
17,276.01–18,920.00	8
18,920.01–20,564.00	9
20,564.01–22,208.00	10
22,208.01 and over	X
No withholding	E

British Columbia Claim Codes

Total claim amount ($)	Claim Code
No claim amount	0
Minimum–8000.00	1
8000.01–9800.00	2
9800.01–11,600.00	3
11,600.01–13,400.00	4
13,400.01–15,200.00	5
15,200.01–17,000.00	6
17,000.01–18,800.00	7
18,800.01–20,600.00	8
20,600.01–22,400.00	9
22,400.01–24,200.00	10
24,200.01 and over	X
No withholding	E

New Terms

taxable income: the amount of income on which you pay tax

Calculating Deductions

Look at the payroll statement below. Notice the gross pay, the various deductions, and the net pay.

To find net income if there are no deductions for union dues or pension plan, follow these steps:

1. Using the gross pay, look up the CPP, the EI, and the income tax (IT) in the appropriate tables. Two income tax tables need to be consulted, one federal and one provincial or territorial.
2. Subtract CPP, EI, and IT deductions from the gross pay to arrive at the net pay.

When an employee contributes to a pension plan or pays union dues, the steps are slightly different. In this case:

1. Using the gross pay, look up the CPP and the EI in the appropriate tables.
2. To find the income tax payable, subtract the amounts for pension plan or union dues from the gross pay. Look up the taxable income, matching it to the claim code for the person.
3. Subtract CPP, EI, IT, pension plan, union dues, and any other deductions to find net pay.

STATEMENT OF EARNINGS AND DEDUCTIONS
SALARY PAYROLL — SALARY BI-WEEKLY

PERIOD ENDING: JANUARY 15   CLAIM CODE 1
BANK ACCOUNT: 123-456-789
BANK: BANK OF MONTREAL

SUMMARY OF EARNINGS   DEDUCTIONS

HOURS   ——
RATE $

REGULAR	2430.00	C.P.P.	98.62
OVERTIME		E.I.	54.68
		FEDERAL TAX	403.90
		B.C. TAX	162.90
		PENSION	145.80
		ADVANCE	
		GROUP INS.	8.50
		SALES	
		CANADA SAVINGS BONDS	255.66
GROSS PAY	2430.00	TOTAL DEDUCTIONS	1130.06
NET PAY	1299.94		

Canada Pension Plan Contributions / Cotisations au Régime de pensions du Canada
Biweekly (26 pay periods a year) / Aux deux semaines (26 périodes de paie par année)

Pay Rémunération From - De	To - À		Pay Rémunération From - De	To - À		Pay Rémunération From - De	To - À		Pay Rémunération From - De	To - À	
1513.10	1523.09	59.49	2233.10 -	2243.09	90.45	2953.10 -	2963.09	121.41	3673.10 -	3683.09	152.37
1523.10	1533.09	59.92	2243.10 -	2253.09	90.88	2963.10 -	2973.09	121.84	3683.10 -	3693.09	152.80
1533.10	1543.09	60.35	2253.10 -	2263.09	91.31	2973.10 -	2983.09	122.27	3693.10 -	3703.09	153.23
1543.10	1553.09	60.78	2263.10 -	2273.09	91.74	2983.10 -	2993.09	122.70	3703.10 -	3713.09	153.66
1553.10	1563.09	61.21	2273.10			2993.09		123.13	3713.10 -	3723.09	
		67.23	2413.10 -	2423.09	98.19	3133.10 -	3143.09	129.15	3853.10 -	3863.09	160.11
1703.10	1713.09	67.66	2423.10 -	2433.09	98.62	3143.10 -	3153.09	129.58	3863.10 -	3873.09	160.54
1713.10	1723.09	68.09	2433.10 -	2443.09	99.05	3153.10 -	3163.09	130.01	3873.10 -	3883.09	160.97
1723.10 -	1733.09	68.52	2443.10 -	2453.09	99.48	3163.10 -	3173.09	130.44	3883.10 -	3893.09	161.40

Employment Insurance Premiums / Cotisations à l'assurance-emploi

Insurable Earnings Rémunération assurable From - De	To - À		Insurable Earnings Rémunération assurable From - De	To - À		Insurable Earnings Rémunération assurable From - De	To - À		Insurable Earnings Rémunération assurable From - De	To - À	
2304.23 -	2304.66	51.85	2336.23 -	2336.66	52.57	2368.23 -	2368.66	53.29	2400.23 -	2400.66	54.01
2304.67 -	2305.11	51.86	2336.67 -	2337.11	52.58	2368.67 -	2369.11	53.30	2400.67 -	2401.11	54.02
2305.12 -	2305.55	51.87	2337.12 -	2337.55	52.59	2369.12 -	2369.55	53.31	2401.12 -	2401.55	54.03
2305.56 -	2305.99	51.88	2337.56 -	2337.99	52.60	2369.56 -	2369.99	53.32	2401.56 -	2402.00	54.04
2306.00 -	2306.44	51.89	2338.00 -	2338.44	52.61	2370.00 -	2370.44	53.33	2402.01 -	2402.44	54.05
		52.50	2365.12 -	2365.55	53.22	2397.12 -	2397.55	53.94	2429.12 -	2429.55	
2333.56 -	2333.99	52.51	2365.56 -	2365.99	53.23	2397.56 -	2397.99	53.95	2429.56 -	2429.99	54.67
2334.00 -	2334.44	52.52	2366.00 -	2366.44	53.24	2398.00 -	2398.44	53.96	2430.00 -	2430.44	54.68
2334.45 -	2334.88	52.53	2366.45 -	2366.88	53.25	2398.45 -	2398.88	53.97	2430.45 -	2430.88	54.69
2334.89 -	2335.33	52.54	2366.89 -	2367.33	53.26	2398.89 -	2399.33	53.98	2430.89 -	2431.33	54.70

Federal tax deductions / Retenues d'impôt fédéral
Effective July 1, 2001 / En vigueur le 1er juillet 2001
Biweekly (26 pay periods a year) / Aux deux semaines (26 périodes de paie par année)
Also look up the tax deductions in the provincial table / Cherchez aussi les retenues d'impôt dans la table provinciale

Pay Rémunération From De	Less than Moins de	Federal claim codes/Codes de demande fédéraux										
		0	1	2	3	4	5	6	7	8	9	10
		Deduct from each pay / Retenez sur chaque paie										
1834. -	1858	320.55	274.95	269.90	259.75	249.65	239.55	229.40	219.30	209.20	199.05	188.95
1858. -	1882	325.85	280.20	275.15	265.05	254.95	244.80	234.70	224.55	214.45	204.35	194.20
1882. -	1906	331.10	285.50	280.45	270.30	260.20	250.10	239.95	229.85	219.75	209.60	199.50
1906. -	1930	336.40	290.80	285.70	275.60	265.50	255.35	245.25	235.15	225.00	214.90	204.80
1930. -	1954	341.65	296.05	291.00			250.55	240.40	230.30	220.20	210.05	
2314. -	2338	425.15	380.55	375.50	365.35	355.25	345.15	335.00	324.90	314.80	304.65	294.55
2338. -	2362	431.45	385.80	380.75	370.65	360.55	350.40	340.30	330.15	320.05	309.95	299.80
2362. -	2386	437.00	391.40	386.35	376.25	366.10	356.00	345.90	335.75	325.65	315.50	305.40
2386. -	2410	443.25	397.65	392.60	382.45	372.35	362.25	352.10	342.00	331.90	321.75	311.65
2410. -	2434	449.50	403.90	398.85	388.70	378.60	368.45	358.35	348.25	338.10	328.00	317.90
2434. -	2458	455.75	410.10	405.05	394.95	384.85	374.70	364.60	354.50	344.35	334.25	324.10

British Columbia provincial tax deductions / Retenues d'impôt de la Colombie-Britannique
Effective July 1, 2001 / En vigueur le 1er juillet 2001
Biweekly (26 pay periods a year) / Aux deux semaines (26 périodes de paie par année)
Also look up the tax deductions in the federal table / Cherchez aussi les retenues d'impôt dans la table fédérale

Pay Rémunération From De	Less than Moins de	Provincial claim codes/Codes de demande provinciaux										
		0	1	2	3	4	5	6	7	8	9	10
		Deduct from each pay / Retenez sur chaque paie										
1858. -	1882	130.50	111.45	109.30	105.00	100.70	96.40	92.10	87.80	83.55	79.25	74.95
1882. -	1906	132.70	113.60	111.45	107.20	102.90	98.60	94.30	90.00	85.70	81.40	77.15
1906. -	1930	134.90	115.80	113.65	109.35	105.05	100.80	96.50	92.20	87.90	83.60	79.30
1930. -	1954	137.05										
2338. -	2362	174.25	155.15	153.05	148.75	144.45	140.15	135.85	131.55	127.25	123.00	118.70
2362. -	2386	176.80	157.75	155.60	151.30	147.00	142.70	138.45	134.15	129.85	125.55	121.25
2386. -	2410	179.40	160.30	158.15	153.85	149.60	145.30	141.00	136.70	132.40	128.10	123.85
2410. -	2434	181.95	162.90	160.75	156.45	152.15	147.85	143.55	139.25	135.00	130.70	126.40
2434. -	2458	184.50	165.40	163.30	159.00	154.70	150.40	146.15	141.85	137.55	133.25	128.95

Small Group Discussion

In a small group, create a list of deductions. Discuss which deductions you think are most important. What are the reasons for your choices? Would your choices vary if your circumstances change?

Example 1

Bob Sloan's bi-weekly salary is $770.00 and his claim code is 1. Find his net pay. He is paid bi-weekly.

Solution

Check the tax tables on the facing page for the deduction amounts:
CPP: $27.32
EI: $17.33
Federal Income Tax: $71.05
B.C. Income Tax: $26.15

Total Deductions: **$27.32 + $17.33 + $71.05 + $26.15 = $141.85**

Net Pay: **$770.00 – $141.85 = $628.15**

Canada Pension Plan Contributions / Cotisations au Régime de pensions du Canada
Biweekly (26 pay periods a year) / Aux deux semaines (26 périodes de paie par année)

Pay / Rémunération From - De	To - À		Pay / Rémunération From - De	To - À		Pay / Rémunération From - De	To - À		Pay / Rémunération From - De	To - À	
737.29	737.51	25.92	754.03	754.26	26.64	770.78	771.00	27.36	787.52	787.74	28.08
737.52	737.74	25.93	754.27	754.49	26.65	771.01	771.23	27.37	787.75	787.98	28.09
737.75	737.98	25.94	754.50	754.72	26.66	771.24	771.47	27.38	787.99	788.21	28.10
737.99	738.21	25.95	754.73	754.95	26.67	771.48	771.70	27.39	788.22	788.44	28.11
738.22	738.44	25.96	754.96	755.19	26.68	771.71	771.93	27.40	788.45	788.68	28.12
738.45	738.68	25.97									
752.87	753.09	26.59	769.62	769.84	27.31	786.36	786.58	28.03	803.10	803.33	28.75
753.10	753.33	26.60	769.85	770.07	27.32	786.59	786.81	28.04	803.34	803.56	28.76
753.34	753.56	26.61	770.08	770.30	27.33	786.82	787.05	28.05	803.57	803.79	28.77
753.57	753.79	26.62	770.31	770.54	27.34	787.06	787.28	28.06	803.80	804.02	28.78

Employment Insurance Premiums / Cotisations à l'assurance-emploi

Insurable Earnings / Rémunération assurable From - De	To - À		Insurable Earnings / Rémunération assurable From - De	To - À		Insurable Earnings / Rémunération assurable From - De	To - À		Insurable Earnings / Rémunération assurable From - De	To - À	
768.23	768.66	17.29	800.23	800.66	18.01	832.23	832.66	18.73	864.23	864.66	19.45
768.67	769.11	17.30	800.67	801.11	18.02	832.67	833.11	18.74	864.67	865.11	19.46
769.12	769.55	17.31	801.12	801.55	18.03	833.12	833.55	18.75	865.12	865.55	19.47
769.56	769.99	17.32	801.56	801.99	18.04	833.56	833.99	18.76	865.56	865.99	19.48
770.00	770.44	17.33	802.00	802.44	18.05	834.00	834.44	18.77	866.00	866.44	19.49
770.45	770.88	17.34									
796.67	797.11	17.93	828.67	829.11	18.65	860.67	861.11	19.37	892.67	893.11	20.09
797.12	797.55	17.94	829.12	829.55	18.66	861.12	861.55	19.38	893.12	893.55	20.10
797.56	797.99	17.95	829.56	829.99	18.67	861.56	861.99	19.39	893.56	893.99	20.11
798.00	798.44	17.96	830.00	830.44	18.68	862.00	862.44	19.40	894.00	894.44	20.12
798.45	798.88	17.97	830.45	830.88	18.69	862.45	862.88	19.41	894.45	894.88	20.13

Federal tax deductions / Retenues d'impôt fédéral
Effective July 1, 2001 / En vigueur le 1er juillet 2001
Biweekly (26 pay periods a year) / Aux deux semaines (26 périodes de paie par année)
Also look up the tax deductions in the provincial table / Cherchez aussi les retenues d'impôt dans la table provinciale

Pay / Rémunération From - De	Less than / Moins de	0	1	2	3	4	5	6	7	8	9	10
					Deduct from each pay / Retenez sur chaque paie							
514. -	522	78.40	32.75	27.70	17.60	7.45						
522. -	530	79.55	33.95	28.90	18.80	8.65						
530. -	538	80.75	35.15	30.10	20.00	9.85						
538. -	546	81.95	36.35	31.30	21.20	11.05	.95					
546. -	554	83.15	37.55	32.50								
754. -	762	114.25	68.65	63.60	53.45	43.35	33.25	23.10	13.00	2.90		
762. -	770	115.45	69.85	64.80	54.65	44.55	34.45	24.30	14.20	4.10		
770. -	778	116.65	71.05	66.00	55.85	45.75	35.65	25.50	15.40	5.30		
778. -	786	117.85	72.25	67.20	57.05	46.95	36.85	26.70	16.60	6.50		
786. -	794	119.05	73.45	68.40	58.25	48.15	38.05	27.90	17.80	7.65		
794. -	802	120.25	74.65	69.55	59.45	49.35	39.20	29.10	19.00	8.85		

British Columbia provincial tax deductions / Retenues d'impôt de la Colombie-Britannique
Effective July 1, 2001 / En vigueur le 1er juillet 2001
Biweekly (26 pay periods a year) / Aux deux semaines (26 périodes de paie par année)
Also look up the tax deductions in the federal table / Cherchez aussi les retenues d'impôt dans la table fédérale

Pay / Rémunération From - De	Less than / Moins de	0	1	2	3	4	5	6	7	8	9	10
					Deduct from each pay / Retenez sur chaque paie							
538. -	546	31.75	12.70	10.55	6.25	1.95						
546. -	554	32.25	13.15	11.00	6.70	2.40						
546. -	554	32.75										
738. -	746	43.35	24.25	22.15	17.85	13.55	9.25	4.95	.65			
746. -	754	43.80	24.75	22.60	18.30	14.00	9.70	5.40	1.15			
754. -	762	44.30	25.20	23.05	18.75	14.45	10.20	5.90	1.60			
762. -	770	44.75	25.65	23.50	19.20	14.95	10.65	6.35	2.05			
770. -	778	45.20	26.15	24.00	19.70	15.40	11.10	6.80	2.50			

Example 2

Paula Dumont works a 40-hour work week and earns $8.00 an hour with time and a half for overtime. Over the last two weeks, she has worked 44 hours each week. She pays union dues of $6.80 and a dental plan deduction of $2.75 every two weeks. Her claim code is 2 and she is paid bi-weekly. Calculate her net pay.

Solution

Paula's gross pay for one week is:

Regular pay   40 h x $8.00 = $320.00
Overtime pay   8 h x $8.00 x 1.5 = $96.00
Total gross pay $320.00 + $96.00 = $416.00

For two weeks, Paula's gross pay is:
$416.00 x 2 weeks = $832.00

Her claim code is 2, so Paula's deductions are:
CPP $29.99
EI $18.72

To find her taxable income, deduct her union dues:
$832.00 – $6.80 = $825.20

Her income tax is:
Federal $73.15
Provincial $26.75 (British Columbia)

Her total deductions, including union dues and dental plan are:
$29.99 + $18.72 + $73.15 + $26.75 +$6.80 + $2.75 = $158.16

Her net pay is:
$832.00 – $158.16 = $673.84

Mental Math

1. Find 50% of $1500.00.

2. If 25% is deducted for income tax, how much is left from $1000.00?

Hints

To calculate savings of 10%, multiply by 0.10 or move the decimal point one place to the left.

Canada Pension Plan Contributions
Biweekly (26 pay periods a year)
Cotisations au Régime de pensions du Canada
Aux deux semaines (26 périodes de paie par année)

Pay Rémunération From - De	To - À		Pay Rémunération From - De	To - À		Pay Rémunération From - De	To - À		Pay Rémunération From - De	To - À	
804.27 -	804.49	28.80	821.01 -	821.23	29.52	837.75 -	837.98	30.24	854.50 -	854.72	30.96
804.50 -	804.72	28.81	821.24 -	821.47	29.53	837.99 -	838.21	30.25	854.73 -	854.95	30.97
804.73 -	804.95	28.82	821.48 -	821.70	29.54	838.22 -	838.44	30.26	854.96 -	855.19	30.98
804.96 -	805.19	28.83	821.71 -	821.93	29.55	838.45 -	838.68	30.27	855.20 -	855.42	30.99
805.20 -	805.42	28.84	821.94 -	822.16	29.56	838.69 -	838.91	30.28	855.43 -	855.65	31.00
805.43 -	805.65	28.85									
			831.48 -	831.70	29.97	848.22 -	848.44	30.69	864.96 -	865.19	
814.96 -	815.19	29.26	831.71 -	831.93	29.98	848.45 -	848.68	30.70	865.20 -	865.42	31.42
815.20 -	815.42	29.27	831.94 -	832.16	29.99	848.69 -	848.91	30.71	865.43 -	865.65	31.43
815.43 -	815.65	29.28	832.17 -	832.40	30.00	848.92 -	849.14	30.72	865.66 -	865.88	31.44

Employment Insurance Premiums
Cotisations à l'assurance-emploi

Insurable Earnings Rémunération assurable From - De	To - À		Insurable Earnings Rémunération assurable From - De	To - À		Insurable Earnings Rémunération assurable From - De	To - À		Insurable Earnings Rémunération assurable From - De	To - À	
768.23 -	768.66	17.29	800.23 -	800.66	18.01	832.23 -	832.66	18.73	864.23 -	864.66	19.45
768.67 -	769.11	17.30	800.67 -	801.11	18.02	832.67 -	833.11	18.74	864.67 -	865.11	19.46
769.12 -	769.55	17.31	801.12 -	801.55	18.03	833.12 -	833.55	18.75	865.12 -	865.55	19.47
769.56 -	769.99	17.32	801.56 -	801.99	18.04	833.56 -	833.99	18.76	865.56 -	865.99	19.48
770.00 -	770.44	17.33	802.00 -	802.44	18.05	834.00 -	834.44	18.77	866.00 -	866.44	19.49
770.45 -	770.88	17.34									
798.45 -	798.88	17.97	830.45 -	830.88	18.69	862.45 -	862.88	19.41	894.45 -	894.88	20.13
798.89 -	799.33	17.98	830.89 -	831.33	18.70	862.89 -	863.33	19.42	894.89 -	895.33	20.14
799.34 -	799.77	17.99	831.34 -	831.77	18.71	863.34 -	863.77	19.43	895.34 -	895.77	20.15
799.78 -	800.22	18.00	831.78 -	832.22	18.72	863.78 -	864.22	19.44	895.78 -	896.22	20.16

Federal tax deductions
Effective July 1, 2001
Biweekly (26 pay periods a year)
Also look up the tax deductions in the provincial table

Retenues d'impôt fédéral
En vigueur le 1er juillet 2001
Aux deux semaines (26 périodes de paie par année)
Cherchez aussi les retenues d'impôt dans la table provinciale

Pay Rémunération From De	Less than Moins de	0	1	2	3	4	5	6	7	8	9	10
						Deduct from each pay Retenez sur chaque paie						
514. -	522	78.40	32.75	27.70	17.60	7.45						
522. -	530	79.55	33.95	28.90	18.80	8.65						
530. -	538	80.75	35.15	30.10	20.00	9.85						
538. -	546	81.95	36.35	31.30	21.20	11.05	.95					
546. -	554	83.15	37.55									
			73.45	68.40	58.25	48.15	38.05	27.90	17.80	7.65		
794. -	802	120.25	74.65	69.55	59.45	49.35	39.20	29.10	19.00	8.85		
802. -	810	121.45	75.85	70.75	60.65	50.55	40.40	30.30	20.20	10.05		
810. -	818	122.65	77.00	71.95	61.85	51.75	41.60	31.50	21.40	11.25	1.15	
818. -	826	123.85	78.20	73.15	63.05	52.95	42.80	32.70	22.60	12.45	2.35	
826. -	834	125.05	79.40	74.35	64.25	54.10	44.00	33.90	23.75	13.65	3.55	

British Columbia provincial tax deductions
Effective July 1, 2001
Biweekly (26 pay periods a year)
Also look up the tax deductions in the federal table

Retenues d'impôt de la Colombie-Britannique
En vigueur le 1er juillet 2001
Aux deux semaines (26 périodes de paie par année)
Cherchez aussi les retenues d'impôt dans la table fédérale

Pay Rémunération From De	Less than Moins de	0	1	2	3	4	5	6	7	8	9	10
						Deduct from each pay Retenez sur chaque paie						
538. -	546	31.75	12.70	10.55	6.25	1.95						
546. -	554	32.25										
		47.00	28.45	26.30	22.00	17.70	13.40	9.15	4.85	.55		
818. -	826	48.00	28.90	26.75	22.45	18.20	13.90	9.60	5.30	1.00		
826. -	834	48.45	29.35	27.20	22.95	18.65	14.35	10.05	5.75	1.45		
834. -	842	48.90	29.85	27.70	23.40	19.10	14.80	10.50	6.25	1.95		
842. -	850	49.40	30.30	28.15	23.85	19.55	15.30	11.00	6.70	2.40		
850. -	858	49.85	30.75	28.60	24.30	20.05	15.75	11.45	7.15	2.85		

Project Activity

Select one of the three careers you are investigating. Choose one that pays by the hour, or calculate the hourly rate of pay. How many hours of work are there in a typical work week? What is the difference between being paid every two weeks and being paid twice a month?

Create a simulated pay statement that includes the following: name, hourly pay rate, hours worked, and gross income. Deduct amounts for income tax, CPP, and EI. Calculate and show the net pay someone working a 35-hour work week for two weeks will earn.

Notebook Assignment

1. Using the appropriate weekly deduction tables, find the net pay for the following situation. Assume the only deductions are CPP, EI, and income tax.

   a) Gross Pay = $300.00   Claim Code = 0

   b) Gross Pay = $326.50   Claim Code = 3

   c) Gross Pay = $410.00   Claim Code = 1

   d) Gross Pay = $309.76   Claim Code = 5

   e) Gross Pay = $505.89   Claim Code = 6

   f) Gross Pay = $321.32   Claim Code = 4

   g) Gross Pay = $435.75   Claim Code = 2

   h) Gross Pay = $372.96   Claim Code = 1

2. Jack Anderson's weekly salary is $395.00. Find his net pay if his claim code is 2 and if his only deductions are CPP, EI, and income tax.

3. Paul Wieler works a 40-hour week and receives $11.75 per hour. Time and a half is paid if he works more than 40 hours a week. Last week he worked 44 hours. Find his net pay if his only deductions are CPP, EI, and income tax (Code 1). He is paid weekly.

4. Agatha Crystal works the following hours during the week of July 13th: M–8; T–7.5; W–10.5; TH–8.5; F–8. Her company pays daily time and a half overtime based on a regular eight-hour day. Her regular rate is $9.00 an hour. Calculate her net pay using Code 2, assuming her only deductions are CPP, EI, and income tax. She is paid weekly.

5. Find Al Passey's net pay for the week. His claim code is 7, his weekly salary is $385.00, and he pays union dues of $3.80, a dental plan premium of $1.85, and the usual CPP, EI, and income tax deductions. He is paid weekly.

6. The following people work for the Ajax Company. Their regular rate of pay is $14.10 an hour. Time and a half is paid if employees work more than 40 hours. Find the workers' net pay. They are paid bi-weekly.

   a) Melissa works for 43 hours. Her claim code is 1. She has bi–weekly deductions as follows: group insurance of $1.76, dental plan of $3.85, and union dues of $6.95.

   b) Emiko works for 40 hours. Her claim code is 3. She has the following bi-weekly deductions: group insurance of $2.09, dental plan of $3.85, and union dues of $6.95.

   c) Louis works in the office and earns a salary of $350.00 a week. His claim code is 2. His bi-weekly deductions are: group insurance of $1.86 and dental plan of $3.85.

   d) Ivan works for 40.5 hours. His claim code is 2. He pays group insurance of $1.76, dental plan of $3.85, and union dues of $6.95 for each pay period.

   e) Maureen works for 42 hours. Her claim code is 4. She pays group insurance of $1.76 and union dues of $6.95 each pay period.

7. Henry usually finds 40% of his pay goes to deductions. How much will his weekly take-home pay be if he makes $12.10 an hour and works 40 hours?

8. List six examples of possible payroll deductions. Explain one situation in which an employee would be happy to have paid into Employment Insurance.

9. Why is a pension plan deduction sometimes called a "good" deduction?

Extension

10. Andrée works part-time and is paid semi-monthly. For her wages, she estimates her CPP contribution to be about 3% of her gross pay, her EI contribution to be about 2%, and her income tax about 20%. If she is paid $500.00 semi-monthly, what are her total deductions, and how much is her take-home pay? Describe two methods of finding Andrée's total deductions.

11. Michelle Wong earns an annual salary of $60,000. She is paid monthly. Virginia Stephens is paid $2307.69 every two weeks. Should they pay the same income tax? Why or why not? Find the amount of income tax each would pay if they are both claim code 1.

New Terms

semi-monthly: twice a month; twenty-four times a year.

Exploration 7

· · · · · · · · · · · · · · · · · · · ·

Making Career Choices

Suppose you are trying to decide which post-secondary courses to take. You have found out which courses match your interests and abilities based on your high school courses and marks. As you consider the careers these courses may lead to, think about which job is likely to pay the most, but also consider which career you would find most satisfying in the long run.

The career you choose will have an impact on your lifestyle. When choosing a career, people often consider questions such as: Do I want to work in the evenings or at night? Is weekend work required? Is the job seasonal? Will it pay me enough to live the way I want?

Small Group Discussion

In a small group, list ten features that are important to consider when making a career choice. Have one person in your group record the ideas. Discuss and come to an agreement on the three most important things that make a career desirable. Have one person list the three things and record one reason that describes why each is important.

Classroom Activity

Have one person from your group report to the whole class on the top three features of a good career. List the features from each group on the board and note where a feature is selected by more than one group. As a class, use the lists to vote on the most important features of a career choice.

Goals

In this exploration, you will select/create problem-solving strategies to explore the financial and lifestyle implications of career selection.

New Terms

seasonal employment: work that occurs at specific times of the year, for example, fishing guide.

Career Connection

Name: Aaron Kusugak

Job: artist/hunter/student

Current wages: approximately $2000 a month selling his artwork during tourist season

Education: currently in grade 12

Keyword search: Inuit art carving Arviat

Mental Math

1. Which job pays more per week, a job that pays $12.00 an hour for a 20-hour week or a job that pays $10.00 an hour for a 25-hour week?

Example 1

Ingrid is trying to decide whether to take an office assistant program or licensed practical nurse program at college. What financial questions should she consider? What lifestyle questions should she consider? List the questions she might ask a career counsellor before she decides. Propose a way that she could make her decision.

Solution

Questions Ingrid might ask include:

1. How much does each program cost and how long does it last?
2. Is there any financial assistance available to help with the costs?
3. What are the chances of getting a suitable job after completing the program?
4. What is the usual income for each job?
5. What work expenses does each job require?
6. Does the job require unusual hours of work, travel, or work in remote areas?
7. Will each choice provide job satisfaction?
8. Do jobs in these areas have room for career advancement?

Ingrid could list the pros and cons of each job and decide on the job with the most "pros" and fewest "cons." She could assign a point for each "pro" and select the job with the most points. After completing her research, Ingrid has the following answers to her questions.

Factor	Job #1 Office Assistant			Job #2 Practical Nurse		
	Pro	Con	(Point)	Pro	Con	(Point)
Cost of course	affordable		1	affordable		1
Length of course	one year		1	one year		1
Student assistance		none		available		1
Chances of a job		difficult		good		1
Usual income		less		more		1
Work expenses	none		1		uniforms	
Unusual conditions	none		1		shifts and	
					weekends	
Job satisfaction		little		strong		1
Career advancement		little		good		1
Total points			4			7

Ingrid chooses the practical nurse option.

Project Activity

Research the educational requirements for the three career options you have chosen. Estimate the cost of any education or training programs you need to take to get a job in this area. Add this information to your project file.

Notebook Assignment

1. Suppose you are qualified to work as both a school library aide and as a school custodian. Two jobs come up, one of each type. The custodial position will be the after-school shift. The library aide will earn $12.86 an hour and the custodian will earn $14.12, which includes an additional 50 cents an hour for working evenings. Calculate the weekly income for each job. Assume a 30-hour work week for each job. Create a list of advantages and disadvantages for each job and assign points to each. Which of the two jobs would be better for you? Why?

2. Michelle Calliou is a commercial pilot searching for work. She is considering two job openings. One is based in northern Manitoba and the other is based in the Yukon. The Manitoba job is full-time, but will require that she spend half her time selling tickets and delivering luggage. This job pays $25 an hour. The Yukon job is part-time, requiring 20 hours a week. The work is all piloting, with no ground work. It pays $30 an hour.

   Create a list of questions that Michelle could ask the employer during an interview for each of these jobs that will help her decide which one she prefers. Make a list of advantages and disadvantages of each job. Create a way to rate the value of each job based on this list. Imagine that you are Michelle and rate each job to find which would be better for you, based on the information given. Justify your answer.

3. Jesse wants to learn about retail sales by getting a part-time job in a store. He is considering one job that pays $9.50 an hour selling sports equipment. This job is for 8 hours on Saturdays. Another job at a sports clothing store requires 4 hours Friday night and 4 hours Saturday afternoon. It pays $8.50 an hour but also pays a bonus of $100 if Jesse sells $1000 worth of clothing in one 4-hour shift. Both jobs are 8 hours a week in total. Which job pays better if Jesse is able to earn a bonus once a month? Which would be the better job from your perspective? Explain why.

4. What are three aspects of a job, other than income, that would be important to you in choosing a part-time after school job? Rate each aspect from most important to least important and explain your choices.

5. Suppose a construction company is looking for summer help. The company pays $12 an hour and is looking for secondary school graduates with construction experience to start apprenticeship programs with them. A grocery store is looking for summer help and pays $8.50 an hour. The store expects some of its summer student staff to continue working in part-time jobs over the winter. Compare the money earned at each job based on the information given. How long would a store worker have to work before she caught up with the income of the construction worker? Which job would be better for you? Explain your answer.

Extension

6. Pierre is interested in photography and is saving to take a photography course at college. He has found a job in a camera shop for the entire summer that he can continue at part-time in the winter months. The job pays the minimum wage. Before he makes his decision, a sawmill employer phones and offers him a summer job. The job pays $19 an hour for 36 hours a week but it will end in the fall when school starts. Describe how Pierre could choose between these jobs. Put yourself in Pierre's place and use the method to come to a decision. Justify your answer.

Problem Analysis

Crossing the River

A peasant is walking her dog, a chicken, and some grain to market. She has to cross a river to get to the market. There is a boat which will hold the peasant and either the dog or the chicken or the grain at one time. The problem is that, if left alone, the dog will eat the chicken. If the chicken is left alone, it will eat the grain.

How does the peasant transport herself and the three items across the river without losing any of them? What is the minimum number of trips she can make to transport herself and all the items across the river?

Games

Addit

This is a game for two people. The goal is to find a winning strategy.

Starting from zero, the players alternately add 1, 2, or 3 to a total. The player who is able to add to obtain exactly 31 wins. Play several games.

Describe verbally or in written form the strategy you used to win the game.

Variations

1) Add to obtain a different final number.
2) Add 1, 2, 3, 4, 5, etc.
3) Subtract from 31 by 1, 2, 3, etc. The person who subtracts to obtain zero wins (or loses).
4) The person who adds last and obtains 31 loses (that is, the person who obtains a total of 30, wins).

Exploration 8

Changing Earnings

During your working life, the amount you earn is likely to change occasionally. You may earn more because you receive a raise or get a new job with a higher rate of pay. Your wages may drop if your employer has to reduce his or her expenses or if you choose to job-share or work part-time. You might also take a new job that pays less than your old job.

Career Connection

Name: Ethan Chan

Job: chef's assistant

Current wages: $10.50 an hour with a 10% raise due in 2 weeks

Education: grade 12; enrolled in culinary arts training at Vancouver Community College, Vancouver

Career goal: chef

Keyword search: Canada culinary arts

Goals

In this exploration, you will investigate the impact of changing earnings.

New Terms

job-share: to split a job with another person; each person does part of the work and receives part of the salary.

Example 1

A mechanic was earning $630.00 a week. Last week, he received a 10% raise. What is the dollar value of the raise? What is the mechanic's new salary?

Solution

Calculate 10% of the original salary:
$630.00 x 0.10 = $63.00

The mechanic's raise is $63.00. Add his raise to his old salary to find his new salary:
$630.00 + $63.00 = $693.00

Example 2

A waiter was earning $8.75 an hour. The boss gave the waiter a raise of $0.50 an hour. Find the percent rate of increase.

Solution

Divide the increase by the old salary and multiply by 100. Round off to two decimal places.

$0.50 ÷ $8.75 = 0.0571428
0.0571428 x 100 = 5.71428% or 5.71% to 2 decimal places
The percent rate of increase is 5.71%.

Technology

On a scientific calculator you can calculate a 10% raise by using the percent button:

$630 x 10% = $63.00

Mental Math

Summer is paid $8.00 an hour. She receives a 5% raise. How much is her raise?

Example 3

Alexis earns $12.00/hour and receives a 4% raise. What is her new salary?

Solution

$12.00 x 0.04 = $0.48
$12.00 + $0.48 = $12.48

You could also multiply her old salary by 1.04:
$12.00 x 1.04 = $12.48

Project Activity

Select one of the careers you are investigating. List three events that could cause income to increase, and two that might cause it to decrease. Explain how an annual budget might help a person adjust to pay changes.

Notebook Assignment

1. Complete this table in your notebook.

	Present Salary	Percent Rate of Increase	Increase ($)	New Salary
a)	$7.65 an hour	2%		
b)	$310.00 a week	11%		
c)	$1087.25 a month	3.5%		
d)	$14.95 an hour	1.5%		
e)	$20,800.00 a year		$572.00	
f)	$15,000.00 annually			$17,750.00

Hints

1. To change a percent to a decimal fraction, divide by 100. For example,

   45% = 45 ÷ 100 = 0.45

2. To change a decimal fraction to a percent, multiply by 100. For example,

   0.45 x 100 = 45%

2. Suppose that you are paid $13.55 an hour. After three months, you receive a raise of 2%. What is your new hourly rate?

3. Last year a secretary earned $21,900. He improved his qualifications by taking two courses and his employer increased his salary by 4.6%. What is his new salary?

4. A fast food outlet gave its employees a 3.25% raise. The average wage rate before the raise was $8.65 an hour. Find the new average hourly rate of pay.

5. An employee receives a weekly salary of $350. He receives a raise of 1.2%. What is his new salary?

6. James Martin's annual salary at his first job after graduation was $13,104. After one year, his employer gave him a $4\frac{1}{2}$% increase in his salary. Calculate his new salary.

7. A wholesaler employed William Green as a salesman, agreeing to pay him $1200.00 a month and to increase his salary by 4% every six months. How much will William Green's monthly salary be at the end of one year?

8. Complete this table in your notebook. Round to the nearest tenth of a percent.

	Present Salary	Amount of Increase	Percent Rate of Increase
a)	$6.00 an hour	$0.30	
b)	$6.75 an hour	$0.52	
c)	$280.00 a week	$19.80	
d)	$320.00 a week	$40.00	
e)	$1700.00 a month	$350.00	
f)	$2100.00 a month		2.4%
g)	$13,480.00 a year	$600.00	
h)	$22,800.00 annually		4.4%

9. A construction worker was earning $17.05 an hour. The company decided to raise her salary by $1.00 an hour. What was her percent rate of increase?

10. The workers at a foundry were given a pay increase of $5250 over a two-year period. If the initial average salary was $20,000, what was the percent rate of increase?

11. Six months ago, an employee of a fast-food outlet was earning $255.00 a week. Now that employee is earning $305.00 a week. Find the percent rate of increase in the employee's pay.

12. A camp counsellor earned a weekly salary of $250.00. He received a raise and his salary increased to $275.00 a week. What was his percent rate of increase in pay?

13. Pat Delaney received a salary of $1500 a month. Pat's salary was increased to $1850 a month. Find the percent rate of increase.

14. Jean Brown worked as a clerk after graduating from high school. She earned $900 a month. After two years, her earnings were $1100 a month. What was the percent rate of increase in her salary over the two-year period?

15. Jean-Luc Thibodeau earns $800,000 as a hockey player. Next year his salary will be $950,000. Calculate the percent rate of increase in Jean-Luc's annual salary.

16. Suppose you were taking courses at night and as a result earned a 10% raise. How could you spend it? List three ways of spending your increase. Which of the three ways is most positive in the long run?

Extension

17. Two teachers decide to job-share. Each will work half-time. Between them they will share one high school teaching job. List advantages and disadvantages of a 50:50 job share.

Exploration 9

Balancing a Budget

Income and expenses can change. You may get a raise or change jobs and find that you earn more or less money. Your expenses may change as prices rise or unexpected expenses occur that must be paid. When your income and/or expenses change, you need to adjust your budget so that you have enough money to meet your financial needs and goals.

This exploration includes an activity that simulates the creation of a budget for a student working part-time. You will create a list of weekly expenses for yourself and then use this to develop a budget.

BUDGET SIMULATOR GAME

Rules

The game is played in groups of four using one regular six-sided die. A turn represents one week. Each turn includes three rolls of the die. The first roll gives a number you will add to your province's or territory's minimum wage to arrive at your hourly wage. For example, if you roll a "3" and your minimum wage is $7.50, then your hourly wage will be $10.50. The second roll is the number of hours you work in a week at a part-time job. The third roll multiplied by 5 represents an unexpected expense you will have to pay that week. If you roll a "6," you will have an unexpected $30.00 expense. The object of the game is to create a balance of $1000 in your savings account. You start the game with $500 in your account.

If a player's final balance is less than zero, he or she is out of the game. If a player makes a mistake in his or her calculations and fails to correct it before the next player rolls the die, any opposing player may call "challenge!" If the opposing player points out a mistake correctly, the original player is out. If the opposing player is wrong about the challenge, he or she is out of the game.

The last player remaining or the first player to reach a balance of $1000 wins.

Goals

In this exploration, you will develop and balance a budget that matches your expected income.

Example 1

Cecile finds her current weekly expenses include $15.00 for books and CDs, $20.00 for clothes, $10.00 for savings, and $25.00 for recreation. If she is playing the budget simulator game and rolls a 2, a 6, and a 3, how can she adjust her budget so she will not have to spend her savings? Assume the minimum wage is $7.50.

Solution

Cecile's income for the week is based on $7.50 plus $2.00 for an hourly wage of $9.50. She works 6 hours that week so her income is $57.00. Her current budget is $70.00 a week. Cecile has an unexpected expense of $15.00. Cecile could reduce her expenses as follows to balance her budget: books and CDs $10.00, clothes $20.00, savings $6.00, recreation $6.00. She must add the unexpected expense of $15.00.

Project Activity

Prepare a wish list based on what you would like to spend. How much income would be required to support the expenses you have listed? Next, prepare a realistic budget based on the income of the career you have chosen to investigate in-depth. Include the following expenses in your budget: transportation, accommodation, food, recreation, entertainment, clothing, and miscellaneous expenses.

Notebook Assignment

1. Play three rounds of the Budget Simulator Game. Record your results in a table in your notebook each time you throw the die.
   Before you start the game, create a list of your usual expenses. Your list might include clothes, entertainment, or recreation. Estimate your total weekly expenses. Make a list of 3 types of unexpected expenses you might have.

Use a table like the one below to record your results.

Name

	Week 1	Week 2	Week 3
Starting balance:	$500		
INCOME			
Hourly Wage:			
Hours Worked:			
Weekly Income:			
EXPENSES			
Regular expenses: (note any changes you make to stay in budget)			
Unexpected expenses:			
Total weekly expenses:			
FINAL BALANCE:			

2. Shelby earns $125.00 a month babysitting. If she lives at home but is saving for college, how much can she spend on recreation if she needs to save $900.00 a year?

3. Indira wanted to save 25 percent of her net pay for trades school. If she saved $500.00, how much was she paid?

Chapter Review

. . . .

1. James Chang earns $8.15 an hour. If he works a total of twelve hours one week, what is his gross pay?

2. Ryan Porter works at a mill on Saturdays doing clean-up. His pay rate is $18.50 an hour for the first 8 hours and then time and a half for any overtime hours. If he works a 12-hour shift not including lunch hour, what is his gross pay?

3. Lisa Una filled out a time card that showed she was at work from 08:00 to 16:00. How many hours did she work if there is a half-hour lunch break? How much money would she earn if her pay rate is $9.54 an hour?

4. Complete a payroll record for Ilia Daniel. Include deductions for income tax, CPP, and employment insurance. Ilia earns $4000 a month, is paid semi-monthly, and his claim code is 3.

5. Sadie Curry works at a gas station earning $8.40 an hour. If she gets a 5 percent raise what is her new wage?

6. John Edwards is offered a raise that increases his hourly wage from $11.25 to $12.25. Another company offers him his original wage plus a 10% bonus. Assume he would work the same number of hours at each job. Which is a better offer? What is the difference in gross pay?

7. Sharon O'Reilly earns $12.50 an hour and works a 35-hour week. What is Sharon's weekly gross pay? If she saves 10 percent of her gross pay, how much will she save in one year?

8. Mary Bruce works at a grocery store. She works a 40-hour week at $12.50 an hour and then works an extra 8-hour shift at time and a half. Find Mary's gross earnings. What would her annual earnings be if she worked these hours all year?

9. Complete a time card for William Whitaker. He is a short order cook in a school cafeteria. He works each morning Monday through Friday from 8:00 am to 12:00 noon. He is paid time and a half for any other time he works. He is docked a quarter of an hour's pay for every quarter of an hour or part thereof that he arrives late or leaves early.

Time Card

Employee Number: **83837**

Name: **WILLIAM WHITAKER**

Signature: *William Whitaker*

Week Ending: **JUNE 24**

Date	Morning In	Morning Out	Afternoon In	Afternoon Out	Overtime In	Overtime Out	Hours Reg	Hours OT	Total Hours
M	7:59	12:01							
T	8:02	12:00							
W	7:55	11:55							
TH	8:27	12:03							
F	8:00	11:32							
S									
SU									
Total							___	___	___

	HOURS	RATE	AMOUNT	POSITION
REGULAR		$9.60		Cook
OVERTIME				

10. Complete a time card for Megan Metcalfe, who teaches at a music school. She works various shifts during the week. Her afternoon shift begins at 1:00 pm and ends at 5:00 pm. Her evening shift begins at 6:00 pm and ends at 9:00 pm. She is paid time and a half for any other time she works. She is penalized a quarter of an hour's pay for every quarter of an hour or part thereof that she arrives late or leaves early.

Time Card

Employee Number: **7896**

Name:　　　　　**MEGAN METCALFE**　　　Signature　*Megan Metcalfe*

Week Ending:　　**NOVEMBER 2**

Date	Afternoon		Evening		Overtime		Hours		Total
	In	Out	In	Out	In	Out	Reg	OT	Hours
M	12:58	5:02							
T			5:59	8:31					
W	2:27	5:00	5:59	8:46					
TH			6:18	9:04					
F	1:09	4:48							
S					8:35	12:02			
SU									
Total							____	____	____

	HOURS	RATE	AMOUNT	POSITION
REGULAR		$15.00		Instructor
OVERTIME				

11. Romeo Lombardo is a corrections officer. He works from 8:00 am to 5:00 pm. His lunch hour is from 12:00 pm to 1:00 pm and he is not paid for that time. He is paid time and a half for Saturday work. He is docked a quarter of an hour's pay for each quarter of an hour or part thereof that he arrives late or leaves early. Complete Romeo's time card.

Time Card

Employee Number: **4747**

Name:	**ROMEO LOMBARDO**	Signature	*Romeo Lombardo*

Week Ending: **OCTOBER 12**

Date	Morning		Afternoon		Overtime		Hours		Total
	In	Out	In	Out	In	Out	Reg	OT	Hours
M	8:00	12:02	12:57	5:05					
T	7:57	11:34	12:58	5:01					
W	7:59	12:03	1:18	5:00					
TH	8:06	12:00	12:59	4:50					
F	7:55	11:58	1:00	5:03					
S					9:15	12:00			
SU									
Total									

	HOURS	RATE	AMOUNT	POSITION
REGULAR		$16.95		Corrections Officer
OVERTIME				

12. Complete a time card for Juan Valdez, who works in an espresso bar. Juan starts work at 13:00 and finishes at 22:00. He takes an hour for dinner from 17:00 to 18:00, for which he is not paid. He receives double time for any Saturday or Sunday hours he works. Juan is docked a quarter of an hour's pay for every quarter of an hour or part thereof that he arrives late or leaves early.

Time Card

Employee Number: **9494**

Name: **JUAN VALDEZ**   Signature *Juan Valdez*

Week Ending: **OCTOBER 12**

Date	Afternoon		Evening		Overtime		Hours		Total
	In	Out	In	Out	In	Out	Reg	OT	Hours
M	13:00	17:01	18:00	22:02					
T	12:57	17:02	17:55	21:31					
W	12:59	17:03	18:07	22:03					
TH	13:08	17:00	17:59	21:56					
F	13:19	17:00	17:56	21:59					
S					12:58	16:33			
SU									
Total							___	___	___

	HOURS	RATE	AMOUNT	POSITION
REGULAR		$7.95		Server
OVERTIME				

13. Hugh Jennings is a barber. His regular hours are from 8:00 am to
12:00 pm in the morning and from 1:00 pm to 5:00 pm in the
afternoon Mondays through Fridays. Any hours worked beyond this
time are paid at time and a half. He is docked a quarter of an hour's
pay for every quarter of an hour or part thereof that he arrives late or
leaves early. His claim code is 5. He contributes $4.50 each week for
medical and dental insurance. Complete a time card for Hugh and
find his net weekly pay.

Time Card

Employee Number: **686899**

Name: **HUGH JENNINGS**   Signature *Hugh Jennings*

Week Ending: **SEPTEMBER 21**

Date	Morning		Afternoon		Overtime		Hours		Total
	In	Out	In	Out	In	Out	Reg	OT	Hours
M	7:56	12:01	1:14	5:00					
T	8:00	12:02	12:55	5:04					
W	7:56	11:50	1:30	5:02					
TH	7:55	12:03	12:55	5:04	5:57	8:36			
F	8:00	12:02	12:58	4:32					
S									
SU									
Total							——	——	——

	HOURS	RATE	AMOUNT	POSITION
REGULAR		$10.50		Barber
OVERTIME				

14. Gabriel Gagnon has just started working for an automobile dealership. His regular hours are from 13:00 to 17:00 and from 18:00 to 22:00 Monday through Friday. Any hours worked beyond this time are paid at time and a half. He is penalized a quarter of an hour's pay for every quarter of an hour or part thereof that he arrives late or leaves early. His claim code is 3. Gabriel pays $3.23 for group insurance and $5.50 to a charitable organization each week. Complete a time card for Gabriel and find his net weekly pay.

Time Card

Employee Number: **14647**

Name: **GABRIEL GAGNON**

Signature *Gabriel Gagnon*

Week Ending: **JUNE 15**

Date	Afternoon		Evening		Overtime		Hours		Total
	In	Out	In	Out	In	Out	Reg	OT	Hours
M	13:00	17:00	18:03	21:02					
T	12:56	16:35	18:25	22:04					
W	12:58	17:02	17:58	22:02					
TH	12:59	17:01	17:55	21:58					
F	12:57	17:01	17:55	21:58					
S					09:00	12:03			
SU									
Total							___	___	___

	HOURS	RATE	AMOUNT	POSITION
REGULAR		$11.95		Car Salesman
OVERTIME				

15. Tyrone Desrochers is a footwear manager in a department store. His regular hours are from 8:00 am to 5:00 pm Monday through Friday. If he works any hours beyond this time, he is paid time and a half, with hours on Sunday paid double time. His lunch hour is from 12:00 noon to 1:00 pm, and he is not paid for that time. He is docked a quarter of an hour's pay for every quarter of an hour or part thereof that he arrives late or leaves early. His claim code is 6. He contributes $4.50 for medical and dental insurance as well as $32.75 to a pension fund each week. Complete a time card for Tyrone and find his net pay.

Time Card

Employee Number: **111315**

Name: **TYRONE DESROCHERS**   Signature: *Tyrone DesRochers*

Week Ending: **FEBRUARY 17**

Date	Morning		Afternoon		Overtime		Hours		Total
	In	Out	In	Out	In	Out	Reg	OT	Hours
M	8:00	12:06	12:56	4:42					
T	7:59	12:02	12:55	5:02	5:57	8:49			
W	7:58	11:03	12:57	4:30	6:03	9:13			
TH	8:00	11:47	12:59	5:00					
F	8:02	12:00	1:14	4:05					
S									
SU									
Total							___	___	___

	HOURS	RATE	AMOUNT	POSITION
REGULAR		$14.90		Dept. Manager
OVERTIME				

Project Presentation

In this exploration you will organize the material from your project file into a poster presentation on the career option that interests you the most. Your poster should contain the following information:

1. A "Help Wanted" ad for the job that indicates the amount of income.
2. A description of the educational requirements for the career.
3. A list of expenses required if you work in that career.
4. A sample pay statement.
5. A wish list of what you would like to spend and what you are likely to earn.
6. A realistic budget, in which your expenses match predicted income.

Extension

Create a real-life budget for yourself. Be realistic. Include any income you earn from odd jobs, paid employment, or as an allowance. List expenses you are responsible for such as recreation, clothing, or transportation. Include an amount for savings and identify a possible future use for the savings. List two expensive items you would like to buy and calculate how long it would take to save for these items.

Case Study

In this case study, you will calculate net pay and develop a balanced budget for John Miller. John works as a surveyor's assistant. He earns $22.00 an hour. John works 37.5 hours a week.

1. John's goal is to save 10 percent of his gross income for a college course he wants to take. Find his monthly gross earnings and calculate how much money he will save after one year of work. If he received a $1.00 an hour raise halfway through the year, what would his savings for college be?

2. Using the appropriate government deduction tables, find John's take-home pay for 2 weeks (without the raise). Show his deductions as they would be indicated on his paycheque stub.

3. Using John's monthly take-home pay, create a balanced monthly budget. He is single, has a dog, and rents an apartment that he shares with a co-worker. Explain the reasoning you used to arrive at your estimates for food, accommodation, transportation, and other expenses.

Chapter 2

Personal Banking

"Freedom Fifteen"

Think about operating your own business next summer or part-time during the school year. Perhaps you play in a band and have just been hired for your first paid gig. Maybe there is a need for someone to split and deliver firewood in your area, or to provide lawn-mowing and gardening services. You may be getting calls to babysit neighbourhood children.

These might be great ways to earn money while you are still a student. You may be able to find a part-time or summer job at a business in your community. No matter how you earn money, you will need a bank account to help you keep track of the money you earn and spend. You will need to deposit paycheques, make withdrawals, and use a bank card for transactions at stores or automated teller machines (ATMs). Using a bank account at a financial institution will help manage your income and expenses.

Chapter Goals

After you complete this chapter, you will be able to research different types of bank accounts, list the costs and benefits of accounts, write cheques, fill out withdrawal and deposit slips, and use bank cards and ATMs. You will be able to keep track of money in your account and check for errors in your statements by completing account reconciliations.

New Terms

automated teller machine (ATM): a self-service banking machine that lets you conduct routine banking transactions. This is sometimes referred to as an automated banking machine (ABM).

bank card: a plastic card with a magnetic strip that allows you access to bank services or to make a direct payment.

Chapter Project

In this project, you will develop a banking plan for a student-run business. You will pick a small or part-time business that may be needed in your community. Choose an idea that matches your own skills and knowledge.

In the project, investigate the banking needs of your business. You will develop a banking plan that would help you manage your business financially. In your project file, you will collect:

1. a collage or drawing showing your business idea
2. a list of income and expenses for your business
3. a sample transaction record
4. a chart comparing different bank accounts and a paragraph that explains which type of bank account would best fit your business needs

You will complete the project with a presentation on the banking needs of your business. Work with a partner to prepare some of the items for your file, exchanging account information with each other and checking each other's calculations. You could complete the whole project with a partner if there is someone in your class who shares your business interest and skills. Occasionally, use small groups to brainstorm ideas and discuss the advantages and drawbacks of certain options. If your banking plan is workable, perhaps you will use it to create your own business!

Hints

For information on Canadian financial services, research the Canadian Bankers Association web site at www.cba.ca.

Career Connection

Name: Stephen Edwards

Job: guitarist in a jazz trio

Current wages: variable: around $50/gig

Education: completed grade 9 in June; returning to grade 10 in September

Background skills and knowledge: school music and private guitar lessons

Career goal: web designer

Keyword search: web design courses Canada

Project Activity

In a small group, construct a list of possible small-business ideas. Record your favourite idea on a title page in your file, then create a collage showing pictures or sketches of the service or product you plan to provide.

Exploration 1

Using Bank Accounts

Banks and other financial institutions such as credit unions and trust companies offer a variety of accounts with many different features. Some accounts are best for saving money and others are best for people who have many transactions to make. Transactions can be made using an automated teller machine (ATM), the telephone, the internet, or in person at your bank.

Today, most bank transactions can be done electronically and paper forms are not always needed. In many cases, some paperwork is still needed and it may be more convenient. No matter how transactions are made, it is important to keep track of them so you know your financial position.

Small Group Activity

In a small group, make a list of advantages and disadvantages of having a bank account. Decide within your group if there may be situations in which not having a bank account would be the best choice for an individual.

Whole Class Discussion

Each group reporter should list the advantages and disadvantages of bank accounts that their group identified. Create a list that includes all the advantages and disadvantages that the class identified.

Example 1—Making a Deposit

Lynn Topp decides to deposit two cheques on March 15, 2001. One is for $236.32; the other is for $176.25. She also wants to deposit some cash: one $5.00 bill, three $20.00 bills, four $1.00 coins, six $2.00 coins, thirteen quarters, and eighteen nickels. She withdraws $50.00 in cash. Her account number is 077-44563-248. Write out a deposit slip for Lynn.

Goals

In this exploration, you will learn how to deposit and withdraw money from an account using forms like those provided by banks and other financial institutions. You will learn to write a cheque.

Solution

A completed deposit slip is shown below. Here are the steps Lynn should follow:

a) List each cheque separately in the space provided. If you need more room, you can list extra cheques on the back of the form.
$236.32
$176.25

b) Enter the number of bills and the amount they add up to:
1 x $5.00 = $5.00
3 x $20.00 = $60.00

c) Find the total of the coins:
4 x $1.00 = $4.00
6 x $2.00 = $12.00
13 x $0.25 = $3.25
18 x $0.05 = $0.90
$4.00 + $12.00 + $3.25 + $0.90 = $20.15

d) Add the total of the bills and the coins:
$5.00 + $60.00 + $20.15 = $85.15

e) Write the totals in the appropriate boxes and add them together to find the subtotal:
$236.32 + $176.25 + $85.15 = $497.72

f) Enter the amount Lynn wants returned in cash where it says "Withdrawal":
$50.00

g) Find the total by subtracting $50.00 from the subtotal to arrive at the final deposit:
$497.72 – $50.00 = $447.72

h) Finally, fill in the date and account number and sign the deposit slip.

DEPOSIT

BANK OF EVERMORE
BLUE HARBOUR, B.C.

Personal Account

Date	March 15, 2001
Account Number	077-44563-248
Name	Lynn Topp

INITIALS	
Depositor	Bank Employee
L.T.	A.B.

Signature for cash withdrawal. (Please sign in the presence of bank employee.)

Lynn Topp

CHEQUES

236	32
176	25
412	57

CASH

1	X5	5.00
	X10	
3	X20	60.00
	X50	
	X100	
	Coins/Other Cash	20.15
	Total Cash	85.15
	Total Cheques	412.57
Subtotal	$	497.72
Withdrawal	$	50.00
TOTAL	$	447.72

Hint

Always fill in bank forms completely. Include the amount of cents in a transaction and write out the complete date. If you are writing a cheque, include the full name of the person or business to whom the cheque is written. Sometimes you may need to look back at records from months ago to find and correct an error or to clarify an expense. You might forget the details of a transaction, so it is wise to write them down clearly.

Example 2—Withdrawing Cash

Mary Francis can withdraw cash from her account by filling out a withdrawal slip or by presenting her bank card to the teller.

Complete a withdrawal form showing Mary Francis withdrawing $20.00 from her account 345-234-67 on March 15, 2001.

Solution

Here are the steps needed to complete Mary Francis' withdrawal form.

a) Write in the date.
b) Indicate your home branch location.
c) Write in the amount of money you want to withdraw in both words and numerals.
d) Write in the account number.
e) Sign the withdrawal form.

BANK OF EVERMORE
BLUE HARBOUR, B.C.

WITHDRAWAL

Date
March 15, 2001

Your Home Branch Location
Blue Harbour

Received from Bank of Evermore
Twenty —————————— ^xx^/100 Dollars

$ *20.00*

Your Account Number
| 3 | 4 | 5 | – | 2 | 3 | 4 | – | 6 | 7 |

Signature (Please sign in the presence of bank employee.)
Mary Francis

Example 3—Writing a Cheque

John Doe writes a cheque in the amount of $165.81 to Revy on March 15, 2001.

Solution

A completed cheque is shown below. Here are the steps you follow to write out a cheque.

a) Write the date.
b) Enter the name of the person or company on the cheque.
c) Enter the amount of the cheque in numerals.
d) Write out the dollar amount of the cheque in words. The cents are written in numerals where it says "/100." If the written amount doesn't fill in the line, draw a line across to the cents.
e) Sign the cheque.

JOHN DOE
20 ANY STREET
CITY, PROVINCE POSTAL CODE

March 15 2001

Pay to the order of

Revy $ _165.81_

one hundred sixty-five ———————————— _81_/100 DOLLARS

BANK OF EVERMORE
BLUE HARBOUR, B.C.

FOR _Building Supplies_

John Doe
Signature

26167 001 1234 567

Hints

1. It is wise to deposit or cash cheques promptly because financial institutions do not accept them indefinitely. A cheque more than six months old is considered "stale" and your bank will no longer accept it. Such cheques are considered "stale dated."

2. It is recommended that you draw a line after the written dollar amount. This prevents anyone from changing the amount.

Career Connection

Name: Jim Greene

Job: fishing guide

Current wages: $10 an hour, plus tips

Education: completed grade 11 in June; returning to grade 12 in September

Background skills and knowledge: excellent fishing skills; knowledge of local area fish resources; driver's licence

Career goal: guide outfitter

Keyword search: fishing guide

FISHING GUIDE AVAILABLE

July and August

I know all the hot spots!

Call Jim Greene, 555–4567.

Project Activity

Develop a list of earnings and expenses for your small business. For instance, if you are a musician, you might earn money playing gigs at your high school dances or at community events such as fairs. You might have to spend money on costume items, guitar strings, or transportation to your gigs.

Beside each item on your list, indicate how you might receive or pay the money, for example, a cheque, a web payment, cash, and so on. List the types of transactions you would need to handle the banking.

Notebook Assignment

Using blackline masters, complete the following assignment. Use the current date for all transactions.

1. Complete a withdrawal slip that shows Henri Charles withdrawing $25.00 cash from account number 246-919-34.

2. Fill out a deposit slip with the following information about Morris Stein. Morris has four cheques to deposit. They are for $285.00, $85.00, $98.97, and $127.83. He wishes to deposit the cheques and keep $100.00 cash. His account number is 538-610-7.

3. Suppose you want to deposit the following amounts in your chequing account: five $1.00 coins, four $5.00 bills, two $10.00 bills, one $20.00 bill, nineteen quarters, and one cheque for $64.95. Make up a deposit slip using account number 3-785-11.

4. Chad Allen wants to deposit 2 dimes, 18 one-dollar coins, 4 twenty-dollar bills, and a cheque for $64.20, and to withdraw $100.00 from his savings account 2892146. Fill in a deposit slip for Chad.

5. Fill in a deposit slip with the following information about Inga van Damme. She deposits three cheques: $64.20, $136.50, and $29.98 into her chequing account #8649843. She also withdraws $125.00 in cash.

6. Fill in a deposit slip using the following information about Ranj Panikkar. He deposits 200 pennies, 50 nickels, 100 dimes, and cheques for $46.94, $78.00, and $192.80 into his savings account #1411-613-08. He withdraws $150.00 in cash.

7. Write cheques for John Graham that pay the following expenses on account 4567.

    a) Mike's Bike Shop for $70.00
    b) Northern Stores for $125.78
    c) Jeans & Tops for $7.50

8. Write the following cheques:

    a) February 4, 2001 to J&M Department Store for $48.72
    b) August 27, 2001 to State-of-the-Art Electronics for $158.95
    c) June 1, 2001 to the Manitoba Humane Society for $105.42
    d) April 30, 2001, to the Minister of Finance for $1573.60

9. Find the errors in the following cheques, which were written over a two-week period. There may be more than one error on each cheque.

JOHN DOE
20 ANY STREET
CITY, PROVINCE POSTAL CODE

December 26 2001

Pay to the order of
    A. Baro

$ *12.00*

twelve ——————————————— xx /100 DOLLARS

ANY BANK
YOUR TOWN
PROVINCE

John Doe

Signature

26167 001 1234 567

JOHN DOE
20 ANY STREET
CITY, PROVINCE POSTAL CODE

December 31 2001

Pay to the order of
    B. Baro

$ *25.79*

twenty-five ——————————————— 97 /100 DOLLARS

ANY BANK
YOUR TOWN
PROVINCE

John Doe

Signature

26167 001 1234 567

JOHN DOE
20 ANY STREET
CITY, PROVINCE POSTAL CODE

January 2 2001

Pay to the order of
    C. Baro

$ *34.10*

thirty-four ——————————————— 10 /100 DOLLARS

ANY BANK
YOUR TOWN
PROVINCE

John Doe

Signature

26167 001 1234 567

10. Imagine you are going shopping after school, but first you want to go to the bank. There, you want to deposit a paycheque for $149.76 and withdraw $50.00 cash. Then you want to visit a store where you bought a leather jacket on a lay-away plan and write a cheque for $122.76. Complete the forms necessary for these transactions.

11. List possible drawbacks of carrying cash to buy things, and drawbacks of using cheques or bank debit cards.

Extension

12. Suppose your bank account has a balance of $219.21. You are shopping in the mall and find three items you want to buy. The prices include all taxes.

    a) paintball supplies $75.68
    b) video game $80.88
    c) bicycle parts $150.26

    Do you have enough money to buy all the items you want? How much money would you need to buy all the items? If you had to choose items depending on your bank balance, what would you buy? Explain how you made your choice.

Technology

Bank cards are often called debit cards. With a debit card, money is automatically withdrawn from your bank account when you buy something.

Exploration 2

Keeping Records

Careful record-keeping is important. Accurate and up-to-date records let you know how much money you have and how you are spending and earning money.

An important part of record-keeping for a bank account is your transaction record book. Each account needs to have a complete record of money that has been deposited into and withdrawn from the account. In addition to the amounts, you usually list the source of any income and the items you have bought. You also record transfers between accounts and any other transactions.

When you write a cheque, fill in a complete entry in the record book and calculate the account balance. This helps you to avoid overdrawing your account. If you do not have enough funds in the account to cover a cheque, it will be returned marked "NSF" (Not Sufficient Funds). Banks typically charge a $20.00 penalty fee for returned NSF cheques and businesses that receive NSF cheques may also charge a penalty, so keep your balance up to date. If you do have enough funds, then the bank accepts the cheque and debits your account. The cheque is then considered cancelled.

Goals

In this exploration, you will learn how to keep records of financial transactions such as deposits and withdrawals.

New Terms

overdraw: to take out more money than is in your account.

Example 1

David Hartley had a balance of $231.18 in his account. On September 30, he wrote cheque #344 for $198.00 to Sears. On the same day he received a paycheque for $488.90. October 1, he wrote cheque #345 for $385.00 to Lane's Rental Group for his apartment rent. What is his balance?

Solution

To find his balance, record these transactions in a transaction record book like the one shown below.

Enter the cheque numbers in the first column, the dates in the second column, and a description of what was being paid or deposited in the third column. Under Payment/Debit, write what is paid out, and under Deposit/Credit, write the amount deposited. To find the balance, begin with the opening balance and subtract withdrawals and add deposits. The closing balance is $137.08.

Transaction Record

Cheque #	Date	Description	Payment/ Debit	√	Deposit/ Credit	Balance 231.18
344	30/09	Sears	198.00			33.18
DEP	30/09	paycheque			488.90	522.08
345	01/10	Lane's Rental Group	385.00			137.08

Project Activity

You will use the list of transactions you created in the last exploration to develop a sample transaction record. Enter your transactions and find the balance. Exchange your sample cheque book record with your partner and check each other's work.

With your partner, brainstorm ideas about why it is a good idea to keep accurate and complete business records. Add a paragraph to your project file that explains why recording your business transactions would be a wise idea.

Notebook Assignment

1. Monique runs a paper and catalogue delivery route. She has a transaction record book in which she records her business transactions. Examine the transaction record below and find Monique's closing balance.

Cheque #	Date	Description	Payment/ Debit	√	Deposit/ Credit	Balance 112.36
100	01/09	Howie's Hardware	25.99			
101	20/09	John's Garage	45.59			
DEP	26/09	paycheque			254.32	
102	27/09	COOP	52.99			

Transaction Record

2. Brock Welding has $2397.50 in a chequing account. On May 3rd, $625.00 was deposited to the account. Brock Welding wrote the following cheques to pay some bills: May 7, #45, Auto Oil for $76.00; May 8, #46, BC Hydro for $67.40; May 8, #47, Telus for $24.90; and May 15, #48, Honda Leasing for $217.00. Find the new balance.

3. The balance in Mary Wong's account on September 8 is $998.43. She wrote the following cheques: September 9, #243, The Bay for $48.00; September 13, #244, Esso for $43.87; September 20, #245, B.C. Hydro for $66.98. On September 25, Mary deposited $200.00. On September 30, she wrote another cheque, #246, to Dale's Rental Agency for $475.00. Enter Mary's transactions in a transaction record and find her new balance.

4. Complete a transaction record for Mike Rarog and find his new balance. His opening balance on February 5 was $837.92. He wrote the following cheques: February 10, #162, Manitoba Hydro, $58.74; February 10, #163, Manitoba Telecom Services, $38.52; February 14, #164, VISA, $194.71; February 18, #165, Sam's Sports Hut, $89.66. He made the following deposits: February 17, $185.92; February 20, $300.00.

5. Complete a transaction record for Arielle Daniel and find her new balance. Arielle's opening balance on October 25 was $78.72. She wrote the following cheques: October 26, #72, Wayne's Gas Bar, $67.25; October 31, #73, C & B Rental Agencies, $400.00; November 4, #74, Baron's Department Store, $12.75; November 7, #75, Medical Ethics Association, $75.00. She also made the following deposits: October 28, $402.96; November 6, $90.82; November 10, $153.72.

6. Complete a transaction record for Kathy Kristensen. Her opening balance on December 1 was $426.97. She wrote the following cheques: December 4, #208, J & M Department Store, $67.25; December 7, #209, I Computer Store, $398.88; December 10, #210, Fast Gas Bar, $32.75; December 14, #211, Value Foods, $86.12. She also made the following deposits: December 2, $49.63; December 6, $250.00; December 11, $48.50. On December 15, Kathy withdrew $100.00 in cash. Find her closing balance.

Technology

Spreadsheets or personal finance software packages such as Quicken can help you manage your financial transactions.

7. Complete a transaction record for Khalid Bajwa. His opening balance on May 27 was $592.84. He wrote the following cheques: May 29, #98, Harrod's, $57.00; June 1, #99, Minister of Finance, $407.82; June 4, #100, World Wide Cable, $32.75; June 8, #101, Telus, $86.12. Khalid also made these deposits: June 2, $629.50; June 7, $80.00. He withdrew $400.00 in cash on June 5.

Extension

8. Your account has an opening balance of $345.78. You write one cheque to pay for a new CD ($17.99 plus tax) and another for a new pair of jeans ($49.99 plus tax). You then want a snack. Having no cash, you go to a bank machine and withdraw $10.00. Finally, you write a cheque for $75.64 (this price includes tax) for new work boots. Find your final balance.

Exploration 3

Using a Bank Card

Have you ever needed to pay for something when you had no cash with you? Perhaps you feel uncomfortable carrying a large amount of cash but want to be able to buy things when it is convenient. You may be too young to have a credit card, or you may not want one. In such situations, many consumers choose to use bank cards for their transactions.

Bank cards can be used as debit cards. A customer can buy items such as clothes or gasoline, and pay directly from his or her account using the bank card as long as the store uses the debit card network.

Bank cards can also be used to access automated teller machines (ATMs). ATMs are located in bank buildings, shopping malls, airports, convenience stores, and other public places. Most ATMs are easy to use if you follow the written instructions on the screen. You may use ATMs operated by financial institutions other than your own because they are linked to each other on a computer network. There is usually an extra fee for using a machine that does not belong to your bank.

Bank cards have encoded strips that enable customers to use an ATM or to make purchases in stores that accept debit cards. You need a Personal Identification Number (PIN) as well as your card to use a bank card. Your bank will issue you a PIN when it issues your card. To access your account, you slide your card into a slot and enter your PIN on the keypad. It is wise to keep your PIN a secret.

Goals

In this exploration, you will learn how to use a bank card as a debit card or to access your accounts through ATMs, and how to keep track of your bank card transactions.

Technology

Some ATMs print a receipt for each transaction, even if you make several at one time. Others print a receipt that includes all the transactions made at one time.

Example 1

Look at the receipt printed by an ATM after a customer has made a transaction. How much did the customer withdraw? How much was left in the account after the withdrawal? When was the withdrawal made? Why is the cardholder number printed this way? Why is it a good idea to keep your ATM receipts?

BANK OF EVERMORE
CARD NUMBER: 4518******5582
DATE: TIME: ATM:
06/01/02   12:09   1234567
Savings Account
Withdrawal $ 50.00
Account Balance $ 310.59
Transaction Record VA41-9039

Solution

The customer withdrew $50.00. The account balance is $310.59. The withdrawal was made January 6, 2002. The cardholder number is not printed in full so that other people cannot find out your number. It is not a good idea to discard your ATM receipts because you need them to record your transactions.

Example 2

The following is part of a bank statement for the account of Ryan Morrison. What is Ryan's starting balance? How much did he withdraw from his account in total? How much was deposited? What is his final balance?

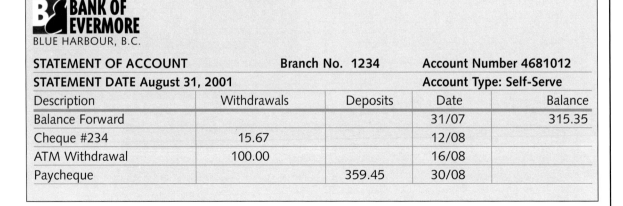

BANK OF EVERMORE
BLUE HARBOUR, B.C.

STATEMENT OF ACCOUNT		Branch No. 1234	Account Number 4681012	
STATEMENT DATE August 31, 2001			Account Type: Self-Serve	
Description	Withdrawals	Deposits	Date	Balance
Balance Forward			31/07	315.35
Cheque #234	15.67		12/08	
ATM Withdrawal	100.00		16/08	
Paycheque		359.45	30/08	

Solution

Ryan's starting balance is $315.35. The amount withdrawn in total is:

$15.67 + $100.00 = $115.67

The amount deposited is $359.45. Ryan's final balance is:

$315.35 − $115.67 + $359.45 = $559.13

Example 3

Examine the debit card receipt from Blockbuster Video. What do you notice about the cardholder number? Why might it not be a good idea to discard debit card receipts?

```
Blockbuster Video #62519
1022 Kingsway Vancouver BC

CARD NUMBER: 4617513055827582
ACCOUNT TYPE: SAVINGS
DATE/TIME: 2002/10/04 17:34:51
RECEIPT No. 1234567
PURCHASE AMOUNT $9.10

Approved Auth. #704489
```

Solution

The cardholder number is printed in full on the debit card receipt. It is not a good idea to discard debit card receipts for two reasons. First, you need them for your records. Second, someone might use your card number to make a counterfeit bank card.

Mental Math

1. A person withdraws $50.00 from an account that had $225.00 in it. How much is left?

2. Tom deposits $24.00 in an account. The new account balance is $144.00. How much did he have before he made the deposit?

3. Jillian deposits a $50.00 cheque, withdraws $25.00, and has $100.00 left in her account. How much was in her account before these transactions?

Small Group Activity

List advantages and disadvantages of using debit cards. Describe two transactions an individual might make with the assistance of a bank teller. Describe doing the same transactions and purchases using a bank card. How are they the same, and how are they different? Which is better? Why?

Notebook Assignment

1. Examine the ATM receipt below. How much money did the customer withdraw? How much is left in the account after the withdrawal? What type of account is it? When was the withdrawal made?

```
BANK OF EVERMORE
CARD NUMBER: 5419******4762
DATE:          TIME:        ATM:
30/07/02       11:46        1234567

Chequing Account

Withdrawal $ 50.00
Account Balance $ 275.39

Transaction Record VD41-9039
```

2. Taylor makes a bill payment of $35.50 to the phone company using an ATM. She withdraws $20.00. Create an ATM receipt that shows that she made the transactions and had $140.25 left in her savings account after these transactions.

Hint

Always keep your ATM receipts until you have updated your transaction record and reconciled your bank statement. If your bank has made an error, your ATM receipt is proof of the transaction.

3. James gets off work late at night. He has his paycheque with him and wants to deposit the cheque and withdraw some cash. What are his options?

4. Howard does all his banking using an ATM. He has $900.00 in his chequing account. On Friday, November 16, 2001, Howard deposits a paycheque for $1200.00 into his account. Next he withdraws $250.00 cash, and then he pays two bills for $234.00 and $150.00. Show Howard's ATM receipts in the order he made the transactions.

5. Describe a transaction you might make either with the assistance of a bank teller or with your bank card at an ATM. How are they the same? How are they different? Which method do you prefer? Explain your preference.

6. List three advantages and three disadvantages of using an ATM.

Extension

7. Timothy is travelling in the United States and uses his bank card to obtain $50.00 US in cash. In addition to the $50.00, he is charged a $1.00 US service charge for the withdrawal. The day he withdraws the cash, $1.00 Cdn is worth $0.66 US. How much in Canadian dollars will be deducted from his account?

Problem Analysis

Networks

Part A

Try to draw each of the figures on the right using a continuous line without drawing any arc or segment twice.

For example:

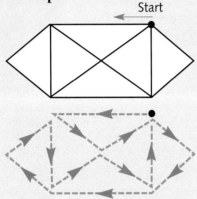

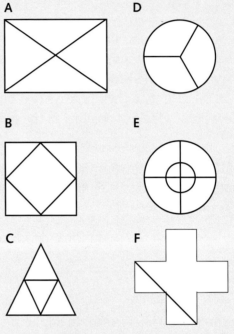

For each figure, count the number of edges (arcs or segments) meeting at a vertex. Use this to help you find a rule that works for any network.

Part B

A famous network problem is the Königsberg Bridges problem. The drawing below shows the river that runs through the city of Königsberg. There are two islands in the river connected to each other and to the mainland by a series of bridges. Years ago, the citizens of the city, out for a Sunday afternoon stroll, would try to take a walk during which they would cross over each bridge exactly once and end up back at their starting point. To determine if this is possible, draw the Königsberg bridges as a network.

Hint: Taking a Sunday afternoon walk is the same as drawing the arcs or segments in Part A.

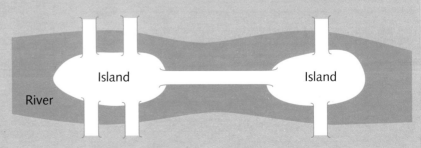

Games

The Game of Nab

This game for two people is played on a triangle of circles. Players decide who is to make the first move. Take turns. Each move consists of drawing a segment through the diameters of adjacent circles. As few as one and as many as five circles can be "crossed off" in one turn. A player cannot draw a diameter through a circle that already has one. A player must draw diameters in a straight "line." The player who draws the last diameter loses.

This is an example of a **legal** move. The line crosses through four adjacent circles.

This is an example of an illegal move. The line crosses through a previously drawn diameter.

This is an example of an illegal move. The diagonal line drawn is tangent to circles on the game board.

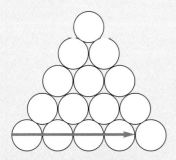
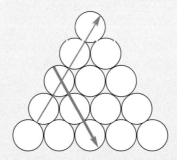
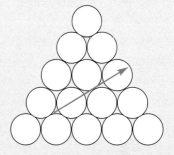

This is an example of a **legal** move. This line crosses through three adjacent circles.

This is an example of an illegal move. The line drawn changes direction to cross off three more circles.

This is an example of an illegal move. The vertical line drawn is tangent to circles on the game board.

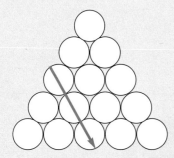
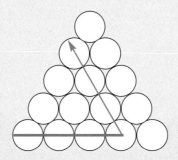
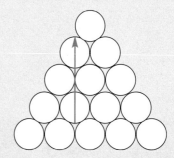

Play the game using a game board like the one shown. Try to find a strategy so you can always win.

Exploration 4

Reconciling a Bank Statement

Every month your bank may send you a statement that lists all your transactions. You need to reconcile this statement with your transaction record book so that you know that neither you nor the bank has made any errors. Reconciling your statement means checking that the entries the bank has listed correspond to your own entries.

The balance on the statement may not match your transaction record book, because you probably will have made some further transactions after the date the statement was issued. One way to reconcile the bank statement with your transaction record book is to account for any transactions made after the statement date. To do this, subtract any deposits and add any withdrawals. You will likely need to enter a service charge from the statement on your transaction record. Then your transaction record balance as of the statement date should match the bank statement.

Your bank statement usually has a reconciliation form printed on the back that you can use to reconcile your account.

Goals

In this exploration, you will learn to reconcile a bank statement with your transaction record book.

New Terms

reconcile: to make one account record consistent with another.

service charge: a fee that the bank charges to your account for its services.

Example 1

There are 3 errors and/or omissions in the transaction record below. Compare the transaction record to the bank statement for this account. Identify the errors/omissions in the transaction record. Assume the bank statement is correct.

BANK OF EVERMORE
BLUE HARBOUR, B.C.

STATEMENT OF ACCOUNT		Branch No. 1570	Account Number 569495	
STATEMENT DATE May 30, 2001			Account Type: Self-Serve	
Description	Withdrawals	Deposits	Date	Balance
Balance Forward			01/05	825.43
Deposit		85.00	04/05	910.43
Cheque #237	100.00		04/05	810.43
Cheque #238	139.09		08/05	671.34
Cheque #239	75.00		08/05	596.34
Deposit		450.00	09/05	1046.34
Cheque #240	217.87		12/05	828.47
Cheque #241	25.00		21/05	803.47
Cheque #242	550.00		28/05	253.47
Cheque #243	48.93		30/05	204.54

Transaction Record

Cheque #	Date	Description	Payment/ Debit	√	Deposit/ Credit	Balance
						825.43
	04/05	deposit			85.00	910.43
237	04/05	cash	100.00			810.43
238	08/05	J & M Dept. Stores	139.90			670.53
239	08/05	Humane Society	75.00			595.53
	09/05	deposit			400.00	995.53
241	21/05	L. Bicks	25.00			970.53
242	23/05	rent	550.00			420.53
243	28/05	groceries	48.93			371.60

Solution

The three errors/omissions in the transaction record are:
a) May 8: The debit amount should be $139.09.
b) May 9: The deposit amount should be $450.00.
c) Cheque #240 in the amount of $217.87 has been left out of the transaction record.

Example 2

Denise Lacroix's bank statement and her transaction record are shown below. Why isn't the balance the same on both items?

BANK OF EVERMORE
BLUE HARBOUR, B.C.

STATEMENT OF ACCOUNT   Branch No. 1570   **Account Number 569495**

STATEMENT DATE September 25, 2001   **Account Type: Self-Serve**

Description	Withdrawals	Deposits	Date	Balance
Balance Forward				20.51
Deposit		600.00	11/09	620.51
Cheque #98	450.50		20/09	170.01
Cheque #99	30.00		22/09	140.01
Deposit		15.00	22/09	155.01
Service Charge	9.50		25/09	145.51

Transaction Record

Cheque #	Date	Description	Payment/ Debit	√	Deposit/ Credit	Balance
						20.51
DEP	11/09	paycheque		√	600.00	620.51
98	16/09	Ski & Sport Shop	450.50	√		170.01
99	17/09	Telus	30.00	√		140.01
DEP	18/09	deposit cheque		√	15.00	155.01
100	24/09	gas	14.95			140.06
101	25/09	Shopper's Drug Mart	5.03			135.03
DEP	26/09	deposit			87.00	222.03
102	27/09	oil for car	4.95			217.08
103	28/09	Safeway	17.93			199.15

Hint

Remember to record service charges listed on your bank statement in your transaction record.

Solution

The balances are not equal for several reasons. First, there are some outstanding cheques. A cheque is outstanding if you have written it but the recipient has not yet cashed it. Since it has not been cashed, your bank has not deducted the money from your account. Cheques #100, #101, #102, and #103 are outstanding.

Second, a deposit of $87.00 was made after the statement was printed.

Third, the bank subtracted $9.50 from the account. This is a service charge the bank takes for handling the account.

You can find the correct balance in the account by checking off all the items that appear on both the statement and the cheque book record. This means you have checked that your transactions have cleared your bank account and are complete. You can also complete the reconciliation form on the back of your account statement. Look at the completed example below.

BANK OF EVERMORE
BLUE HARBOUR, B.C.

STATEMENT OF RECONCILIATION

Bank Statement	Transaction Record
FINAL BALANCE shown on this statement	FINAL BALANCE shown in transaction record
$ 145.51	$ 199.15
ADD DEPOSITS made after the statement date	SUBTRACT WITHDRAWALS which are not shown in transaction record
$87.00	Service charge $9.50
SUBTOTAL $ 232.51	
SUBTRACT WITHDRAWALS made after the statement date	
$14.95	
$5.03	
$4.95	
$17.93	
FINAL BALANCE $ 189.65	FINAL BALANCE $189.65

Career Connection

Name: Michel Gagnon

Job: ski instructor at Fernie, B.C.

Current wages: $11.70 an hour

Education: grade 12; Canadian Ski Instructors Alliance Level 1 training

Background skills and knowledge: expert skier

Career goal: ski school manager at a ski resort

Keyword search: CSIA ski instructor

Hint

If you make a mistake while writing a cheque, void the cheque and mark it in your transaction record as a void cheque. That way you will know that there isn't a cheque with that number that has not been cashed.

Notebook Assignment

1. Compare the following monthly account statement with its transaction record. The bank statement is correct, but there is one error or omission in the transaction record. Locate the error or omission and make the necessary change in the transaction record (sometimes called a cheque record).

BANK OF EVERMORE
BLUE HARBOUR, B.C.

STATEMENT OF ACCOUNT Branch No. 1234 **Account Number 4681012**

STATEMENT DATE February 28, 2001 **Account Type: Self-Serve**

Description	Withdrawals	Deposits	Date	Balance
Balance Forward			01/02	362.54
Deposit		400.00	01/02	762.54
Cheque #183	25.16		04/02	737.38
Cheque #181	32.27		05/02	705.11
Cheque #184	465.00		09/02	240.11
Deposit		400.00	15/02	640.11
Cheque #186	126.50		20/02	513.61
Cheque #185	84.25		22/02	429.36
Cheque #187	19.98		28/08	409.38

Transaction Record			Payment/	√	Deposit/	Balance
Cheque #	Date	Description	Debit		Credit	362.54
DEP	01/02	deposit			400.00	762.54
181	03/02	Photocopies for Less	32.27			730.27
182	03/02	M. Fenster	82.60			647.67
183	03/02	Wholesome Foods	25.16			622.51
184	04/02	Q + R Rental Agency	465.00			157.51
DEP	15/02	deposit			400.00	557.51
185	17/02	Budget Dept. Store	84.25			473.26
186	19/02	Zack's Electronics	126.00			347.26
187	25/02	Terry's Photos	19.98			327.28
DEP	02/03	deposit			400.00	727.28

2. Compare the following monthly account statement with its transaction record. There is one error or omission in the transaction record. Locate the error or omission and make the necessary change in the cheque register.

BANK OF EVERMORE
BLUE HARBOUR, B.C.

STATEMENT OF ACCOUNT   Branch No. 1234   **Account Number 46997720**

STATEMENT DATE January 31, 2001   **Account Type: Chequing**

Description	Withdrawals	Deposits	Date	Balance
Balance Forward			01/01	527.84
Cheque #156	50.00		04/01	477.84
Cheque #158	232.17		04/01	245.67
Cheque #157	28.75		08/01	216.92
Cheque #159	31.03		08/01	185.89
Deposit		450.00	10/01	635.89
Cheque #161	78.29		18/01	557.60
Cheque #163	42.80		18/01	514.80
Cheque #162	64.20		20/01	450.60
Cheque #164	95.80		28/01	354.80

Transaction Record

Cheque #	Date	Description	Payment/ Debit	√	Deposit/ Credit	Balance 527.84
156	02/01	L. Patterson	50.00			477.84
157	03/01	Mastercard	28.75			449.09
158	03/01	Baron's Dept. Store	232.17			216.92
159	06/01	High Teck Hair	31.03			185.89
	10/01	deposit			450.00	635.89
160	16/01	Smith Photos	28.00			607.89
161	17/01	Centra Gas	78.29			529.60
162	17/01	Manitoba Hydro	64.20			465.40
163	17/01	Manitoba Telecom	42.80			422.60
165	01/02	home insurance	260.00			162.60

3. Reconcile this account using the bank statement and transaction record below.

BANK OF EVERMORE
BLUE HARBOUR, B.C.

STATEMENT OF ACCOUNT   Branch No. 1579   Account Number 5333499

STATEMENT DATE August 30, 2001   Account Type: Chequing

Description	Withdrawals	Deposits	Date	Balance
Balance Forward			20/06	1175.39
Cheque #66	40.00		26/06	1135.39
Deposit		850.00	30/06	1985.39
Cheque #67	25.92		14/07	1959.47
Cheque #68	104.00		15/07	1855.47
Cheque #69	346.00		15/07	1509.47
Cheque #70	177.54		09/08	1331.93
Cheque #71	68.56		12/08	1263.37
Cheque #72	23.16		16/08	1240.21
Cheque #73	40.00		19/08	1200.21
Cheque #74	35.20		19/08	1165.01
Service Charge	11.60		30/08	1153.41

Transaction Record

Cheque #	Date	Description	Payment/ Debit	√	Deposit/ Credit	Balance
						1175.39
66	25/06	cash	40.00			1135.39
DEP	30/06	deposit			850.00	1985.39
67	08/07	Shopper's Drug Mart	25.92			1959.47
68	08/07	Autopac	104.00			1855.47
69	08/07	car payment	346.00			1509.47
70	07/08	eaton's	177.54			1331.93
71	09/08	B.C. Hydro	68.56			1263.37
72	12/08	Telus	23.16			1240.21
73	13/08	Sears	40.00			1200.21
74	16/08	IGA	35.20			1165.01
75		Void Cheque				1165.01
76	23/08	Esso	35.00			1130.01
77	24/08	Radio Shack	27.95			1102.06
78	24/08	Future Shop	16.36			1085.70
DEP	30/08	deposit			700.00	1785.70
DEP	01/09	deposit			30.00	1815.70

4. Using the bank statement and transaction record below, complete a reconciliation statement.

BANK OF EVERMORE
BLUE HARBOUR, B.C.

STATEMENT OF ACCOUNT		Branch No. 1579	Account Number 5113400	
STATEMENT DATE November 29, 2001			Account Type: Self-Serve	
Description	Withdrawals	Deposits	Date	Balance
Balance Forward			01/11	127.18
Deposit		520.15	01/11	647.33
Cheque #346	425.00		07/11	222.33
Cheque #347	57.66		10/11	164.67
Deposit		80.89	10/11	245.56
Cheque #348	42.38		12/11	203.18
Cheque #350	103.56		15/11	99.62
Deposit		420.15	15/11	519.77
Cheque #349	144.34		16/11	375.43
Cheque #352	125.00		25/11	250.43
Cheque#353	36.15		29/11	214.28
Service Charge	14.75		29/11	199.53

Transaction Record

Cheque #	Date	Description	Payment/ Debit	√	Deposit/ Credit	Balance 127.18
	01/11	deposit			520.15	647.33
346	01/11	rent	425.00			222.33
347	06/11	Big Eagle Foods	57.66			164.67
348	10/11	hydro	42.38			122.29
	10/11	deposit			80.89	203.18
	12/11	deposit			420.15	623.33
349	12/11	car repair	144.34			478.99
350	15/11	Thiessen's General Store	103.56			375.43
351	15/11	Void Cheque				375.43
352	20/11	bike repair	125.00			250.43
353	25/11	Revy	36.15			214.28
354	31/11	Big Eagle Foods	54.76			159.52
	31/11	deposit			45.00	204.52

5. Fill out a statement of reconciliation for the following bank statement and transaction record.

BANK OF EVERMORE
BLUE HARBOUR, B.C.

STATEMENT OF ACCOUNT		Branch No. 1571	Account Number 53243496	
STATEMENT DATE September 10, 2001			Account Type: Self-Serve	
Description	Withdrawals	Deposits	Date	Balance
Balance Forward				350.00
Deposit		452.51	21/08	802.51
Cheque #98	102.90		23/08	699.61
Cheque #99	141.12		24/08	558.49
Cheque #100	24.88		24/08	533.61
Cheque #101	56.70		25/08	476.91
Deposit		215.00	27/08	691.91
Deposit		280.00	30/08	971.91
Cheque #102	125.45		05/09	846.46
Service Charge	8.75		09/09	837.71

Transaction Record						
Cheque #	Date	Description	Payment/ Debit	√	Deposit/ Credit	Balance 350.00
DEP	21/08	deposit			452.51	802.51
98	21/08	Esso (gas, oil, and lube)	102.90			699.61
99	22/08	OK Tires	141.12			558.49
100	22/08	Telus	24.88			533.61
101	22/08	BC Hydro	56.70			476.91
DEP	27/08	deposit			215.00	691.91
DEP	30/08	deposit			280.00	971.91
102	01/09	Pete's Shack	125.45			846.46
103	03/09	ICBC	211.11			635.35
DEP	06/09	deposit			2000.00	2635.35
104	07/09	Sears	854.00			1781.35
105	07/09	Chevron (gas, oil)	57.10			1724.25
106	08/09	eaton's	146.58			1577.67

6. Reconcile the monthly account statement below to the corresponding transaction record.

BANK OF EVERMORE
BLUE HARBOUR, B.C.

STATEMENT OF ACCOUNT		Branch No. 1234	Account Number 973-X0J-12	
STATEMENT DATE November 30, 2001			Account Type: Chequing	
Description	Withdrawals	Deposits	Date	Balance
Balance Forward			01/11	1567.24
Deposit		48.26	03/11	1615.50
Cheque #147	348.78		10/11	1266.72
Deposit		728.35	16/11	1995.07
Cheque #148	43.60		20/11	1951.47
Deposit		149.90	23/11	2101.37
Cheque #149	1252.95		23/11	848.42
Cheque #151	54.55		30/11	793.87
Cheque #150	19.21		30/11	774.66
Cheque #152	42.78		30/11	731.88
Service Charge	5.50		30/11	726.38

Transaction Record

Cheque #	Date	Description	Payment/ Debit	√	Deposit/ Credit	Balance
						1567.24
DEP	09/11	deposit			48.26	1615.50
147	09/11	Econo Airlines	348.78			1266.72
DEP	16/11	deposit			728.35	1995.07
148	18/11	For-Life Health Insurance	43.60			1951.47
149	20/11	computer upgrade	1252.95			698.52
DEP	23/11	deposit			149.90	848.42
150	28/11	World Wide Cable	19.21			829.21
151	28/11	Centra Gas	54.55			774.66
152	28/11	Manitoba Hydro	42.78			731.88
153	28/11	Manitoba Telecom	37.32			694.56
DEP	01/12	deposit			724.32	1418.88
154	03/12	car repairs	385.46			1033.42

7. Reconcile the monthly account statement below to the transaction record for that account.

BANK OF EVERMORE
BLUE HARBOUR, B.C.

STATEMENT OF ACCOUNT		Branch No. 4056		Account Number 278-902XJ	
STATEMENT DATE August 31, 2001				Account Type: Self-Serve	
Description	Withdrawals	Deposits	Date		Balance
Balance Forward			01/08		523.87
Deposit		475.00	01/08		998.87
Cheque #52	23.96		07/08		974.91
Cheque #53	78.24		10/08		896.67
Deposit		73.21	12/08		969.88
Cheque #55	38.56		16/08		931.32
Cheque #56	158.20		20/08		773.12
Cheque #58	148.37		22/08		624.75
Deposit		450.00	26/08		1074.75
Cheque #59	28.62		27/08		1046.13
Cheque #60	26.17		29/08		1019.96
Cheque #61	100.00		31/08		919.96
Service Charge	5.00		31/08		914.96

Transaction Record

Cheque #	Date	Description	Payment/ Debit	√	Deposit/ Credit	Balance
						523.87
DEP	01/08	deposit			475.00	998.47
#52	05/08	H & D Hardware	23.96			974.91
#53	09/08	Advance Tickets (concert)	78.24			896.67
#54	10/08	R. Mills (music lessons)	80.00			816.67
DEP	12/08	deposit			73.21	889.88
#55	14/08	Artist's Supplies (paints)	38.56			851.32
#56	18/08	Kozy Clothing (jacket)	158.20			693.12
#57	19/08	Rosie's Flowers	37.24			655.88
#58	19/08	J&M Dept. Stores (gift)	148.37			507.51
#59	23/08	Fantastic Dry Cleaning	28.62			478.89
DEP	26/08	deposit			450.00	928.89
#60	28/08	Well-Read Books	26.17			902.72
#61	28/08	cash	100.00			802.72
#62	30/08	VISA	395.25			407.47

8. Reconcile the monthly account statement below to the transaction record for the account.

BANK OF EVERMORE
BLUE HARBOUR, B.C.

STATEMENT OF ACCOUNT		Branch No. 4056	Account Number 444-678-1	
STATEMENT DATE September 28, 2001			Account Type: Self-Serve	
Description	Withdrawals	Deposits	Date	Balance
Balance Forward			01/09	212.85
Deposit		645.15	03/09	858.00
Cheque #256	435.00		08/09	423.00
Cheque #257	79.63		11/09	343.37
Deposit		648.23	16/09	991.60
Cheque #260	29.04		16/09	962.56
Cheque #259	36.94		17/09	925.62
Cheque #258	23.16		17/09	902.46
Cheque #261	94.20		20/09	808.26
Cheque #263	127.89		28/09	680.37

Transaction Record

Cheque #	Date	Description	Payment/ Debit	√	Deposit/ Credit	Balance
						212.85
DEP	03/09	deposit			645.15	858.00
256	06/09	rent	435.00			423.00
257	10/09	groceries	79.63			343.37
258	14/09	Centra Gas	23.16			320.21
259	14/09	Manitoba Hydro	36.94			283.27
260	14/09	Manitoba Telecom	29.04			254.23
DEP	16/09	deposit			648.23	902.46
261	18/09	Baron's Dept. Store	94.20			808.26
262	22/09	music lessons	56.00			752.26
263	24/09	roller blades	127.89			624.37
264	27/09	groceries	61.16			563.21
DEP	30/09	deposit			647.21	1210.42
265	01/10	subscription	45.98			1164.44
DEP	03/10	deposit			50.00	1214.44

9. Reconcile the monthly account statement below to the corrected
transaction record for this account.

BANK OF EVERMORE
BLUE HARBOUR, B.C.

STATEMENT OF ACCOUNT		Branch No. 1579	Account Number 5113400	
STATEMENT DATE July 31, 2001			Account Type: Self-Serve	
Description	Withdrawals	Deposits	Date	Balance
Balance Forward			01/07	1522.71
Cheque #90	231.80		04/07	1290.91
Cheque #92	25.00		06/07	1265.91
Deposit		484.24	09/07	1750.15
Cheque #94	36.12		26/07	1714.03
Cheque #97	104.86		29/07	1609.17
Cheque #96	42.73		30/07	1566.44
Cheque #95	15.00		31/07	1551.44
Service Charge	5.00		31/07	1546.44

Transaction Record

Cheque #	Date	Description	Payment/ Debit	√	Deposit/ Credit	Balance 1522.71
90	02/07	Econo Airlines	231.80	√		1290.91
91	03/07	E. Cadlof	25.00			1265.91
92	05/07	P. Anders	25.00	√		1240.91
DEP	09/07	deposit		√	484.24	1725.15
93	12/07	music lesson	28.00			1697.15
94	24/07	J&M Dept. Stores	36.12	√		1661.03
96	24/07	Outdoor Supplies	42.73	√		1618.30
97	25/07	Value Foods	(104.68)	√		1513.62
DEP	03/08	deposit			482.53	1996.15
98	04/08	Bob's 24-Hour Shops	88.23			1907.92
		Correction: #95 omitted	15.00			1892.92
		Correction				
		#97 should be $104.86	.18			1892.74

Extension

10. Suppose you completed a reconciliation and found that you could not balance the bank's statement with your records. When you rechecked the bank statement you found that a transaction for a purchase from a local store had been debited from your account twice. List several reasons why this might have happened. Describe what you could do to correct the situation. Would you visit the store to explain the problem, or would the bank be the place to start? What records would be good to have with you? Why might it be a good idea to photocopy the records before you gave them to the bank or store? Would it be a good idea to report something like this to the police?

Exploration 5

Choosing the Best Account

A typical bank offers many types of accounts. It can be a challenge to find out which accounts offer the best features at the best price for your needs. Banks will often help customers select an account if they are able to explain what type of transactions they need or want to make. If you write a lot of cheques, for example, you may need a different type of account than a person who writes few cheques.

Banks charge monthly service fees for their accounts. Many accounts have a flat rate that covers a certain number of transactions of various types. Extra charges are added for transactions over that number. Some accounts are inexpensive, but require you to keep a minimum balance in the account to receive the low service charge.

Whole Class Activity

Brainstorm a list of transactions for which students are most likely to use a bank account. Describe the features of a bank account that would meet the needs of most students. As a class, decide what a reasonable service charge might be for such an account.

Goals

In this exploration, you will research bank accounts to find the most efficient and cost-effective accounts for various situations.

Value Account

Ideal if you prefer self-serve banking but do not have many transactions. Self-serve transactions include all transactions that don't need a bank teller to carry them out. These include writing cheques, ATM withdrawals and deposits, automated telephone or computer web transfers, and debit card transactions.

Monthly Fees and Rebates
- $3.95. If you maintain a $1000.00 balance, the monthly fee is waived.

Transactions
- 10 self-serve included, additional are $0.50 each
- 4 full-serve included, additional are $1.00 each

Record-Keeping Options
- monthly statement $2.00 a month or FREE passbook
- cheque return $2.00 per cheque
- additional fee waived for a credit card

Self-Serve Account

Good if you have an active account, pay bills by phone, and use the web and ATMs.

Monthly Fees and Rebates
- $6.95; maintain a $1500.00 balance and the monthly fee is waived

Transactions
- 20 self-serve included, additional are $0.50 each
- full-serve transactions are $1.00 each

Record-Keeping Options
- monthly statement $2.00 a month or FREE passbook
- cheque return $2.00 per cheque

STUDENTS
- full-time post-secondary students save 50% on the monthly fee
- no annual fee for a credit card

New Terms

full-serve transaction: when a teller performs a transaction.

self-serve transaction: when you perform a transaction at an ATM, by telephone, or on the web.

waive: in certain circumstances, a bank will not collect a service fee. In that case, the bank is said to waive the fee.

ull-Serve Account

If you like full-service, this is the account for you.

Monthly Fees and Rebates
- $9.95; if you maintain a $2000.00 balance, the monthly fee is waived

Transactions
- 25 self-serve or full-serve included; additional are $0.25 each

Record-Keeping Options
- monthly statement $2.00 per month or FREE passbook
- cheque return $2.00 per cheque
- additional fee waived for credit card

avings Account

If you make very few transactions, this is the best choice for you.

Debit Transactions
- 2 free, $1.25 each after that

Additional Fees
- bill payments and Interac™ purchases are $1.25 each plus an additional $1.25 debit fee

Record-Keeping Options
- monthly statement or passbook $1.00; free when minimum monthly balance is $1000.00

Additional Features
- daily interest that grows with your balance

Example 1

Françoise is trying to pick a bank account from the brochures shown previously. She is a college student and has $8000.00 in savings. Her monthly expenses are $2000.00. She estimates that she will need to write about 10 cheques each month and use her bank card for about 12 transactions. Which account would be her best choice?

Solution

Françoise could set up a table and enter the service charges she would likely be charged.

The table below shows that for some of the accounts the monthly fee would be zero, because she has the minimum balance for at least some of the months. For example, in the case of the value account, Françoise will have more than the required $2000 minimum balance for the first three months. Françoise also noticed that the self-serve account offers students a reduction of 50% on the monthly fees charged.

For Françoise, the least expensive account is the self-serve account.

	Month 1		Month 2		Month 3		Month 4		Total
Account	Monthly Fee	Transaction Charges	Monthly Fee	Transaction Charges	Monthly Fee	Transaction Charges	Monthly Fee	Transaction Charges	Charges for 4 Months
Value	$0	12 x $0.50 = $6.00	$0	12 x $0.50 = $6.00	$0	12 x $0.50 = $6.00	$3.95	12 x $0.50 =$6.00	$27.95
Self-Serve	$0	2 x $0.50 = $1.00	$0	2 x $0.50 = $1.00	$0	2 x $0.50 = $1.00	$3.48	2 x $0.50 = $1.00	$7.48
Full-Serve	$0	$0	$0	$0	$0	$0	$9.95	$0	$9.95

Technology

Many banks offer an account selector on their web sites. To use the account selector, you must know approximately what your minimum balance will be and how many transactions of each type you would normally use. Often, account selectors will generate a bar graph that shows the total service charges for each account.

Career Connection

Name: Françoise LeClaire

Job: student

Career goal: GIS technician

Education: grade 12 graduate; enrolled in a GIS technician course at the British Columbia Institute of Technology

Anticipated wages: $18.61 an hour

Keyword search: geographic information systems course Canada college

This GIS technician is working at a field camp in the Finlayson Lake area as part of the Yukon Geology Program.

Project Activity

For your small business, make a chart like the one made by Françoise. Using your own list of transactions, decide which type of bank account will best meet your needs. Add your chart and a statement justifying your choice to your project file.

Hints	New Terms	Technology
Bank web sites often explain their accounts and service charges.	**Interac™:** a computer network that gives people access to their money through banking machines and direct payment.	Visit www.interac.ca for information on the Interac network.

Notebook Assignment

Use the account descriptions shown previously to answer the following questions.

1. Gerard writes 25 cheques and makes 5 deposits each month. He keeps a monthly balance of no less than $5000. Which is the best account for him? State any assumptions you make. Calculate the costs of each and justify your choice.

2. Billy keeps as small a balance in her chequing account as possible. She has a savings account that pays interest based on a high minimum balance. However, Billy uses her chequing account for many things and makes an average of 60 self-serve transactions a month. Which account is best for her? Justify your answer.

3. What type of bank transactions would most students make? Collect information on different types of personal banking accounts. If possible, investigate different banks or other financial institutions. Information on accounts can be found on web sites, using banks' toll-free numbers, or by visiting financial institutions.

4. Use the information from question 3 to create a brochure that could be used by the bank. List the costs and benefits of each account.

Extension

5. A bank offers its customers two types of accounts. One type has a service charge of $15.00 a month and unlimited no-cost transactions. The other account charges $5.00 a month plus an additional $0.50 a transaction. At what number of transactions would the second account cost the same as the first account? Explain your reasoning.

Exploration 6

Internet and Telephone Banking

Suppose you were at work on a job in Yellowknife, NT and your bank branch was in Brandon, MB. How could you pay your bills? What if your band plays at Crofton Days on Vancouver Island, but you live in Surrey, BC and you need to transfer money from your savings account to your chequing account to cover an automatic withdrawal? What if you were visiting the United States and remembered a cell phone bill you had forgotten to pay? What if you were unable to go to your bank during business hours and wanted to check your account balance?

All of these situations can be handled by using a telephone or a computer. Most banks offer both telephone banking and internet banking services.

Keeping track of transactions that are made using the computer or telephone can sometimes be difficult because there is no paper receipt. Banks usually provide confirmation numbers for transactions that are done on the telephone or on the internet. Confirmation numbers should be recorded in your transaction record book.

Goals

In this exploration, you will learn about telephone and internet banking.

Example 1

Sean paid a $24.35 cable television bill from his chequing account using telephone banking. How could he record this transaction if his opening balance is $246.50?

Solution

Sean should write the transaction in his transaction record book as a debit, and record the confirmation number provided by the bank. He could use a code such as "TEL" to indicate that it is a telephone transaction. His bank will indicate that it was a telephone transaction on his monthly statement.

Transaction Record

Cheque #	Date	Description	Payment/ Debit	√	Deposit/ Credit	Balance
						246.50
TEL	05/08	cable tv bill (#12423)	24.35			222.15

Example 2

Michelle transferred $50.00 from her savings account to her chequing account using internet banking. Her savings account's opening balance is $624.80 and her chequing account's opening balance is $154.18. Show the transaction records for both accounts.

Solution

Michelle should record this transfer in the records for both accounts. She could record the debit from her savings account like this:

Transaction Record SAVINGS ACCOUNT #763-012

Cheque #	Date	Description	Payment/ Debit	√	Deposit/ Credit	Balance
						624.80
WWW	05/11	transfer to chequing (#4277)	50.00			574.80

She could record the deposit to her chequing account in her transaction record like this:

Transaction Record CHEQUING ACCOUNT 4J2-783-27						
Cheque #	Date	Description	Payment/ Debit	√	Deposit/ Credit	Balance 154.18
WWW	05/11	transfer from savings (#4283)			50.00	204.18

Small Group Activity

Research which bills can be paid using internet or telephone banking services. Many bank statements show electronic transactions occurring 1 or 2 business days after they are actually made. Why does this happen?

Hints

Financial institutions use various codes to identify transaction types. For example, some use WWW to show that a transaction was made on the internet. The codes your bank uses can be found on your account statement or you can ask for a list at your financial institution.

Notebook Assignment

1. On September 30, Steven paid his $45.56 gym fee by using telephone banking. How could he record this transaction?

2. On October 23, Leanne transferred $50.00 from her chequing account to her savings account using internet banking. How could she record this? Show both transaction records.

3. List three reasons for making sure that you record internet and telephone transactions as you make them.

4. Explain why you should record confirmation numbers for internet and telephone banking transactions.

5. Glenn visited his bank on December 11 and deposited a cheque for $450.00 into an account that had a previous balance of $210.00. Later that evening, he used the internet to pay two bills: $50.00 for locker rental and $40.00 for his cable internet account. The next morning he went shopping and bought new gym shorts for $23.00. He paid for them using his debit card. Next, he wrote cheque #354, dated December 12, 2002, for $56.78 to pay for new CDs. Create a transaction record that records these transactions and shows the final balance.

Extension

6. List several types of transactions you might make using the following: internet banking, telephone banking, debit card transaction, an ATM deposit, and a cheque. Create a transaction record form that shows each transaction. Include confirmation numbers where needed.

Chapter Review

1. Match each of the following terms (listed as 1 to 13) with its definition (listed as a to m).

1. interest rate
2. minimum monthly balance
3. deposit
4. PIN
5. cancelled cheque
6. service charge
7. cheque register
8. withdrawal
9. interest
10. ATM
11. minimum deposit
12. cheque
13. NSF cheque

a) money taken out of an account
b) a fee paid for using a service
c) a cheque written on an account that does not have enough money to cover the cheque
d) a cheque that has been cashed
e) the least amount of money that has been in a bank account during a month
f) a token amount of money given as a sign of good faith when opening a bank account
g) the percentage used to calculate the interest to be paid
h) the fee paid for the use of money
i) a book with space for you to note the details of every transaction in your chequing account
j) a unique identification number entered by a customer when using an ATM
k) a written order for payment of a certain amount of money
l) a self-service banking machine
m) money put into an account

2. Find five mistakes to avoid when using an automated teller machine as indicated in the following picture.

3. Terry Lynn is depositing the following items into her chequing account 22-763-4: twenty $2.00 coins; five $10.00 bills; twenty quarters; four dimes; six pennies; and three cheques for $14.67, $53.26, and $5.64. Fill in a deposit slip for her.

4. Fill in a deposit slip using the following information for Ida Chow. She is depositing 20 dimes, 4 one-dollar coins, 3 five-dollar bills, and three cheques for $24.20, $100.00, and $29.50 into her savings account 211-843-521. She withdraws $50.00 in cash at the same time.

5. Write out the following cheques:

    a) February 14, 2002, to Flowers for All Occasions for $39.90
    b) June 27, 2003, to the Folk on the Rocks for $88.00

6. Complete a transaction record for the following transactions. The balance on September 7 is $898.43. The following cheques were written: September 9, #43 for $47.00 to The Bay; September 13, #44 for $124.50 to Beaver Lumber. The following deposits were made: September 10, $110.50; September 14, $75.00; September 20, $41.80.

7. Complete a transaction record with the following transactions. The opening balance on September 1 was $822.34.

Cheques

Sept. 04	Cheque #26	Sports Wear	$54.90
Sept. 04	Cheque #27	Value Foods	$64.95
Sept. 10	Cheque #28	K. Tetley	$200.00
Sept. 21	Cheque #29	Holme's Rental Agency	$535.00
Sept. 23	Cheque #30	CD Music	$26.92
Oct. 2	Cheque #31	Fit Physiotherapy	$31.00

Deposits

Sept. 5	$535.00
Oct. 2	$250.00

8. Each month Wendy Chang reconciles her bank statement with her own records. The balance in Wendy's transaction record is $383.22. She has determined that she has an outstanding deposit of $203.14, and that cheque #361 for $109.20 and internet bill payment #98J24B for $123.56 are outstanding. Does her transaction record agree with her bank statement? Find the actual amount in her chequing account by completing a statement of reconciliation.

BANK OF EVERMORE
BLUE HARBOUR, B.C.

STATEMENT OF ACCOUNT		Branch No. 1570		Account Number 569495	
STATEMENT DATE April 30, 2001				Account Type: Chequing	
Description	Withdrawals	Deposits	Date		Balance
Balance Forward			31/03		141.16
Deposit		203.14	01/04		344.30
Cheque #353	63.10		08/04		281.20
Deposit		203.14	09/04		484.34
Deposit		80.89	10/04		565.23
Cheque #354	12.38		13/04		552.85
Cheque #355	25.00		14/04		527.85
Deposit		203.14	16/04		730.99
Cheque #356	33.56		19/04		697.43
Cheque #357	36.15		20/04		661.28
Cheque #358	27.96		23/04		633.32
Cheque #359	57.66		26/04		575.66
Cheque #360	144.34		28/04		431.32
Cheque #362	18.48		29.04		412.84
Service Charges	14.75		30/04		398.09

9. Reconcile the following bank statement with its cheque register. There are two errors and/or omissions in the cheque register. Before filling out the statement of reconciliation, make the necessary changes in the cheque register.

BANK OF EVERMORE
BLUE HARBOUR, B.C.

STATEMENT OF ACCOUNT		Branch No. 100		Account Number 52273XJ
STATEMENT DATE January 31, 2001				Account Type: Self-Serve
Description	Withdrawals	Deposits	Date	
Balance Forward			01/01	430.64
Cheque #126	107.22		04/01	323.42
Cheque #127	25.00		07/01	298.42
Deposit		863.91	16/01	1162.33
Cheque #129	523.37		23/01	638.96
Cheque #130	64.20		23/01	574.76
Cheque #132	37.28		27/01	537.48
Service Charge	4.50		31/01	532.98

Transaction Record

Cheque #	Date	Description	Payment/ Debit	√	Deposit/ Credit	Balance
						430.64
126	02/01	Kathy's Clothing	107.22			323.42
127	06/01	W. Wallace	25.00			298.42
DEP	16/01	deposit			863.19	1161.61
128	20/01	Paul's Custom Tailors	112.95			1048.66
129	21/01	rent	523.37			525.29
130	21/01	cleaning company	64.00			461.29
131	22/01	Dr. Payne	82.28			379.01
132	25/01	Foods-to-Go Deli	37.28			341.73
133	31/01	McPhillips Gallery	44.12			297.61
DEP	02/02	deposit			200.00	497.61

10. Use a blank cheque form to write a cheque from yourself to Frankie's CD House in the amount of $27.49. Use today's date.

11. Raquel's bank charges $4.95 each month plus $0.50 a transaction. On average, she makes 25 transactions a month. Wilfred's bank charges $1.00 for each transaction but has no monthly charge. How many transactions would Wilfred need to make for his account to be more expensive than Raquel's?

12. Yanu's bank balance is $75.50. He deposits a cheque for $72.34. If Yanu uses his bank card to buy books for $39.99, what is his new bank balance?

Project Presentation

Develop a presentation about the banking needs of your small business using the items in your file:

- a list of possible transactions for your business
- a sample chequebook record
- a paragraph explaining the need for accurate record-keeping
- the type of bank account that would best fit your business needs

Your presentation may take any form you choose. It could be an oral presentation to the class, or a recording on audiotape or videotape. You could develop a poster presentation that includes the materials from your file and summarizes them in a flow chart. You could prepare a short written report entitled "Banking Needs of My Business." Another possibility is to create a Power Point presentation.

   If you have worked on this project with a partner, include a statement in your presentation about the benefits of having a business partner.

Case Study

• • • • • • • • • • • • • • •

Casey Williams–Student Entrepreneur

Casey Williams operates a mountain bike repair shop at his home. He is an excellent cyclist and has learned over the years to repair and tune up bicycles like an expert. Show Casey's transactions for each of the following:

1. Casey makes out cheque #204 on June 15, 2002 for $27.31. This cheque is to pay for parts he has ordered from an internet supplier, Pedals R Us. Using a cheque template, complete the cheque for Casey.

2. Casey wants to deposit a cheque for $123.32, two $20.00 bills, and five $1.00 coins into his chequing account 268983-4 on June 16, 2002. Fill out a deposit slip showing his deposit.

3. Bring Casey's transaction record book up to date by entering the transactions in questions 1 and 2. The starting balance is $300.27. Enter Casey's final balance in the transaction record.

Transaction Record

Cheque #	Date	Description	Payment/ Debit	√	Deposit/ Credit	Balance 300.27
205	17/06	Mountain Tires	128.96			
DEP	18/06	deposit			206.46	
206	21/06	Mountain Bike Association	50.00			
207	22/06	Overland Bikes & Helmet	286.23			
DEP	24/06	deposit			75.29	
DEP	25/06	deposit			196.96	
208	01/07	Cross Country 2001 Registration Fees	75.00			
DEP	02/07	deposit			1500.00	

4. Reconcile Casey's monthly statement with his transaction record in question 3.

BANK OF EVERMORE
BLUE HARBOUR, B.C.

STATEMENT OF ACCOUNT		Branch No. 107		Account Number 268983-4
STATEMENT DATE July 10, 2002				Account Type: Chequing
Description	Withdrawals	Deposits	Date	Balance
Balance Forward				300.27
Deposit		168.32	16/06	468.59
Deposit		206.46	18/06	675.05
#204	27.31		19/06	647.74
#205	128.96		20/06	518.78
Deposit		75.29	24/06	594.07
Deposit		196.96	25/06	791.03
#207	286.23		25/06	504.80
Deposit		1500.00	02/07	2004.80
Service Fees	4.50		10/07	2000.30

5. Casey has used his account for both his business and personal banking. He wants to open a new chequing account just for his business transactions. He estimates that he will write 12 cheques, make 10 deposits, and use his bank card 8 times in an average month. Using the information about bank accounts provided in this chapter, choose the account that will be best for his business. Explain why you made this choice.

Chapter 3
....
Spreadsheets

Power Tools

Think of a spreadsheet program as an extremely quick and powerful tool that can track, calculate, organize, and analyze large quantities of data. Do you know any people who use spreadsheets in their jobs? If so, how do they use them? Can you think of a way you could use a spreadsheet in your everyday life?

Small businesses often rely on spreadsheets to do payroll, inventory, budgets, supply orders, and bookkeeping. Imagine that you own a small, trendy coffee shop. How might you use spreadsheets to help you run your business efficiently and effectively? Through a number of activities, this chapter will show you many ways that spreadsheets can be used.

While this chapter specifically uses Microsoft Excel, there are several other spreadsheet programs that are equally useful, such as Lotus 1-2-3, Quatro Pro, Appleworks, and Microsoft Works.

Chapter Goals

In this chapter, you will learn how to create spreadsheets in Microsoft Excel using various formatting options, formulas, and functions. You will use spreadsheets to solve problems and answer "what if" questions. Finally, you will identify where spreadsheets could be used effectively.

Chapter Project

Your project in this chapter is to plan a new neighbourhood coffee shop.
You will collect and record a variety of related information in your project
file. You will research prices for a variety of food items to sell in your
coffee shop. Once you have developed a plan, you will calculate the daily
profit of your coffee shop.

Career Connection

Name: Carole Johnson

Job: assistant manager of small
restaurant

Current wages: $9.50 per hour

Education: grade 12; community
college hospitality program

Career goal: restaurant owner

Keyword search: food service
hospitality Canada college

Refilling sugar servers at the Miss Spuzzum Café.

Project Activity

Begin the project by creating a title page to place in your file.
Add a list of ten to fifteen items you want to sell in your shop.
Include items such as coffee, tea, muffins, cookies, and coffee mugs.

Exploration 1

The Basics of Spreadsheets

Much like a word processing program, a spreadsheet program has special terms and functions. You need to become comfortable with the language of spreadsheets in order to use them effectively. Once you have learned the basics, you will be able to start designing your own spreadsheets.

Example 1

A spreadsheet is a computerized chart with vertical columns and horizontal rows. The boxes inside a spreadsheet are called cells. How many columns, rows, and cells does the following spreadsheet have? In which cell is the number 182?

Solution

This spreadsheet has 6 columns and 8 rows. That means there are 48 cells. Notice that columns are identified by letters and rows are identified by numbers. These are used to determine the cell address. The number 182 is located in cell D4.

	A	B	C	D	E	F
1						
2						
3						
4				182		
5						
6						
7						
8						

Three types of information can be entered into a cell: labels, values, and formulas. Labels are words that identify a column, row, or cell. Think of a label as a title. Values are numbers that are entered into a cell, such as 182 in Example 1. Formulas are mathematical expressions. These are the most powerful part of a spreadsheet. A formula can do a calculation involving many cells and display the answer in the cell containing the formula. The formula itself only appears in the formula bar at the top of the spreadsheet. In Exploration 3, you will learn how to work with formulas in spreadsheets.

Goals

In this exploration, you will learn the names for the parts of a spreadsheet and how to enter data into one.

Example 2

The following spreadsheet calculates term marks for four students. Do cells B5, C1, and E2 contain labels, values, or formulas?

	A	B	C	D	E	F
1	NAME	Assignments (120 marks)	Project (80 marks)	Tests (60 marks)	FINAL MARK	
2	Crystal	88	75	31	75	
3	Marie	72	58	39	65	
4	Stefan	103	64	48	83	
5	David	49	42	51	55	
6						
7	CLASS AVERAGE				70	
8						
9						
10						

Solution

While it is difficult to determine whether these cells contain labels, values, or formulas without seeing the spreadsheet on a computer, we can make reasonable guesses about what the cells contain based on what we already know. Since cell B5 has the number 49 in it, this cell probably contains a value. Since cell C1 has words in it, this cell likely contains a label. Although cell E2 appears to contain the number 75, it is possible that there is a formula that calculates Crystal's final mark. The label provides a hint that this column performs a calculation. To be sure, we would have to put the cursor in cell E2 and see what is revealed in the formula bar at the top of the spreadsheet.

Example 3

Open a new spreadsheet and complete the following instructions. In cell A1, type "Courses for." In cell A2, enter your name. In the cells as shown in column A, enter the courses you are currently taking. In cell B4, type "Grades." Enter an estimated letter grade for each course in the cells in column B. In cell C4, type "Absences." In the cells in column C, enter the number of times you estimate that you have been absent from each of your courses.

Solution

Your spreadsheet should look something like the following.

	A	B	C	D
1	Courses for			
2	"Your Name"			
3				
4		Grades	Absences	
5	English	C	2	
6	Mathematics	B	1	
7	Science	C-	5	
8	Social Studies	C+	2	
9	French	A	1	
10	Physical Education	B	2	
11	Technology Education	B	2	
12	Information Technology	C+	3	
13				
14				

Hints

Notice that the grades are on the left side of the column and the absences are on the right side of the column. This is because the computer automatically aligns labels on the left and aligns values on the right. In the next exploration, you will learn how to change the alignment of any column, row, or cell.

Project Activity

For your project file, open a blank spreadsheet and immediately save it as a file. Pick a file name that you would like to use for your coffee shop.

Enter a label in cell A1 that indicates the name of your coffee shop.

In the remainder of column A, enter the ten to fifteen menu items that you chose earlier to sell.

Research retail prices in your community for the various menu items you plan to sell. Enter a label in cell B1 that says "Prices." Decide how much each item will sell for in your coffee shop. Enter these values in the appropriate places in column B.

Label cell C1 "Costs." Based on your research, decide on the approximate cost for each of your menu items and input these values in the appropriate places in column C.

In a paragraph, explain and justify your decisions for the costs and prices of each of your menu items. Use a word processor to prepare your paragraph.

Print your spreadsheet and add it to your project file, along with any research you have completed, and the paragraph you have written.

Notebook Assignment

1. Use the spreadsheet below to answer the following questions in your notebook.

	A	B	C	D	
1	NAME	WEEKLY HOURS	RATE OF PAY	GROSS PAY	
2	Kanaka	40	$8.95	$358.00	
3	Tyler	45	$6.55	$294.75	
4	Renée	38	$7.85	$298.30	
5	Tanya	39	$8.40	$327.60	
6	Simran	42	$5.95	$249.90	
7	Sinead	35	$8.60	$301.00	
8					
9	TOTAL			$1,829.55	
10					
11					
12					

   a) How many columns, rows, and cells does this spreadsheet contain?
   b) In which cell is Simran's gross pay located?
   c) Try to determine whether cells A9, B4, C5, D3, and D9 contain labels, values, or formulas. Explain your guesses and assumptions for each.
   d) Explain why the label GROSS PAY is on the left side of column D and all the numbers underneath it are on the right side of column D.

Extension

2. What mathematical formula could be used to calculate the amount in cell D9?

Exploration 2

The Style File

One of the advantages of spreadsheets is that they can be much easier to read and more eye-catching than other methods of organizing data. Through the use of merging, wrapping, justifying, and formatting, a spreadsheet can look extremely polished. Fonts, borders, colours, and clip art can make a spreadsheet unique and professional at the same time. In this exploration, you will discover creative ways to make your spreadsheets stand out.

Career Connection

Name: Larry Ostrikoff

Job: sales representative in music store

Current wages: $7.50 an hour plus 10% commission

Education: grade 12, business diploma

Career goal: manager of music store

Keyword search: Canada music store merchandising

Shelf restocking and CD selection at a music store.

Goals

In this exploration, you will learn a variety of formatting options that can make spreadsheets appear more organized and attractive.

Hint

To highlight a group of cells, place your cursor at the start of the selection. If you have a PC, hold down the left button of your mouse, drag it to the end of the selection, then release the left button. On a Macintosh, place your cursor at the start of the selection, hold down your mouse button, and drag to the end of the selection. Then release your mouse button.

Example 1

Create a spreadsheet like the one below.

	A	B	C	D	E	F
1	Music for You				INVOICE#:	
2	Box 2130				34510	
3	Whitehorse, YK					
4	Y1A 5M5					
5						
6	Cat. No.	Name	Unit Price	Quantity	Total	
7	23487	Puff Daddy	19.99	15	299.85	
8	65897	Eve 6	14.99	8	119.92	
9	56897	Garth Brooks	16.99	7	118.93	
10	12897	Janet Jackson	15.99	12	191.88	
11	36587	Van Halen	9.99	8	79.92	
12						
13	SUBTOTAL				810.50	
14	GST				56.74	
15	TOTAL				867.24	
16						
17						
18						
19						

Make the following formatting changes.

a) Change the store's name and address to a different font in a larger size.

Solution

To change the font, highlight cells A1, A2, A3, and A4. Choose the Format option from the upper menu bar. Then choose Cells and then Font. You have lots of options here for font, style, size, effects, and colour. For now, change the store's name and address to a different font and increase their size.

b) Merge all the cells that contain the store's name and address.

Solution

There may not be enough room in column A to fit in all of the address. Merging cells gives you more room. Highlight cells A1 and B1. Choose the Format option from the upper menu bar. Then choose Cells and then Alignment. This menu allows you to change the orientation, alignment, and control of the text. Check off the box that says Merge cells. This should spread out the title of the store into cells A1 and B1. Repeat this process for cells A2 and B2, A3 and B3, A4 and B4.

c) Adjust the column and row sizes so that everything is easily readable.

Solution

You probably noticed that you cannot read some of the information in your spreadsheet, because the columns and/or rows are too small. To adjust the size of column D, for example, position your cursor on the line that divides column D and E at the very top of the spreadsheet. If you've got it positioned properly, your cursor should look as it does here.

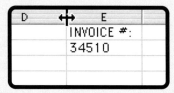

   Click, hold, and drag the cursor over to the right until you can see all the information in column D.

   To adjust the size of row 15, let's say, position your cursor on the line that divides rows 15 and 16 on the very left of the spreadsheet. Again, if you've got it positioned properly, your cursor should look as it does here.

   Click, hold, and drag the cursor down until you can see all the information in row 15. Adjust the remaining columns and rows, so that you can see all the information in your spreadsheet clearly.

d) Align all the catalogue numbers.

Solution

You can change the contents of any cell, so that it lines up on the left, right, or exactly in the middle. To make all the catalogue numbers (Cat. No.) line up on the left, highlight all the cells from A7 to A11. One way is to select Format, Cells, Alignment, Horizontal, and then choose Left. A shorter way is to click on the button shown here. It is at the top of your spreadsheet in the toolbar and looks like a bunch of small horizontal lines lined up on the left. All the category numbers should now be aligned above each other.

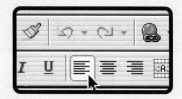

e)   Centre all the quantity numbers.

Solution

Highlight all the cells from D7 to D11. Use either of the two methods from the previous question to centre all the quantity numbers.

f)   Make the items in row 6 bold italic.

Solution

An easy way to select all the items in row 6 is to click directly on row 6 at the very left of your spreadsheet. This will highlight the entire row. To bold and italicize, either go into Format, Cells, Font, and choose Bold Italic, or simply click on the B and I buttons in the toolbar.

g)   Make all dollar amounts appear with dollar signs.

Solution

Highlight cells C7 to C11. Either go into Format, Cells, Number, and choose Currency, or simply click on the $ button in the toolbar. Do the same for cells E7 to E11.

h)   Make a double-lined border all the way around the store's name and address.

Solution

To put borders around any cells, simply highlight the cells, and choose Format, Cells, Border, and choose the double-lined outline border.

i)   Colour rows 7 to 11 yellow.

Solution

Highlight all of rows 7 to 11 on the very left of your spreadsheet. Either go into Format, Cells, Patterns, and choose the appropriate colour, or simply click on the button that looks like a paint bucket in the toolbar.

j)   Insert a picture.

Solution

From the Insert option on your toolbar, choose Picture and Clip Art. Click on a picture that fits your store. Once the clip art has been inserted, click and drag it to wherever you want.

The spreadsheet will look something like the following.

	A	B	C	D	E	F
1	Music for You				INVOICE #:	
2	Box 2130				34510	
3	Whitehorse, YK					
4	Y1A 5M5					
5						
6	Cat. No.	Name	Unit Price	Quantity	Total	
7	23487	Puff Daddy	$19.99	15	$299.85	
8	65897	Eve 6	$14.99	8	$119.92	
9	56897	Garth Brooks	$16.99	7	$118.93	
10	12897	Janet Jackson	$15.99	12	$191.88	
11	36587	Van Halen	$9.99	8	$79.92	
12						
13	SUBTOTAL				$810.50	
14	GST				$56.74	
15	TOTAL				$867.24	
16						

Project Activity

"Beautify" the spreadsheet you made for your coffee shop. Add unique formatting. (Don't forget to include a picture!) Print this version and place it in your project file.

Hints

Clip art is often included with your office software and there are internet sites that specialize in clip art as well. Try typing "clip art" in an internet search engine to locate sites.

Notebook Assignment

1. In your notebook, describe the steps you would take to make Spreadsheet A look like Spreadsheet B.

SPREADSHEET A

	A	B	C	D	E	F
1	Chequing Acc #486795552			Bank of Yukon		
2						
3						
4	Description	Debits	Credits	Date	Balance	
5	Balance forwa			6/01/2001	348.92	
6	Deposit		659.08	6/04/2001	1008	
7	Cheque 129	127.34		6/09/2001	880.66	
8	ATM withdraw	7693		6/14/2001	803.73	
9	Cash withdraw	100.00		6/18/2001	703.73	
10	Maintenance f	9.50		6/20/2001	694.23	
11	Cheque 130	575.00		6/25/2001	119.23	
12	Deposit		418.92	6/29/2001	538.15	
13						
14						
15						

SPREADSHEET B

	A	B	C	D	E	F
1						
2	Chequing Account				Bank of Yukon	
3	#486795552					
4						
5						
6						
7	Description	Debits	Credits	Date	Balance	
8	Balance forward			6/01/2001	$348.92	
9	Deposit		$659.08	6/04/2001	$1,008.00	
10	Cheque 129	$127.34		6/09/2001	$880.66	
11	ATM withdrawal	$76.93		6/14/2001	$803.73	
12	Cash withdrawal	$100.00		6/18/2001	$703.73	
13	Maintenance fee	$9.50		6/20/2001	$694.23	
14	Cheque 130	$575.00		6/25/2001	$119.23	
15	Deposit		$418.92	6/29/2001	$538.15	

2. After you have described at least seven formatting steps in question 1, choose a partner. Trade descriptions with your partner to make sure you have written clear instructions. Check to see whether you have missed any steps.

Extension

3. Explore some of the other formatting options available with your spreadsheet program. Describe two of the best options that you discovered.

Exploration 3

Smart Spreadsheets

Up until now, you haven't had an opportunity to see the real power of spreadsheets. In this exploration, you will be given a number of spreadsheets with formulas provided. Once you input them, you will see how quickly and easily a spreadsheet can perform numerous and very complex calculations.

Spreadsheet formulas always begin with an equal sign (=). Spreadsheet formulas use the following symbols to represent different mathematical functions:

+   addition
−   subtraction
*   multiplication
/   division
^   exponent (for example, 3^2 means 3^2)
( ) brackets (used for order of operations)

Goals

In this exploration, you will begin to experiment with formulas in spreadsheets. You will be provided with a template to solve spreadsheet problems that require the use of formulas.

Hint

Microsoft Excel uses the correct order of mathematical operations. The order is as follows:

    brackets
    exponents
    division
    multiplication
    addition
    subtraction

Example 1

Create a spreadsheet that calculates term marks for four students.

	A	B	C	D	E	F
1	NAME	Assignments (120 marks)	Project (80 marks)	Tests (60 marks)	FINAL MARK	
2	Crystal	88	75	31	?	
3	Marie	72	58	39	?	
4	Stefan	103	64	48	?	
5	David	49	42	51	?	
6						
7	CLASS AVERAGE				?	

a) The formula in cell E2 is =(B2+C2+D2)/260*100. Explain in words how the spreadsheet calculates Crystal's final mark.

b) What number will be produced by the formula you entered in cell E2?

c) Based on the formula in cell E2, what should be the formula in cell E3? Fill in the appropriate formulas for cells E4 and E5.

d) The formula in cell E7 is =AVERAGE(E2:E5). How does the spreadsheet program calculate the class average or mean?

e) What is the class average (that is, what number should appear in cell E7)?

f) How could you write another formula to calculate class average?

Solution

a) The spreadsheet program finds the sum of Crystal's assignments, projects, and tests and divides it by a total of 260 marks. Then it converts the number to a percent by multiplying by 100.

b) Crystal's final mark is 75% (rounded to a whole number).

c) Similarly, the formula in cell E3 calculates Marie's final mark by adding together her assignments, projects, and tests and then dividing by the total number of possible marks. Again, this result is changed to a percent by multiplying by 100. The formula in cell E3 would be =(B3+C3+D3)/260*100. Cells E4 and E5 contain similar formulas, with cell addresses indicating the fourth and fifth row.

d) The formula in cell E7 is a special spreadsheet function, which calculates the class average by adding the numbers in cells E2, E3, E4, and E5 and then dividing by 4.

e) The class average is 69.5%, rounded up to 70%.

f) Another formula to calculate the class average would be:
=(E2+E3+E4+E5)/4

Career Connection

Name: Darcy Cummins

Job: apprentice mechanic

Current wages: $16.00 an hour

Education: grade 12, one year of trade school

Career goal: owner of automotive repair shop

Keyword search: Canada college mechanic courses

Mental Math

1. If you received a mark of 16 out of 20 on Test A and 10 out of 20 on Test B, what is the average of your test scores?

2. Estimate the total cost of a $9.99 CD including 7% GST and 8% PST.

Example 2

A hardware store in Manitoba uses a spreadsheet to determine its daily sales of bolts. Different sizes of bolts have different prices but this template calculates the total sales easily.

	A	B	C	D	E	F
1	BOLT TYPE	QUANTITY	PRICE	AMOUNT		
2	1/4 inch	37	$0.06	$2.22		
3	3/8 inch	28	$0.08	$2.24		
4	1/2 inch	21	$0.10	$2.10		
5	3/4 inch	19	$0.14	$2.66		
6	1 inch	11	$0.18	$1.98		
7						
8	SUBTOTAL			$11.20		
9	PST			$0.78		
10	GST			$0.78		
11	TOTAL			$12.76		
12						
13						
14						

a) If the formula in cell D2 is =B2*C2, what must be the formula in cell D3?

b) If the formula in cell D8 is =SUM(D2:D6), explain what this formula does.

c) If the taxes are 7% PST and 7% GST, what formula would you put in cell D9 to calculate PST?

d) What formula must be in cell D11?

Solution

a) The formula in cell D3 is very similar to the one in cell D2. To calculate the amount for 3/8 inch, the formula would be =B3*C3.

b) The formula in cell D8 is a special spreadsheet function, which finds the sum of all the amounts in cells D2, D3, D4, D5, and D6. Another (longer) way to calculate this would be the formula =D2+D3+D4+D5+D6.

c) To calculate 7% PST, the formula would be =D8*0.07.

d) To calculate the final total, the formula in cell D11 would be =D8+D9+D10.

Notebook Assignment

1. Give a correct formula for each of the following:
   a) Add G5 and H5.
   b) Divide C6 by 2.
   c) Subtract B6 from B7.
   d) Multiply G7, H7, and J7.
   e) Sum all cells from E5 to E9.
   f) Multiply B4 by 7%.
   g) Divide C5 by D5.
   h) Average all cells from D3 to D10.
   i) Subtract 8 from the sum of F5 and F6.
   j) Divide the product of B2 and B3 by 2.

2. For the following spreadsheet what is a formula for cell B10? What value would be computed for cell B10?

	A	B	C	D	E	F	G
1	Monthly Expenses						
2							
3	Expense Title	AMOUNT					
4	Clothes	$50.00					
5	Movies	$20.00					
6	Bus Fare	$32.50					
7	Gum, etc.	$3.75					
8	Gifts	$27.60					
9							
10	TOTAL						
11							
12							
13							
14							
15							

3. Describe how to use the square root function (SQRT) in a spreadsheet.

4. Using the spreadsheet below, answer the following questions.

	A	B	C	D	E	F
1	Small	14				
2	Medium	32				
3	Large	51				
4	Extra Large	19				
5						
6	Total					
7						
8						

a) If the formula in cell B6 is =SUM(B1:B4), explain what this formula does.

b) What number will appear in B6 once the formula has been entered?

c) What is another formula that would calculate the same value?

5. Using the spreadsheet below, answer the following questions.

	A	B	C	D	E	F
1	2001					
2	Sales	$27,000				
3	Expenses	$19,000				
4	Profit					
5						
6						
7						
8						
9						

a) If the formula in cell B4 is =B2-B3, explain what this formula does.

b) What number will appear in B4 once the formula has been entered?

6. Using the spreadsheet below, answer the following questions.

	A	B	C	D	E	F	G
1	Quantity	10					
2	Price	$2.35					
3	Subtotal						
4	Tax						
5	Total						
6							
7							

    a) If the formula in cell B3 is =B1*B2, explain what this formula does.

    b) If the formula in cell B4 is =0.14*B3, explain what this formula does.

    c) If the formula in cell B5 is =B3+B4, explain what this formula does.

    d) What numbers will appear in cells B3, B4, and B5?

7. Use the spreadsheet template below. Give a formula for each of the following cells: E5, E9, B12, C12, D12, and E12.

	A	B	C	D	E	F
1	PETS & FRIENDS STORE					
2	Aug-03					
3						
4	ANIMAL	BEGINNING INVENTORY	BOUGHT	SOLD	ENDING INVENTORY	
5	Dogs	1	2	2		
6	Cats	5	4	3		
7	Fish	100	200	275		
8	Snakes	3	5	2		
9	Hamsters	6	10	12		
10	Birds	15	3	3		
11						
12	TOTAL					

Extension

8. Explore some of the other spreadsheet functions in the Insert menu. Pick any function, give its category and name, and explain what it does.

9. When completing tables requiring calculations, what are the advantages of using computerized spreadsheets over paper-and-pencil techniques?

Exploration 4

Starting from Scratch

The templates that you have used so far have been provided for you. Generally, for simple spreadsheets like these, it is not wise to pay someone to develop them. Instead, design them on your own. To do this, you will need to use the skill of writing formulas you learned in the last exploration.

Career Connection

Name: Marian Dupuis

Job: forestry surveyor in northern B.C.

Current wages: $2585/month

Education: grade 12; course in forest resource technology from New Caledonia College in Prince George, B.C.

Career goal: forest resource manager

Keyword search: forestry technology course Canada college

Goals

In this exploration, you will create your own spreadsheets with appropriate formulas and formatting.

Example 1

A local greenhouse pays double-time for any hours over 40 worked per week during the summer. The weekly payroll for all employees is as follows. How would you create a spreadsheet that calculates the gross pay for each employee and the total weekly gross pay for the company?

	A	B	C	D	E	F	G
1	NAME	HOURS	REGULAR PAY				
2	Sophie	44	$7.85				
3	Marc	51	$8.50				
4	Craig	45	$7.85				
5	Georgia	43	$9.25				
6	Han	55	$11.75				
7							
8							

Solution

A possible solution is as follows. The total weekly gross pay is $2544.30.

	A	B REGULAR HOURS	C REGULAR PAY RATE	D OVERTIME HOURS	E OVERTIME PAY RATE	F	G
1	NAME					GROSS PAY	
2	Sophie	40	$7.85	4	$15.70	$376.80	
3	Marc	40	$8.50	11	$17.00	$527.00	
4	Craig	40	$7.85	5	$15.70	$392.50	
5	Georgia	40	$9.25	3	$18.50	$425.50	
6	Han	40	$11.75	15	$23.50	$822.50	
7							
8	TOTAL PAY					$2,544.30	
9							
10							
11							

The formulas in columns E and F would be the following:

E	F	
Overtime Pay	Gross Pay	
=C2*2	=B2*C2+D2*E2	
=C3*2	=B3*C3+D3*E3	
=C4*2	=B4*C4+D4*E4	
=C5*2	=B5*C5+D5*E5	
=C6*2	=B6*C6+D6*E6	
	=SUM(F2:F6)	

Example 2

Given any rectangle, you can determine the perimeter and area using the following formulas; "*l*" stands for length and "*w*" stands for width.

$$P = 2 (l + w)$$
$$A = l * w$$

A spreadsheet allows you to alter the length and width of any particular rectangle to see the effect on perimeter and area. Create a spreadsheet that will do these calculations for rectangles that measure 8 cm x 3 cm, 6 cm x 5 cm, and 12 cm x 1 cm.

Solution

A possible solution is shown in the following spreadsheet.

	A	B	C	D	E	F	G
1	Length (cm)	Width (cm)	Perimeter (cm)	Area (cm²)			
2	8	3	22	24			
3	6	5	22	30			
4	12	1	26	12			
5							
6							
7							

The formulas in columns C and D would be the following.

C	D	
Perimeter (cm)	Area (cm²)	
=2*(A2+B2)	=A2*B2	
=2*(A3+B3)	=A3*B3	
=2*(A4+B4)	=A4*B4	

Project Activity

Go back to your coffee shop spreadsheet and estimate how many of each menu item you would sell in one week. Enter these numbers in column D.

Create appropriate formulas in columns E and F that calculate the weekly costs and weekly revenues from the sale of these items.

At the bottom of your spreadsheet, use formulas to calculate the total weekly costs and revenues.

Use a formula to calculate the weekly profit in your coffee shop.

Print the resulting spreadsheet and add it to your project file.

Notebook Assignment

1. A teacher records the following marks for five students. The term mark is calculated by averaging the project and test results. The final mark is calculated using 60% of the term mark and 40% of the exam mark. Use formulas to design a spreadsheet that will calculate each student's term mark and final grade.

	A	B	C	D	E	F	G
1	Name	Project	Test	Exam			
2	Teya	70	75	65			
3	Vijay	85	82	75			
4	Anne	75	70	65			
5	Jordan	96	89	82			
6	Stefan	56	65	51			
7							
8							
9							

Mental Math

A rectangle has a length of 4 m and a width of 3 m.
What is the perimeter of the rectangle?

2. Hockey standings in a recent season are as follows. Use a spreadsheet to determine which team is ranked highest, if a win is worth 2 points, a tie is worth 1 point, and a loss is worth 0 points.

	A	B	C	D	E	F	G
1	Eastern Teams						
2							
3		Wins	Losses	Ties			
4	Montreal	32	41	9			
5	Detroit	36	37	9			
6	Chicago	28	43	11			
7	Tampa	27	47	8			
8	New Jersey	35	40	7			
9	Toronto	27	47	8			
10							
11							

Extension

3. In the previous question, determine what would happen to the rankings if a win was worth 3 points and a tie worth 1 point.

4. What are the advantages of using a spreadsheet over a calculator?

Exploration 5

What if . . . ?

A major advantage of spreadsheets is the ability to ask "how" and "what if" questions. How much do I need to invest to have $1000 after one year? How many hours of overtime do I need in order to earn $500? What marks do I need if I want to get a B average in mathematics? What if the interest rate is only 6.5%? Spreadsheets allow you to change a value to see how it affects the overall picture.

Career Connection

Name: Trent Daniels

Job: golf caddy

Current wages: $8.50 per hour

Education: grade 12, enrolled in marketing course at local college

Career goal: car salesman

Keyword search: Canada college marketing

Goals

In this exploration, you will use spreadsheets to answer "what if" questions.

Example 1

Suppose that you want to invest enough money so that, with interest, you will have $10,000 at the end of one year. If you know that your money can earn 9.5% simple interest, use a spreadsheet to determine how much money you need to invest (to the nearest $50) to achieve this goal.

Solution

Make a spreadsheet that calculates the final value of any investment at 9.5% simple interest for one year.

	A	B
1	Initial Value	$8,000.00
2	Interest Rate	0.095
3	Final Value	?
4		
5		

The formula in cell B3 would be =B1+(B1*B2). Experiment with several initial values until your final value exceeds $10,000.

	A	B
1	Initial Value	$8,000.00
2	Interest Rate	0.095
3	Final Value	$8,760.00
4		
5		

	A	B
1	Initial Value	$9,000.00
2	Interest Rate	0.095
3	Final Value	$9,855.00
4		
5		

	A	B
1	Initial Value	$9,150.00
2	Interest Rate	0.095
3	Final Value	$10,019.25
4		
5		

Mental Math

1. How much interest is earned on $100 at 5% after one year?

2. If you put $1000 in a savings account earning 6% simple interest, what is your balance after 1 year?

Example 2

Ann and Marian work at a grocery store. Ann makes $7.50 stocking shelves and Marian makes $8.25 as a clerk operating the cash register. Marian always works 15 hours per week. How many hours would Ann have to work to earn the same as or slightly more than Marian?

Solution

A possible solution is as follows.

	A	B	C	D	E	F	G
1	Name	Hours	Wage	Pay			
2	Marian	15	$8.25	$123.75			
3	Ann	?	$7.50				
4							
5							
6							
7							

Experiment with different values for cell B3 until Ann's pay is the same or slightly more than Marian's. If Ann works 16.5 hours, she earns the same as Marian. If she works 17 hours, she will earn slightly more than Marian.

Project Activity

Experiment with the menu items on your coffee shop spreadsheet, so that your weekly profit is at least $1000.00. Print the spreadsheet and add it to your project file.

Notebook Assignment

1. Rudy has $20.00 and wants to buy a compact disk. Use a spreadsheet to determine the maximum price before tax of a CD he could buy, if the GST is 7% and the PST is 7%.

2. Your four mathematics term marks are 65, 72, 58, and 81, and your final exam is worth 20% of your overall grade. Use a spreadsheet to determine the minimum mark you can get on the exam in order to earn a final grade of 70%.

3. Tenille has $5000 that she wants to invest. She would like her investment to grow to $10,000 so she can buy a car. She thought that investing at a simple interest rate of 5% for 3 years would earn enough to meet this goal.

	A	B	C	D	E
1	Initial Amount	$5,000.00			
2	Rate	0.05			
3	Years	3			
4	Final Value	$5,750.00			
5					
6					
7					
8					

As you can see, she was wrong. Use a spreadsheet to find at least two combinations of time and interest rate, with an investment of $5000, to achieve the amount of $10,000. You are not allowed to use an interest rate greater than 15%.

Extension

4. A salesperson is offered two different salary options for a 40-hour work week.

    a) $12.00 an hour
    b) $7.00 an hour plus 10% commission on weekly sales

    Use a spreadsheet to determine the weekly sales required for the second option to pay the most.

Exploration 6

Saving Precious Time

Entering formulas, especially long ones, can be time-consuming. The formulas from cell to cell may only differ by one letter or number. There are a few ways that a spreadsheet can save you the work of retyping similar formulas. Just as a word-processing program allows you to copy a word, sentence, or paragraph, a spreadsheet program lets you copy and paste the contents of any cell, even mathematical formulas.

Example 1

Recall how you experimented in the previous exploration with different initial values in order to achieve a final value of $10,000. Now determine the amount of initial investment at 10% annual interest you would need in order to have $10,000 at the end of 1 year.

	A	B	C	D	E	
1	Initial Value	$8,000.00	$9,000.00	$9,150.00		
2	Interest Rate	0.10				
3	Final Value	$8,800.00				
4						
5						
6						

1. Use the copy/paste function to copy the interest rate into cells C2 and D2.

2. Use the fill/right function to copy the final value formula into cells C3 and D3.

3. Explain what happened to the final value formulas after they were copied.

Goals

In this exploration, you will learn to save time creating spreadsheets by copying formulas using the copy/paste, fill/right, and fill/down commands.

Solution

1. You want the same interest rate to appear in cells C2 and D2. Highlight cell B2 and choose Edit and Copy from the menu bar. Move your cursor over to cell C2 and choose Edit and Paste from the menu bar. The interest rate should automatically transfer over to cell C2. Since you still have cell B2 ready for copying, simply place your cursor in cell D2 and paste in the interest rate.

2. If you want to copy the same cell multiple times, the Fill command is very handy. Highlight cell B3, C3, and D3. Choose Edit, Fill, and Right from the menu bar. The numbers should appear as follows.

	A	B	C	D	E	F
1	Initial Value	$8,000.00	$9,000.00	$9,150.00	$9,090.00	$9,091.00
2	Interest Rate	0.10	0.10	0.10	0.10	0.10
3	Final Value	$8,800.00	$9,900.00	$10,065.00	$9,999.00	$10,000.10
4						
5						
6						

3. When you highlight cell C3 you should see that the formula shown in the formula bar has changed from =B1+(B1*B2) to =C1+(C1*C2). The spreadsheet automatically adjusted the formula so it matched up with other items in the column. Similarly, the formula in D3 should have changed to =D1+(D1*D2).

You need to invest $9091.00 at 10% in order to have $10,000 after one year.

Example 2

Suppose you need to fence in an area next to your dog's house, like the one shown in the diagram. You have 30 m of fencing and you want to fence in the largest possible area. You have set up a spreadsheet that automatically calculates the length as follows.

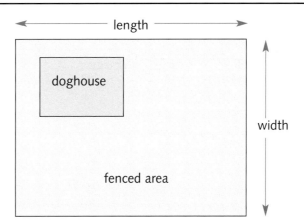

	A	B	C	D	E	F
	Width (m)	Length (m)	Perimeter (m)	Area (m²)		
1						
2	1	14	30	14		
3	2					
4	3					
5	4					
6	5					
7	6					
8	7					
9	8					
10	9					
11	10					
12	11					
13	12					
14	13					
15	14					
16	15					
17						
18						

Since the perimeter is 30 m, half the perimeter is 15 m. The formula in cell B2 could be =15-A2 and the formula in cell D2 would be =A2*B2. Complete the spreadsheet using the fill/down function to determine what length and width to use.

	A	B	C	D	E	F
1	Width (m)	Length (m)	Perimeter (m)	Area (m^2)		
2	1	14	30	14		
3	2	13	30	26		
4	3	12	30	36		
5	4	11	30	44		
6	5	10	30	50		
7	6	9	30	54		
8	7	8	30	56		
9	8	7	30	56		
10	9	6	30	54		
11	10	5	30	50		
12	11	4	30	44		
13	12	3	30	36		
14	13	2	30	26		
15	14	1	30	14		
16	15	0	30	0		
17						
18						
19						

Solution

Highlight cell B2 all the way down to cell B16. Choose Edit, Fill, and Down from the upper menu bar. This should automatically calculate all the lengths that correspond with the widths. You can also do more than one column at the same time. Highlight cell C2 across to D2 and down to D16. Again, choose Edit, Fill, and Down from the upper menu bar. You should get the following results.

If the length and width must each be whole numbers, then a length of 7 m and a width of 8 m or a length of 8 m and a width of 7 m gives the maximum fenced area. Try numbers between 7 and 8.

You should find that a length of 7.5 m and a width of 7.5 m would maximize the fenced area.

Assignment

1. You are working for the owner of a hamburger and hot dog stand. The owner asks you to take a cart to a music festival. You want to make the most money possible. A hamburger yields a profit of $1.50 and a hot dog yields a profit of $0.75. You are limited by the amount of storage. Your cooler only holds 3000 cm^3. You determine that the volume of one hamburger is 30 cm^3 and the volume of one hot dog is 25 cm^3. Create a spreadsheet like the one below.

	A	B	C	D	E
1	# of Hamburger:	# of Hot Dogs	Volume	Profit	
2					
3					
4					
5					
6					

a) What formula should go in cell C2 to calculate the volume of 20 hamburgers and 15 hot dogs?

b) What formula should go in cell D2 to calculate the profit of 20 hamburgers and 15 hot dogs?

c) Enter at least ten other possible combinations of hamburgers and hotdogs.

d) Use the fill/down command to copy the formulas in cells C2 and D2.

e) Which of your ten combinations provides the greatest profit while having a volume of 3000 cm^3 or less?

Hints

Remember you must use whole numbers for the number of hamburgers and the number of hot dogs. You cannot sell half a hamburger!

Extension

2. Pretend that you live in British Columbia and are trying to decide between the following long distance telephone providers. The goal is to keep your long distance telephone bill under $50 per month. You call your sister in Europe once a month and speak for about half an hour. You do the same with your brother in Nunavut. You also call your sister in the United States every two months for a half-hour call. Create a spreadsheet that explores different options for helping you decide which long distance provider would be better for you. Explain how and why you made your choice.

	A	B	C	D	E	F
1	**DASH Long Distance**					
2						
3		In-Province	Canada Out-of-province	U.S.A	Overseas	
4	Rate per minute (¢)	10	14	19	25	
5						
6	**AB&B Long Distance**					
7						
8		In-Province	Canada Out-of-province	U.S.A	Overseas	
9	Rate per minute (¢)	8	12	15	30	
10						

Exploration 7

Handy Uses and Applications

You now realize the power and efficiency of spreadsheets. Spreadsheet programs can help you organize both your personal and professional life. Now that you know the basics of designing your own spreadsheet and creating your own formulas, you can apply your knowledge in a variety of situations.

Career Connection

Name: Jacinda Gedney

Job: caretaker in youth group home

Current wages: $15.00 an hour

Education: grade 12; three years part-time studies in social work

Career goal: social worker

Keyword search: social work course Canada college

A caregiver at a Developmental Disabilities Association group home helps a resident with daily tasks.

Goals

In this exploration, you will identify where spreadsheets could be used effectively.

Example 1

Design a spreadsheet that uses formulas to track your monthly income, expenses, and savings.

Solution

One possible solution is shown below.

	A	B	C	D	E	F
1	MONTHLY BUDGET					
2						
3	Description	Income	Expenses			
4	Allowance	$25.00				
5	Part-time job	$150.00				
6	Clothing		$50.00			
7	Transportation		$20.00			
8	Food		$20.00			
9	Recreation		$30.00			
10	Personal Care		$20.00			
11						
12	Total	$175.00	$140.00			
13	Savings	$35.00				
14						
15						
16						
17						
18						

The formula in cell B12 is =B4+B5, in cell C12 =SUM(C6:C10), and in cell B13 it is =B12-C12.

Example 2

A clothing store is trying to get rid of its summer stock of sweatshirts, t-shirts, tank tops, and shorts. The current prices are as follows:

	A	B	C
1	Sweatshirts	$49.99	
2	T-Shirts	$19.99	
3	Tank Tops	$14.99	
4	Shorts	$29.99	
5			
6			

The manager decides to take 10% of the original price off each week for the next four weeks. Design a spreadsheet that will show the price of each item for each of the next four weeks.

Solution

	A	B	C	D	E	F
1	SUMMER STOCK					
2						
3		Original Price	Week 1	Week 2	Week 3	Week 4
4	Sweatshirts	$49.99	$44.99	$39.99	$34.99	$29.99
5	T-Shirts	$19.99	$17.99	$15.99	$13.99	$11.99
6	Tank Tops	$14.99	$13.49	$11.99	$10.49	$8.99
7	Shorts	$29.99	$26.99	$23.99	$20.99	$17.99
8						
9						
10						

The formulas in columns C, D, E, and F could be the following.

Week 1	Week 2	Week 3	Week 4
=B4*0.9	=B4*0.8	=B4*0.7	=B4*0.6
=B5*0.9	=B5*0.8	=B5*0.7	=B5*0.6
=B6*0.9	=B6*0.8	=B6*0.7	=B6*0.6
=B7*0.9	=B7*0.8	=B7*0.7	=B7*0.6

Project Activity

You could use your coffee shop spreadsheet to manage your inventory. Create a spreadsheet that would allow you to do this efficiently. Ensure that your spreadsheet has all the necessary formulas and formatting. Print your spreadsheet and add it to your project file

Notebook Assignment

1. According to a survey, the percentage of Canadians who read books in 1998 is as follows.

	A	B	C	D
1	Percentage of Canadians who read books			
2				
3		Male	Female	
4	at least a book a week	10%	7%	
5	at least a book a month	20%	16%	
6	at least a book every 3 months	27%	34%	
7	at least a book every 6 months	35%	37%	
8				

   a) Create a spreadsheet using the statistics shown above that predicts how many male and female students in your class should be reading books in each of the categories.
   b) Research the actual reading practices of your classmates.
   c) Compare the survey results to the actual results in your class. Add these to your spreadsheet.
   d) Are these results different? If so, why?

Mental Math

A computer game costs $39.99 but it is on sale for 50% off. What is the sale price of the game?

Technology

Visit www.statcan.ca to find a variety of information on the economic, transportation, leisure, and political habits of Canadians.

Extension

2. **a)** Your grandparents have $5000 they would like to invest for one year. They want to give you the interest their money earns as a gift. They hope to earn at least $500 in interest, but they do not want to put all their money into a single type of investment. They want to put some in a savings account earning 2.5% interest, some in a Canada Savings Bond earning 5% interest, and the rest in a corporate bond earning 13%. Use a spreadsheet to come up with two different investment combinations that will earn at least $500 in interest.

    b) What factors, other than rate of return, should be considered?

    c) What would you recommend to your grandparents?

Hints

Different types of investments give different rates of return, depending on economic factors. Your grandparents feel that by investing in more than one type of investment they are spreading the risk of financial loss.

Problem Analysis

A Ferry Ride

You are waiting for a ferry crossing Kootenay Lake to Balfour, B.C. It arrives fully loaded at 10:00 am with six automobiles on board. Ahead of you in line are a tour bus, a truck camper, a car with a trailer, a truck loaded with lumber, and seven other cars. The vehicles are loaded onto the ferry in two rows, and the ferry is capable of carrying vehicles of any weight. The round-trip ferry schedule allows 50 minutes, which includes time for loading and unloading.

Write down assumptions you must make in order to estimate when you will arrive on the other side of the bay.

Determine, using your assumptions, when you will arrive on the other side of the bay.

Games

Tower of Hanoi

In the city of Hanoi, in a temple, are several monks. The monks are working on a challenge.

On a base there are three columns. On one of the columns are 64 gold disks. The disks each have a different diameter and are stacked so the largest disk is on the bottom as modelled in the following diagram.

The task for the monks is to move the disks to a different column using the following rules:

1. Disks are moved from one column to another.
2. Only one disk can be moved at a time.
3. A larger disk cannot be placed on top of a smaller disk.

Question: What is the minimum number of moves it will take to transfer all 64 disks to another tower?

Hints

A problem such as this can often be solved by using a simpler model. Look at the simpler related problems of moving a one-disk stack, a two-disk stack, a three-disk stack, a four-disk stack, and a five-disk stack.

Make a table of the number of disks and the minimum number of moves required to transfer these disks to another column.

You can build a stack of coins or Cuisenaire rods of different sizes to represent the disks.

Once you have completed your chart, look for a pattern between the number of disks in the stack and the minimum number of moves required.

Write this pattern as a rule. Use your rule to solve for a 10-disk stack and a 64-disk stack.

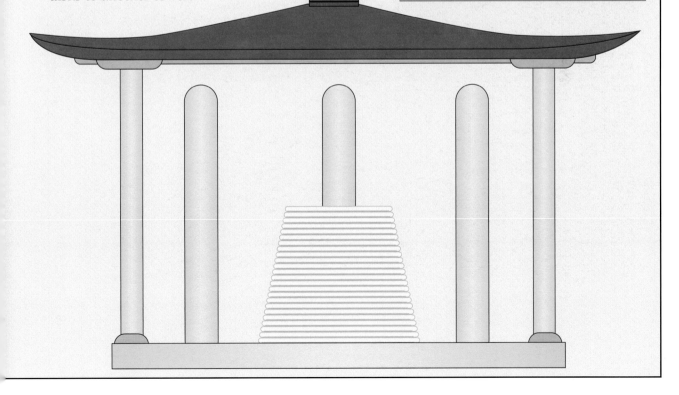

Chapter Review

1. Examine the spreadsheet below and answer the following questions.

	A	B	C	D	E	F
1	NAME	QUIZ 1	PROJECT	QUIZ 2	LAB	TERM
2	Joaquin	59	84	75	49	67
3	Aaron					
4	Pauline					
5	Carlos					
6						
7						
8						

a) How many columns, rows, and cells are shown in the spreadsheet?

b) In which cell is the number 49?

c) Does cell C1 contain a label, value, or formula?

d) What is a possible formula in cell F2?

2. Describe in detail how you would format Spreadsheet A so that it looks like Spreadsheet B. Be sure to mention alignment, colour, typeface, column/row size, currency, borders, and clip art in your description.

SPREADSHEET A

	A	B	C	D	E	F	G
1	Rocking Record Sales			Specializin g	CDs Tapes DVDs Videos		
2	Month	CDs	Tapes	DVDs	Videos		
3	January	48	19	28	39		
4	February	58	24	43	55		
5	March	79	21	57	49		
6	April	103	31	40	77		
7	May	125	35	62	89		
8							
9	Cost Per Item	12.00	3.00	18.00	9.00		
10	Price Per Item	18.00	8.00	25.00	15.00		
11							

SPREADSHEET B

	A	B	C	D	E	F
1	*Rocking Record Sales*			Specializing in:	CDs Tapes DVDs Videos	
2						
3	Month	CDs	Tapes	DVDs	Videos	
4	January	48	19	28	39	
5	February	58	24	43	55	
6	March	79	21	57	49	
7	April	103	31	49	77	
8	May	125	35	62	89	
9						
10	Cost Per Item	$12.00	$3.00	$18.00	$9.00	
11	Price Per Item	$18.00	$8.00	$25.00	$15.00	
12						
13						

3. Examine the spreadsheet below and answer the following questions.

	A	B	C	D	E	F
1	Description	Price	Quantity	Subtotal	Tax	Total
2	Tri-Mode PCS Digital Phone	$24.99	2	$49.98	$7.00	$56.98
3	Dual Mode PCS Digital Phone	$174.99	4	$699.96	$97.99	$797.95
4	Prepaid Cellular Phone	$124.99	5	$624.95	$87.49	$712.44
5	Neoprene Arm Pouch	$24.99	11	$274.89	$38.48	$313.37
6	Neoprene Case	$29.99	11	$329.89	$46.18	$376.07
7						
8	INVOICE TOTAL					$2,256.81
9						
10						
11						

a) What formula should appear in cell D2?

b) What formula should appear in cell E2, if the total tax is 14%?

c) What formula should appear in cell F2?

d) Describe how you would copy the formula in cell D2 down to D6.

e) Describe two possible formulas for cell F8.

4. While vacationing in the Okanagan Valley, you decide to take your parents out to dinner for their anniversary, but you only have $75 to spend. You know that PST and GST are 7% each, and you want to be able to leave a 15% tip on the bill. A good, yet inexpensive restaurant uses the menu shown on the right.

Use a spreadsheet to design a meal for you and your parents that includes an appetizer, entrée, dessert, and beverage for each of you. Keep your total bill under $75, including tax and tip.

Apple Blossom Restaurant

Dinner Menu

Appetizers

Tossed Salad $3.25
Caesar Salad $4.25
French Onion Soup $4.75
Soup of the Day $3.50
Chips & Salsa $2.75

Entrées

Roast Beef $11.75
Baked Chicken $8.50
Fettucine Alfredo $7.50
Vegetable Stir Fry $7.50
Broiled Salmon $13.50

Desserts

Apple Pie $3.25
Tiramisu $4.25
Hot Fudge Sundae $2.75
New York Cheesecake . . . $3.75
Fruit Salad $2.50

Beverages

Pop $1.25
Milk $1.50
Iced Tea $1.75
Milkshake $2.25
Coffee/Tea $0.75

5. The following spreadsheet template is used to determine the payroll for the ABC Toy Company. Complete the spreadsheet. Use appropriate formulas. Use current EI, CPP, federal Income Tax, and provincial Income Tax deduction amounts.

	A	B	C	D	E	F	G	H	I
1	ABC Company Payroll								
2	Two Weeks Ending September 14, 2005								
3									
4	EMPLOYEE	HOURS	RATE	GROSS PAY	EI	CPP	FED. TAX	PROV. TAX	NET PAY
5	Wong	50	$14.50						
6	Gibson	30	$10.25						
7	Lu	40	$16.00						
8	Demski	20	$8.50						
9	Kandia	35	$9.75						
10									
11	TOTAL								
12									

6. The following spreadsheet template is used to budget grocery expenditures for a student living on his/her own. Decide what groceries you need to purchase. You can only spend $125.00 for the two-week period. You must select at least one item from each of the food groups in the Canada Food Guide. Your list must be realistic. Use current prices.

	A	B	C	D	E
1	BUDGETING FOR GROCERIES				
2					
3	$ to Spend	$125.00			
4					
5	ITEM	QUANTITY	PRICE	COST	
6					
7					
8					
9					
10					
11					
12					
13					

Technology

The Canada Food Guide is available on the web at:
http://www.hc-sc.gc.ca/hppb/nutrition/pube/foodguid/index.html.

Project Presentation

Organize the information in your project file into a report. Your report should contain the following items:

- a title page
- spreadsheets you have created
- an explanation of how you arrived at the costs and prices of your menu items
- an explanation of how you calculated the weekly profit for your coffee shop
- detailed examples of other expenses you will likely have in your coffee shop and how each will affect your weekly profit
- one paragraph that identifies
    a) two new things you learned in this chapter
    b) the meaning of two terms learned in the chapter
    c) the career profile in the chapter that most appeals to you

Extension

Assume that you have three part-time and two full-time employees in your coffee shop.

Based on your hours of business, make an initial estimate of how many hours each employee would work on a weekly basis. Research other coffee shops to find out appropriate wages for each of your employees. Find out whether coffee shops pay overtime if employees work more than a certain number of hours a week and how they pay overtime to employees who work on statutory holidays.

Create a spreadsheet that calculates the total weekly wages for employees in your coffee shop. Assume that employees will be paid time and a half if they work more than 40 hours a week.

Based on your costs and revenues, adjust the hours you have scheduled for each of your employees to maximize your profit, while still being able to run the coffee shop efficiently. Write a paragraph that explains your decisions.

Case Study

· · · · · · · · · · · · · · ·

The treasurer for the student council at a local high school needs to create a spreadsheet that will track expenses in order to meet the budget for the upcoming school year. Using last year's budget, as well as this year's donations and fundraising, the class has decided to budget as follows:

School sweatshirts:	$1400
Dances:	$3200
Decorations:	$300
Yearbook:	$3700
Pep rallies:	$500

Create a formatted spreadsheet that documents the budget categories shown above. Be sure to include the name of your high school and a piece of clip art that relates to your school team.

In the month of September, you have the following expenses:

Logo design for sweatshirts:	$35
Prizes for pep rally:	$125
Film for yearbook:	$75
Site license for digital yearbook program:	$50
Banner supplies:	$125
Dance tickets:	$50
DJ:	$300

Enter these expenses in the appropriate places in your spreadsheet. Use formulas to determine how much is left in each of the budget categories at the beginning of October.

Assume that the expenses for October, November, and December are the same as they are for September. How much money would be left in each of the budget categories at the beginning of January? Use your spreadsheet to find the answers.

Chapter 4
Consumer Decisions

Shopping Wisely

How much shopping do you do? What have you bought recently? Was it clothing, a CD, or some other product? Are you happy with your purchase? How much did you pay for it? Could you have purchased it for less? Do you think it was a good buy? Or could the money be put to better use?

This chapter deals with consumer decision-making. Consumer decisions are based on many things, including price. When you compare the various prices of a product in which you are interested, you can be confident you are making a more informed purchase. There are times when shopping can be confusing because of sales and promotions. This chapter explains how you can calculate the cost of a product when it is on sale and determine whether it is a good buy.

This chapter also looks at sales tax. Most items have additional taxes that are added to the advertised price.

The concepts of rate and ratio are introduced. Understanding rate and ratio can help you in many situations, for example, when you are making consumer decisions, drawing scale diagrams, or solving problems in geometry.

Chapter Goals

In this chapter, you will learn to calculate unit price, sales tax, and the savings resulting from sales promotions, as well as to solve problems using rate and ratio.

Technology

A calculator, spreadsheet software, and the internet can be helpful tools when you are making consumer decisions.

Chapter Project

This project requires you to plan a menu for a 3-day camping trip and to determine the cost of the food per person. You may wish to complete this project in a small group.

Choose food for the camping trip that is both nutritious and reasonably priced. Refer to the Canada Food Guide as you plan the menu for the trip. Remember to keep track of the cost of each food item you choose.

When you complete the chapter, your project file will contain the following information:

- the menu for each day of the camping trip
- the number of servings from each food group per person per day (based on the Canada Food Guide)
- the number of servings in each food item
- the cost of each food item
- the cost of one serving of each food item
- the cost per meal per person
- the total cost of food per person

This woman is a cook at a mining camp in the Yukon.

Career Profile

Name: Anna Fiorentino

Job: summer job cooking at a camp in Whiteshell, Manitoba

Current wages: $10.75 an hour

Education: grade 12; professional cooking program at Assiniboine Community College, Brandon, Manitoba

Career goal: chef at a restaurant

Keyword search: Canada college chef certificate

Project Activity

Choose your group of 2-3 persons. Has anyone in your group gone camping before? Obtain a copy of the Canada Food Guide. The Canada Food Guide lists the daily nutritional requirements for Canadians. You can find a copy of the Canada Food Guide on the internet at:

http://www.hc-sc.gc.ca/hpfb-dgpsa/onpp-bppn/food_guide_rainbow_e.html

Exploration 1

Smart Shopping

Have you ever bought a product because it was on sale, or because you thought it would be nice to have? After you have had it for a while, have you found that you do not use it or do not even like it? Most people have made such purchases. However, with careful planning and comparison-shopping, this kind of purchase can be kept to a minimum.

In this exploration, you will examine the kind of shopper you are. Do you buy on impulse or do you plan before you purchase a product? Do you compare products before you buy? Do you check the prices from more than one company? Do you have a budget and stay within it? Do you consider how often you will wear an article of clothing or the lifespan of a product before purchasing it? You will find out what kind of shopper you are by taking a buyer behaviour self-test.

In this exploration, you will also examine the packaging and labels of food items.

Whole Class Activity

To determine the kind of shopper you are, fill out a copy of the buyer behaviour self-test on the next page. How did you rate? What did the self-test tell you about how you shop? Are you happy with the kind of shopper you are?

Goals

In this exploration, you will examine the packaging and labels of food items and become a more informed shopper.

What Kind of Shopper Are You?

Directions: Circle the word that describes you best.

1. **I look at ads to get information about products or services.**

   4 Always   3 Often   2 Rarely   1 Never

2. **I find information about products and services from places other than ads.**

   4 Always   3 Often   2 Rarely   1 Never

3. **I check for the price and quality of different brands at different companies before I buy.**

   4 Always   3 Often   2 Rarely   1 Never

4. **I read the labels and the guarantees given on products and follow any directions given.**

   4 Always   3 Often   2 Rarely   1 Never

5. **I try out a product before buying it, if possible, and ask about items I can't try out.**

   4 Always   3 Often   2 Rarely   1 Never

6. **I make a list and follow it while shopping.**

   4 Always   3 Often   2 Rarely   1 Never

7. **I let manufacturers and retailers know what I like and dislike about their products and services.**

   4 Always   3 Often   2 Rarely   1 Never

8. **I decide what products and services to get before I go out shopping.**

   4 Always   3 Often   2 Rarely   1 Never

9. **I consider what I need and want as well as the price before I decide what to buy.**

   4 Always   3 Often   2 Rarely   1 Never

Add up your scores and rate yourself according to the following scale:

28–36   super shopper
19–27   careful shopper
10–18   poorly prepared shopper
0–9   need-to-improve shopper

Knowing what kind of shopper you are is valuable because it allows you to see how you make consumer decisions. How did you answer question #4? Do you read the labels of products when you are shopping? Reading labels is a good way to find out more about the products you are buying. Most food labels are required by law to have the following information:

a) the legal name of the product

b) the net weight (grams) or liquid volume (millilitres) of the contents

c) the name and address of the manufacturer, packer, or distributor

d) the ingredients; these are listed in order by weight, from most to least, and should include additives such as colouring, flavouring, and preservatives

e) a description of the product's form, such as whole tomatoes, diced tomatoes, or crushed tomatoes

f) special features of the product, such as whether it is low-fat or salt-free

g) nutrition-related information: serving size, number of servings, calories per serving, grams of protein, fat, and carbohydrates per serving, and percentage of the recommended daily allowance in each serving for protein and important vitamins and minerals

Hint

Many people have food allergies. For people with food allergies, checking the ingredients on the labels of food products is extremely important.

Career Connection

Name: George Roussopoulos

Job: part-time clerk at a clothing store

Current wages: $7.65 an hour

Education: currently in grade 10; planning to complete grade 12 and take a college course in fashion design

Background skills and knowledge: designs and sews clothing for his friends

Career goal: fashion designer

Keyword Search: Canada fashion design college certificate

Mental Math

1. If 1 serving of cereal is 30 g, how many servings are there in:

   300 g of cereal

   150 g of cereal

   450 g of cereal

2. If 1 serving of yogurt is 175 g, how many servings are there in:

   350 g

   700 g

   1400 g

3. If 1 serving of juice is 1/2 cup, how many servings are there in:

   1 cup of juice

   2 cups of juice

   1/4 cup of juice

Project Activity

Refer to your copy of the Canada Food Guide.

1. List the four food groups from the Canada Food Guide.
2. List the suggested number of servings from each food group indicated in the Canada Food Guide.
3. Find the number of servings from each food group as indicated in the Canada Food Guide for the following meals:

Breakfast # 1

1	orange
60 g	cold cereal + 1/2 cup milk
1	slice toast
1	tbsp peanut butter

Breakfast # 2

1	glass apple juice
2	slices toast
2	eggs

Lunch #1

1	tuna sandwich
1	glass milk
1	apple
1	chocolate bar

Lunch #2

1	large salad
2	slices pizza
1	cup coffee
2	cookies

Supper #1

200 g	chicken
1	green salad
1 cup	peas and carrots
1 cup	rice
1 scoop	ice cream

Supper #2

1	hamburger
1	large order of fries
1	milkshake

Notebook Assignment

1. One thing that may influence you when you are shopping is the packaging. Good packaging protects the product and makes it easier to handle. It also helps sell the product.

   The shape of a package is one way to make products look appealing. It can fool you into thinking that you are seeing something you are not. Look at the following packages. Which ones look like they contain more? Explain why.

2. The packaging of a product gives you information about its contents. Food producers are required to list certain information on their packaging. Consider the following information given on two boxes of cereal and answer the questions that follow.

Cereal #1

Nutrition Information	
Servings 20	
Per serving 30 g = 160 mL (2/3 cup)	
Energy	110 Cal
	460 kJ
Protein	2.9 g
Fat	0.6 g
Polyunsaturates	0.4 g
Monounsaturates	0.1 g
Saturates	0.1 g
Cholesterol	0 mg
Carbohydrate	25 g
Sugars	4.3 g
Starch	16 g
Dietary Fibre	3.5 g
Sodium	167 mg
Potassium	114 mg

Percentage of Recommended Daily Intake	
Vitamin A	0%
Vitamin D	0%
Thiamine	46%
Riboflavin	4%
Niacin	9%
Vitamin B6	10%
Folacin	8%
Vitamin B12	0%
Pantothenate	7%
Calcium	1%
Phosphorus	9%
Magnesium	15%
Iron	29%
Zinc	9%

Ingredients: whole wheat, corn syrup, sugar, natural flavour, salt

Cereal #2

Nutrition Information	
Per 30 g serving (300 mL, 1 1/4 cup)	
Energy	112 Cal
	470 kJ
Protein	2.1 g
Fat	0.2 g
Carbohydrate	26 g
Sugars	2.3 g
Starch	23 g
Dietary Fibre	0.8 g
Sodium	215 mg
Potassium	30 mg

% of Recommended Daily Intake	
Vitamin A	0%
Vitamin D	0%
Vitamin B1	46%
Vitamin B2	50%
Niacin	8%
Vitamin B6	10%
Folacin	8%
Vitamin B12	0%
Pantothenate	7%
Calcium	0%
Phosphorus	1%
Magnesium	1%
Iron	28%
Zinc	1%

Ingredients: flaked milled corn, sugar/glucose-fructose, malt flavouring, salt, natural colour, vitamins, iron. Contains traces of soybeans

a) Ingredients are listed in order of weight from most to least. List the ingredient that weighs the most in cereal #1. List the ingredient that weighs the most in cereal #2.

b) List the serving size of cereal #1. List the serving size of cereal #2.

c) List the energy per serving of cereal #1. List the energy per serving of cereal #2. Which cereal contains more energy per serving?

d) What percentage of your recommended daily intake of iron is supplied by one serving of cereal #1?

e) How many servings of cereal #2 would you have to eat to meet your recommended daily intake of vitamin B6?

f) In which food group(s) of the Canada Food Guide would you place cereal? In what food group(s) would you place cereal with milk?

3. Consider the following information printed on a can of tuna.

Ingredients
albacore tuna, water, salt, sodium acid pyrophosphate

Delicious Seafoods
1504 20th Ave.
Vancouver B.C.

Net wt.
170 g

Drained wt.
120 g

Nutrition Information	
Per 50 g Serving	
Energy	116 cal/490 kJ
Protein	27 g
Fat	0.6 g
Polyunsaturates	0.4 g
Monounsaturates	0.1 g
Saturates	0.1 g
Cholesterol	33 mg
Carbohydrate	0 g

a) Does tuna contain more protein, fat, or carbohydrate?

b) In what food group of the Canada Food Guide would you place tuna?

c) What is 1 serving size of tuna as listed on the can?

d) There are two weights listed on the can. What are they?

e) How many servings are there in this can of tuna?

f) Which weight did you use to determine the number of servings in the can of tuna?

4. Consider the following information printed on a jar of peanut butter.

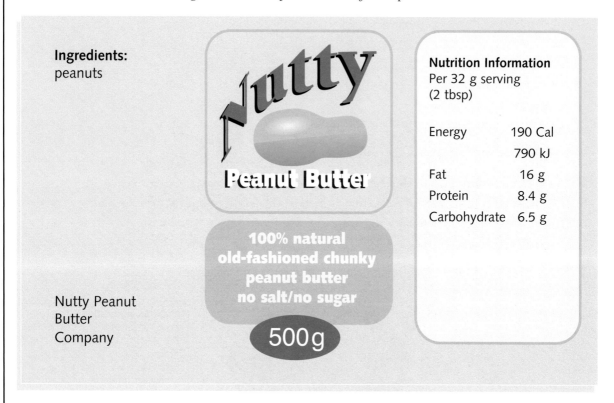

Ingredients:
peanuts

Nutty Peanut
Butter
Company

100% natural
old-fashioned chunky
peanut butter
no salt/no sugar

500 g

Nutrition Information
Per 32 g serving
(2 tbsp)

Energy	190 Cal
	790 kJ
Fat	16 g
Protein	8.4 g
Carbohydrate	6.5 g

a) In what food group of the Canada Food Guide would you place peanut butter?

b) Does peanut butter contain more protein, fat, or carbohydrate?

c) How many tablespoons of peanut butter make up one serving?

d) How many servings could you get from 1.5 kg of peanut butter?

e) How much protein is there in one serving of peanut butter?

Extension

5. Think about three food items that would be appropriate to take on a camping trip. Determine the following information for each food item: serving size, price, and nutritional information. Record this information and bring it to class. You will need this information for your project.

Problem Analysis

Quilting

Quilts are often created using a number of squares or other geometric shapes. These squares can be constructed in a variety of patterns. The pattern shown is called Twelve Triangles.

You have decided to sew a quilt using this pattern. At home you know you have some fabric but you are not sure if you have enough. You want to include at least three different colours in your pattern.

- How much fabric will you need of each colour for a 20 cm square?
- How much fabric would you need to complete the entire quilt?
- What other information do you need in order to solve the problem?

Games

Black Holes

In astronomy, a black hole is a region in space that is so dense and has a gravity so intense that nothing, not even light, can escape. In mathematics, a "black hole" occurs when a repeated process results in a constant or a repeating series of numbers, from which no escape is possible. Try the following example of a mathematical black hole.

Steps	Try 2193
1. Choose any positive four-digit number with different digits	2193
2. Write the largest number that can be formed with these digits.	9321
3. Write the smallest number that can be formed with these digits.	1239
4. Subtract the smaller number from the larger.	9321 – 1239 = 8082
5. Repeat steps 2, 3, and 4 using the previous result.	8820 – 0288 = 8532
6. Continue the process until you cannot go any further.	8532 – 2358 = 6174 7641 – 1467 = 6174

1. What do you notice about the final result when we began with 2193?
2. What happens when you begin with 5288?
3. a) Begin with other positive four-digit numbers. What happens?
   b) Will this happen for any four-digit number? Why do you think so?

Exploration 2

The Cost of One

Suppose you need to buy two litres of milk. You can buy either two 1-litre containers or one 2-litre container. How do you decide which you should buy?

Groceries, as well as other products, are often available in a variety of sizes. One way you can make sure you get the best possible price for a product is by calculating its unit price. The unit price of a product is an expression of the cost of one unit of the product. It can be the cost of one litre of milk, the cost of one T-shirt, or the cost of one kilowatt of electricity. The unit varies depending on the product.

Example 1

Solomon wants to buy natural spring water. His local supermarket in Yellowknife sells natural spring water at $3.75 for 12 bottles. Calculate the unit price of 1 bottle of water.

Solution

In this case, the unit is 1 bottle. Since the cost is $3.75 for 12 bottles, the cost of 1 bottle of natural spring water is:

$3.75 ÷ 12 bottles = $0.31/bottle (rounded to the nearest cent)

Note that $0.31 can also be written as 31¢.

Goals

In this exploration, you will learn to calculate the unit price of a product.

New Terms

unit price: the cost of one unit of a product expressed as cost per unit.

Example 2

Jennifer lives in Ste. Agathe, Manitoba. She wants to buy orange juice. The orange juice comes in two sizes. The smaller size sells at 99¢ for 355 mL while the larger size sells at $1.19 for 500 mL. Which is a better buy?

Solution

The unit is 1 millilitre (1 mL). The smaller size costs 99¢ for 355 mL. The unit price of the smaller size is:

99¢ ÷ 355 mL = 0.279¢/mL (rounded to three decimal places)

The larger size costs $1.19 for 500 mL. The unit price of the larger size is:

119¢ ÷ 500 mL = 0.238¢/mL

Since the unit price of the larger size is less than the smaller size, the larger size is a better buy.

Hints

1. To calculate the unit price, divide the cost of the product by the number of units.

2. To compare the unit price of two items, both prices have to be in the same unit and both quantities must be in the same unit.

Project Activity

In this activity, you will create the charts and/or spreadsheets
you need to prepare for your camping trip. You need to create
the six charts and/or spreadsheets shown below.

Chart #1 Camping Trip Menu

Day	Breakfast	Snack	Lunch	Snack	Supper	Snack
Day #1	None					
Day #2	2 slices toast 30 g cold cereal $1/2$ c. milk 1 banana 1 glass orange juice					
Day #3					None	None

Mental Math

1. Round the following to the nearest cent:
   a) $2.488
   b) $6.642
   c) $0.299

2. Find the unit price of 1 pencil if it costs $1.00 for 4 pencils.

3. Find the unit price of 1 chocolate bar if 10 chocolate bars cost $4.99.

4. Find the unit price of 1 litre of gasoline if 20 litres cost $15.00.

Chart #2 Food Groups Chart

Day	Grain Products	Fruits and Vegetables	Milk Products	Meat and Alternatives	
Day #1	2 slices toast 30 g cold cereal	1 banana 1 glass orange juice	$1/2$ c milk		
Day #2					
Day #3					

Chart #3 Breakfast Chart

Day	Food Item	Serving Size	Package Size	Cost per Package	Cost per Serving	Number of Servings per Person	Cost per Item per person
Day #2	toast	1 slice	20 slices	$1.69	$0.08	2	$0.16
	cold cereal	30 g	525 g	$4.89	$0.28	1	$0.28
	milk	250 mL	2 litres	$2.34	$0.29	1	$0.29
	banana	1 banana	5 per kg	$1.30	$0.26	1	$0.26
	orange juice	125 mL	1.89 L	$2.89	$0.19	2	$0.38
Day #3							
						Total Cost per Person $1.37	

Chart #4 Lunch Chart

Day	Food Item	Serving Size	Package Size	Cost per Package	Cost per Serving	Number of Servings per Person	Cost per Item per person
Day #1							
Day #2							
Day #3							
						Total Cost per Person $ _____	

Chart #5 Supper Chart

Day	Food Item	Serving Size	Package Size	Cost per Package	Cost per Serving	Number of Servings per Person	Cost per Item per person
Day #1							
Day #2							
						Total Cost per Person $ _____	

Chart #6 Snack Chart

Day	Food Item	Serving Size	Package Size	Cost per Package	Cost per Serving	Number of Servings per Person	Cost per Item per person
Day #1							
Day #2							
Day #3							
						Total Cost per Person $ _____	

Create the six charts and/or spreadsheets. Complete the first two charts: the Camping Trip Menu and the Food Groups Chart.

In order to complete these charts, refer to your copy of the Canada Food Guide. Together with your group, decide on a menu for the camping trip. Choose foods that meet the requirements of the Canada Food Guide. You need meals for breakfast, lunch and supper as well as three snacks a day. You do not need breakfast the first day nor supper or a third snack the last day.

Drinking water will be available on the trip so you do not have to bring any water. Keep in mind that you are camping and that you would prefer the food to be lightweight and to create as little garbage as possible. You will have to bring back any garbage.

As you decide on food products for your menu and enter them in the first chart, also enter them in the second chart. This way, you will make sure you have the required number of servings from each food group from the Canada Food Guide. Feel free to make changes in the menu until you are satisfied with the food you have chosen.

Because you are going to need to calculate the cost of the food products you have included in your menu, collect food flyers from various supermarkets or food stores in your area, or you can check local supermarkets or food stores for the prices of these foods.

Notebook Assignment

1. While shopping, Rajeet finds that two boxes of cereal cost $3.50. What is the unit price of a box of cereal?

2. At a fruit and vegetable stand, a dozen apples sells for $2.50. What is the price of one apple?

3. A week later, the fruit and vegetable stand in question 2 changes its price for apples to $2.20 for 1.4 kg. Two other fruit stands in the area sell their apples at 2.4 kg for $3.00 and 4.5 kg for $5.50, respectively. Which stand has the lowest unit price?

4. Carole finds canned peas offered for sale at three cans for $2.00 in one store, five cans for $2.50 in a second, and eight cans for $3.25 in a third. Which store has the lowest unit price?

5. Cola in Store A is four cans for $4.75. Cola in Store B is twelve cans for $8.95. Which store has the less expensive cans of cola? Justify your answer in two different ways.

6. A can of apple juice costs 37¢ at the corner store. The local supermarket has the same juice priced at three cans for $1.09. Do you get a bargain at the supermarket? Justify your answer in two different ways.

7. Nan finds that she can buy oat bran in three stores at the following prices: 89¢ for 500 g, $1.79 for 1.5 kg, and 2.2 kg for $2.98. At which store is the unit price lowest?

8. Exactly the same type of oat bran can be bought at the corner store for the following prices: 79¢ for 250 g, $1.57 for 500 g, or $3.09 for 1.5 kg. Which of these packages has the lowest unit price? How do these prices compare to those in question 7?

Extension

9. Jason wants to buy some T-shirts. His favourite department store sells T-shirts individually, or in packages of two or three. One T-shirt sells for $2.98, a package of two T-shirts sells for $5.49, and a package of three T-shirts sells for $7.89.

   a) Find the unit price when T-shirts are sold in a package of two.
   b) Find the unit price when T-shirts are sold in a package of three.
   c) Which package offers the best unit price?
   d) Suppose Jason wants to buy seven T-shirts. Which combination of packages will be the least expensive?

Hints

Remember that 1000 g = 1 kg.

Exploration 3

● ● ● ● ● ● ● ● ● ● ● ● ● ● ● ● ● ● ●

Sales Taxes: GST and PST

Suppose you are shopping for a CD and see one advertised for $14.95. How much will you have to pay for the CD? Suppose you buy a meal advertised at $5.95 in a food court. How much will you have to pay for the meal? In both cases, you will pay more than the advertised price. In addition to the advertised price, you will have to pay tax.

One tax is the GST. GST stands for Goods and Services Tax and is a federal tax paid everywhere in Canada. The percent rate of the GST is 7%. Examples of goods that are subject to the GST are CDs, portable CD players, and tools. Examples of services subject to the GST are home improvements and haircuts. Many provinces also have a provincial sales tax referred to as the PST. The PST varies from province to province and each province applies their sales tax to different products. The province of Alberta as well as Yukon, Northwest Territories, and Nunavut do not have a PST. Newfoundland and Labrador, New Brunswick, and Nova Scotia combine GST and PST into a "Harmonized Sales Tax" referred to as the HST.

Because of these taxes, when you buy certain products or pay for certain services, the final price will be greater than the advertised price.

Goals

In this exploration, you will learn to calculate the GST, the PST, and the final price of a product.

New Terms

GST: a federal tax calculated on goods and services.

PST: a provincial sales tax calculated on goods and services sold. Different provinces or territories impose PST at different rates and on different items.

HST: a combined federal and provincial tax applied in some provinces.

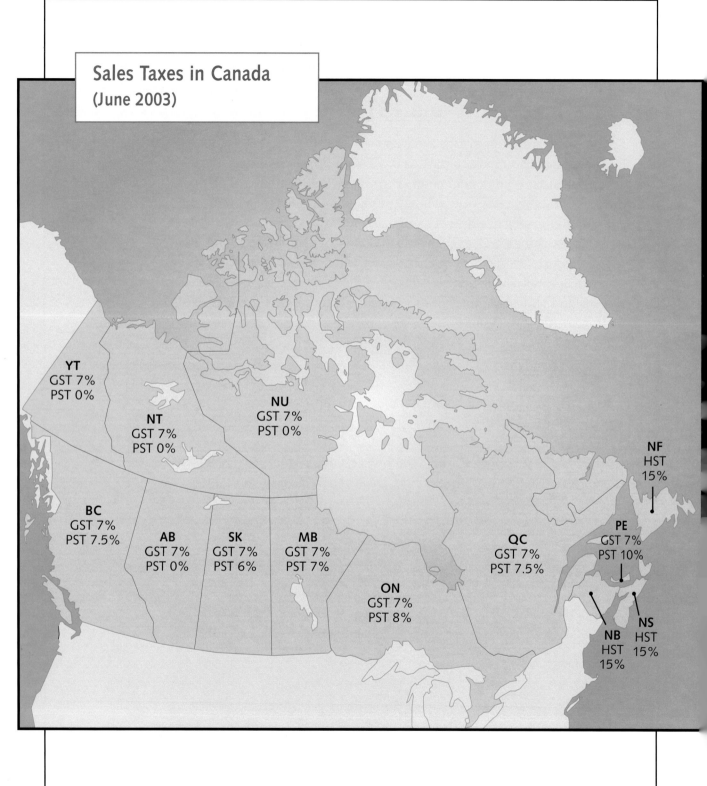

Sales Taxes in Canada
(June 2003)

YT
GST 7%
PST 0%

NT
GST 7%
PST 0%

NU
GST 7%
PST 0%

NF
HST
15%

BC
GST 7%
PST 7.5%

AB
GST 7%
PST 0%

SK
GST 7%
PST 6%

MB
GST 7%
PST 7%

QC
GST 7%
PST 7.5%

PE
GST 7%
PST 10%

ON
GST 7%
PST 8%

NB
HST
15%

NS
HST
15%

Example 1

Marina lives in Nelson, British Columbia.

a) How much tax will she pay when she buys a surround-sound stereo advertised at $2595.00?

b) What will be the final price of the system when taxes are included?

Solution

a) The GST in Canada is 7%. The PST in British Columbia is 7.5%.

GST   = 7% of $2595.00   PST   = 7.5% of $2595.00
         = 0.07 x $2595.00   = 0.075 x $2595.00
         = $181.65   = $194.63

The total tax Marina will pay is:
$181.65 + $194.63 = $376.28

b) The final price Marina will pay is:
$2595.00 + $376.28 = $2971.28

Class Discussion

Many products are advertised for amounts like $1.99, $9.95, $49.95, or $1995.98. Why do you think the amounts often have 9's in them?

If you look at a product that is advertised for $1.99, how can you quickly estimate how much the GST is on that product? Explain.

How can you estimate the GST for products with prices like $9.95, $49.95, or $1,995.98? Explain.

Hints

7% means 7 out of one hundred, 7 hundredths, or 0.07. To find 7% of a number, you can multiply the number by 0.07.

Project Activity

Begin to fill in the Breakfast, Lunch, Supper, and Snack Charts that you created in the last exploration. In this exploration, you will complete three columns in each of these charts.

- In each column titled Food Item, list the foods you have chosen for each meal of the trip.
- In each column titled Serving Size, list the serving size of each of these foods, according to the Canada Food Guide.
- In each column titled Number of Servings per Person, list the number of servings of each food provided per person.

Reminder: Collect food flyers and/or check the prices of foods you have chosen at various food stores in your area.

Notebook Assignment

1. Indicate on which of the following you pay GST and/or PST.

   a) 3 kg apples
   b) haircut
   c) portable compact disk player
   d) box of chocolates
   e) restaurant meal
   f) pair of jeans
   g) jar of peanut butter
   h) electrical repair
   i) book
   j) package of paper towels

Mental Math

1. What is the GST on an item that costs $1.00?

2. What is the GST on an item that costs $10.00?

3. What is the GST on an item that costs $100.00?

4. What is the GST on an item that costs $1000.00?

Technology

The % key on your calculator can be used to find the percent of a quantity. For example, to find 7% of 50, enter 50 x 7 % . The calculator should give an answer of 3.5. If this is not the case, check the instructions for your calculator.

2. Find the GST and the PST of a Toast-r-Oven which sells at $68.88. What will the total cost be to the customer? The Toast-r-Oven is sold in Manitoba.

3. A customer purchases a new suit. The price of the suit is $285.00. What is the cost to the customer after GST and PST are added? The suit is purchased in Ontario.

4. Janet purchases a new compact car. The car has a sticker price of $12,675.00. What does she have to pay for GST and PST, and what is the total of the sticker price plus the taxes? The car is sold in British Columbia.

5. Paul went to an electronics store and bought a CD player advertised at $450.00, a set of speakers at $235.00, and a portable telephone at $189.00. How much did he have to pay altogether including taxes? He bought these items in Nova Scotia.

6. Rocco purchased a propane barbecue for $165.00 and a propane tank for $45.00. How much did he have to pay altogether including taxes? Rocco lives in the Northwest Territories.

7. If a package of four pairs of socks costs $7.16 and a package of three pairs costs $5.19:

   a) Find the unit price of a pair of socks from each package.
   b) Which is a better buy?
   c) Find the after-tax cost of 12 pairs of the less expensive socks. The socks are purchased in Manitoba.

8. If you purchase a VCR with an advertised price of $329.00:

   a) Find the total price you would pay for the VCR in Victoria, British Columbia.
   b) Find the total price you would pay for the VCR in Kugluktuk, Nunavut.
   c) What is the difference in these prices?
   d) Find an alternate way to calculate this price difference.

Extension

9. Aimée lives in northern Manitoba and is interested in purchasing a used snowmobile. She finds one she likes at a dealership for $1299.00. Since both the GST and PST in Manitoba are 7%, she concludes that she will have to pay an extra 14% for her snowmobile.

    a) Find the total of the advertised price and the taxes by multiplying the advertised price by 1.14.

    b) Find the total of the advertised price and the taxes by finding the GST and PST separately and then adding the taxes to the advertised price.

    c) Are the totals the same? Explain.

10. Aimée finds another snowmobile at a second dealership priced at $1224.95. Find the total of the advertised price and the taxes.

Exploration 4

· · · · · · · · · · · · · · · · ·

Sales Promotions

Darren wants to buy a portable CD player. He finds one he likes at an electronics store. When he talks to the salesperson, she tells him that they are having their anniversary sale next week and that everything in the store will be 25% off. Darren calculates how much he will save on the CD player and decides to wait until next week to purchase it.

Stores often have promotions in which they offer discounts on the products they sell. The discount is often expressed as a percent. If you are walking through a department store, you may see signs offering 10%, 25%, or even 50% off regular prices. Other times, promotions involve coupons, two-for-one sales, or free gifts. What types of promotions are offered in your community?

Suppose you want to buy a pair of jeans and Store A usually sells the pair you want at a higher regular price than Store B does. Store A is having a sale and is selling the jeans at 15% off. By calculating the sale price of the jeans in Store A, you will be able to compare the two prices and determine which store offers a better buy.

Goals

In this exploration, you will learn to calculate percent discount, given the regular price and the amount of discount. You will also consider the impact of sales promotions.

Example 1

Sheena buys a tank top that is regularly priced at $15.95 but is on sale for $12.95. How much does she save by purchasing the tank top at the reduced price? Sheena buys the tank top in British Columbia.

Solution

GST on regular price: PST on regular price:
   7% x $15.95   7.5% x $15.95
  = 0.07 x $15.95   = 0.075 x $15.95
  = $1.12   = $1.20

Total cost using regular price and taxes:
  = $15.95 + $1.12 + $1.20
  = $18.27

GST on sale price: PST on sale price:
   7% x $12.95   7.5% x $12.95
  = 0.07 x $12.95   = 0.075 x $12.95
  = $0.91   = $0.97

Total cost using sale price plus taxes:
  $12.95 + $0.91 + $0.97 = $14.83

Sheena's savings are:
  $18.27 - $14.83 = $3.44

There is another way to calculate Sheena's savings. The difference between the regular price and the sale price is:
  $15.95 – $12.95 = $3.00

GST on the difference: PST on the difference:
   7% x $3.00   7.5% x $3.00
  = 0.07 x $3.00   = 0.075 x $3.00
  = $0.21   = $0.23

Sheena saves the difference in price plus the taxes on that difference:
  $3.00 + $0.21 + $0.23 = $3.44

Example 2

Jeremy lives in British Columbia. He wants to buy a computer that regularly sells for $1500.00. One electronics store is selling the computer at a 25% discount. If Jeremy decides to buy the computer at that electronics store, what will be his total cost?

Solution

The discount is 25% of $1500.00:

   0.25 x $1500.00 = $375.00

The sale price is the regular price minus the discount:

   $1500.00 – $375.00 = $1125.00

The GST on the sale price is 7% of $1125.00, and the PST on the sale price is also 7.5% of $1125.00.

   0.07 x $1125.00 = $78.75   0.075 x $1125.00 = $84.38

The total cost using sale price plus taxes is:

   $1125.00 + $84.38 + $78.75 = $1288.13

Note that if the discount is 25% of the regular price, the sale price is 75% of the regular price. You can use this sale price of 75% to solve the example in an alternative way:

   0.75 x $1500.00 = $1125.00

You then find the GST, PST, and total cost as you did in the solution above.

Mental Math

1. Find 10% of $400.00.

2. Find 20% of $400.00.

3. Find 5% of $400.00.

4. Find 15% of $400.00.

Career Profile

Name: Jason Burrows

Job: owner of a skateboard store in Abbotsford, British Columbia

Current wages: $35,000 annual salary

Education: merchandising management course at Capilano Community College, North Vancouver, British Columbia

Background skills and knowledge: building skateboards

Keyword search: Canada community college business program

Project Activity

Create a question involving a sales promotion that relates to the food you have chosen for the camping trip. Answer the question. Then give the question to another classmate to answer.

Mental Math

1. Find 25% of $80.00.
2. Find 5% of $2500.00.
3. Find 10% of $44.99.

Hint

During a promotion, stores sometimes advertise that customers will pay no GST or PST on products they purchase. The store owners must still pay GST and PST on the products. The stores reduce the price on the products so that the final price the customers pay is the total of the reduced price plus the GST and PST.

Notebook Assignment

1. Shauna lives in Dauphin, Manitoba. She collects coupons and uses them when she shops for food at her local supermarket. On one of her recent shopping trips, she purchased the following foods:

   2 L milk for $2.40
   1 dozen eggs for $1.80
   500 g of cottage cheese for $1.99
   3 packages of macaroni and cheese at 3 for $1.09
   525 g package of cereal for $4.59

   Shauna had the following coupons:

   35¢ off 500 g of cottage cheese
   25¢ off 3 packages of macaroni and cheese
   75¢ off the 525 g package of cereal

   a) Calculate the regular cost of the groceries.
   b) Calculate the amount Shauna saves by using coupons.
   c) Does Shauna save more or less than 10% by using coupons? Explain.

2. A supermarket charges $3.89 for a package of Pizza Pops. Claude has a coupon for 45¢ off. During a promotion, the supermarket doubles the value of each coupon.

   a) If Claude uses his coupon, what will he pay for the package of Pizza Pops?
   b) Approximately what percent does Claude save by using his coupon? Explain.

3. Video Village sells a book of 10 coupons for $29.95. Each coupon is good for the rental of one video from Video Village. The coupons are good for a 1-year period. The regular rental price of newly released videos at Video Village is $3.49.

   a) What is the unit price of 1 coupon?
   b) How much money would be saved in a year if all 10 coupons were used? How much tax would also be saved?
   c) Why do you think Video Village sells the coupons?

4. At one sports store, the price of a tennis racket is $49.95. At a second sports store, the regular price of a similar racket is $55.95 but it is on sale at 15% off.

   a) Calculate the sale price before tax of the tennis racket that is on sale.
   b) Which tennis racket is a better buy?

5. Takeshi can purchase the same skateboard at two stores. The price at the first store is $149.95, while the price at the second store is $154.50. The second store is having a promotion advertising that customers pay no tax. The stores are in British Columbia.

   a) Calculate the final cost of the skateboard at the first store.
   b) Which store offers a better buy?

Extension

6. A clothing store is having a sales promotion on sweaters. When you buy two sweaters, the more expensive sweater is at the regular price while the less expensive sweater is 50% off. The clothing store is in the Yukon.

   a) Kelly finds two sweaters she likes, one at $35.95 and the other at $29.95. Find the final cost of these two sweaters, including tax.
   b) Why do you think the store offers this type of promotion?

Exploration 5

Rate

Dieter wants to buy twelve notebooks. He can buy the notebooks in packages of 3 or 4. The cost of 3 notebooks is $3.49 while the cost of 4 notebooks is $4.79. Dieter knows that by calculating the unit price of one notebook, he can determine which one is a better buy.

Unit price is an example of rate. A rate expresses one quantity measured in relation to a second quantity. The second quantity is 1.

Think of a car travelling at 60 km/h. This rate expresses the number of kilometres travelled in 1 hour. Think of a basketball player scoring 18 points per game. The expression "18 points per game" is a rate. It expresses the number of points scored in 1 game. A rate of $8.50 per hour is an expression of the money earned in 1 hour.

Goals

In this exploration, you will learn to solve problems involving rate.

New Terms

rate: one quantity measured in relation to another quantity, for example, km/h.

Example 1

During the hockey season, Jennifer scored 22 goals in 40 games, while Katya scored 31 goals in 55 games. Which player scored more goals per game?

Solution

This question can be answered by calculating the number of goals scored per game. Since Jennifer scored 22 goals in 40 games, her goals-per-game rate was:

22 goals ÷ 40 games = 0.550 goals/game (expressed to 3 decimal places)

Since Katya scored 31 goals in 55 games, her goals-per-game rate was:

31 goals ÷ 55 games = 0.564 goals/game

Since 0.564 is greater than 0.550, Katya scored more goals per game than Jennifer. A rate of 0.564 goals per game means that, on average, Katya scores about one half a goal per game. Another way of looking at this is to say that if she played 1000 games, she would score 564 goals.

Example 2

Kim travelled from Kelowna to Vancouver in 4 hours and 15 minutes. The distance from Kelowna to Vancouver is 331 km. Find Kim's average rate of travel.

Solution

Since each quantity must be in only one unit of measure, write 15 minutes in terms of an hour. Since 15 minutes is 1/4 of an hour, write 4 hours, 15 minutes as 4.25 hours. Kim's average rate of travel is:

331 km ÷ 4.25 hours = 78 km/h (rounded to the nearest whole number)

Hints

When you express a rate you must include the units for both quantities.

Mental Math

Find the hourly rate of pay:

a) $19.00 for 2 hours of work

b) $51.00 for 3 hours of work

c) $64.80 for 8 hours of work

Project Activity

In order to do this part of the project, your group will have to check flyers or visit local supermarkets or grocery stores in your area. Refer to the Breakfast, Lunch, Supper, and Snack Charts you have already started. Complete the following in each of these charts.

- In each column titled Package Size, enter the size of the package of the particular food item (in millilitres, grams, etc.).
- In each column titled Cost per Package enter the cost of each package of food. If there is any tax on the food, add it to the cost.

Did your group do any comparison shopping for the food items it chose? Did your group check prices of different sizes of food items or prices at different stores? What did you find?

Notebook Assignment

1. Express each of the following as a unit rate. Be sure to include correct units in your final answers.

   a) gross pay of $15.50 for 2 hours
   b) 18 doughnuts for 12 people
   c) 48 cans of pop in 4 cases
   d) cost of $3.00 for 6 bagels
   e) 5000 paper clips in 20 boxes
   f) $17.50 for 10 bus tickets
   g) 240 km in 3 hours

Hint

You can express a rate in a number of ways: 65 km/h or 65 kilometres in 1 hour.

Mental Math

Find the unit rate of speed for each of the following:

   a) 150 km in 2 h
   b) 30 km in 1/4 h
   c) 620 km in 10 h

2. Jordy left home at 9:15 am and drove a distance of 350 km. He stopped for half an hour for lunch and arrived at his destination at 1:30 pm.

   a) What is his average speed, excluding the stop for lunch?
   b) What is his average speed, including the stop for lunch?
   c) Do you think the stop for lunch should be included when calculating average speed?

3. Mary leaves Rankin Inlet and flies 1150 kilometres in 2 hours.

   a) Find her average speed for the first two hours of her flight.
   b) Mary's flight will take her 1750 kilometres from Rankin Inlet. If she continues at the same average speed, what is the total number of hours she must travel to reach her destination?

4. Robert's gross pay is $51.00 for 6 hours of work.

   a) What is Robert's hourly rate of pay?
   b) Robert has approximately 10% deducted from his gross pay. Find Robert's net hourly rate of pay.
   c) Robert is saving for skates. He has found a pair he likes at a price of $149.50. What will be Robert's total cost for the skates? Robert lives in Arviat, Nunavut.
   d) How many hours will Robert have to work to be able to afford to buy the skates?

5. Anna takes the bus to and from work each day. She also uses the bus on weekends. On average, Anna uses the bus twice a day. Anna has a choice in how she can pay for the bus rides. A single bus ride costs $1.65, 10 bus tickets cost $16.00, and a monthly bus pass costs $62.00.

   a) How many times would Anna take the bus in March?
   b) How much will it cost Anna for the month of March if she pays cash each time she takes the bus?
   c) How much will it cost Anna for the month of March if she uses bus tickets each time?
   d) How much would Anna save in March by buying a monthly bus pass? Calculate the savings compared to travelling using tickets.
   e) Would she save as much using a bus pass in the month of February? Explain.

6. Marie's boat travels a distance of 115 km on 3 tanks of gasoline.

   a) What is the distance her boat will travel on 1 tank of gasoline?

   b) If Marie reduces her speed by about one-quarter, her boat will be able to go twice as far on the same amount of fuel. If Marie travels at the lower speed, how far can she expect to go on 1 tank of gasoline?

   c) List some factors that may affect the rate of fuel consumption of a boat.

Extension

7. Damien decides he will mow lawns in his neighbourhood during the summer. He calculates it will take 2 hours each time he mows a lawn. He estimates he will have to mow each lawn twelve times during the summer. Damien wants to charge each neighbour a single amount for the entire summer's work.

   a) How much should Damien charge per neighbour for his lawn service over the summer?

   b) What is Damien's hourly rate of pay, based on your answer to a)?

   c) Damien is considering upgrading his family's lawn mower. He is interested in a mower that is advertised for $399.98. How many lawns would he have to mow in order to earn enough to pay for the new mower? Do not forget to add the taxes. Damien lives in British Columbia.

Exploration 6

Ratio

In the last exploration, you worked with rates such as a speed of 60 km/h and a wage of $8.50 an hour. In this exploration, you will look at another type of comparison, a ratio.

You are probably familiar with the term ratio. You use a ratio when you compare the number of games your sports team has won to the number of games it has played. You use a ratio when you compare the length of a room to its width. You also use a ratio when you compare the number of questions you answer correctly on a test to its total number of questions. Can you think of some other examples where you use a ratio?

Did you notice that the two quantities in each ratio are measured using the same unit? A ratio is a comparison between quantities measured using the same unit.

Two out of three teenagers saw The Phantom Menace

Canucks Win 3 Out of 4 Games!

Goals	Hints
In this exploration, you will learn to solve problems using ratios.	**1.** It is not necessary to include units when you express a ratio.
	2. You can reduce a ratio to its lowest terms by dividing each term by the same number. For example, consider the ratio 15:20. You can divide both 15 and 20 by 5 which gives you a ratio of 3:4.

Example 1

Bohdan's soccer team played 16 games and won 9 of them. Express the number of games won to the number of games played as a ratio.

Solution

Bohdan's team won 9 games. They played 16 games. The ratio of number of games won to number of games played is 9 to 16. You can also express a ratio two other ways.

a) You can express the ratio 9 to 16 with the notation 9:16. This is called the colon form.

b) You can express the ratio 9 to 16 using the fraction 9/16. This is called the fraction form.

Example 2

Sam is looking for posters to cover the walls in his room. He finds one poster that is 50 cm by 50 cm. He finds another one that is 21 cm by 67 cm. Find the area of each poster, then compare the area of the first poster to the area of the second using a ratio.

Solution

The formula for the area of a rectangle is length multiplied by width.

$A = l \times w$ $A = l \times w$

$A = 50 \text{ cm} \times 50 \text{ cm}$ $A = 21 \text{ cm} \times 67 \text{ cm}$

   $= 2500 \text{ cm}^2$ $= 1407 \text{ cm}^2$

The ratio of the two areas is 2500:1407.

The ratio is about 2:1. This means that the area of first poster is roughly twice as large as the area of the second one.

Hint

A ratio is a comparison of two quantities. These quantities are called the terms of the ratio. In the ratio 9 to 16, the first term is 9 and the second term is 16. You can express this ratio in the following forms:

9 to 16   **9:16**   **9/16**

Project Activity

Continue filling in the Breakfast, Lunch, Supper, and Snack Charts you have made. Complete the remaining columns in each of these charts.

- In the columns titled Cost per Serving, indicate the cost of 1 serving of each food item chosen.
- In the columns titled Cost per Item per Person, indicate the cost per item per person of each food item.

To find the cost per serving, consider the following examples taken from the sample breakfast included in the Breakfast Chart.

Food Item	Serving Size	Package Size	Cost per Package
Toast	1 slice	20 slices	$1.69
Cold Cereal	30 g	525 g	$4.89

The cost of 1 slice of toast is 169¢ divided by 20, or 8¢ (rounded to the nearest cent). The cost of 1 g of cereal is 489¢ divided by 525, or 0.93¢ (rounded to the nearest hundredth of a cent). The cost of 30 g of cereal is 0.93¢ multiplied by 30, or 28¢ (rounded to the nearest cent).

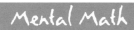

Write the following ratios in their lowest terms:

a) 3:12

b) 6:8

c) 50:75

d) 50:50

Career Connection

Name: Rodel Estaban

Job: volunteer coach of a little league soccer team in Kamloops, British Columbia

Current wages: none

Education: grade 10

Background skills and knowledge: knowledge of soccer; experience coaching

Career goal: fitness instructor

Keyword search: Canada college fitness instructor

Notebook Assignment

1. Which of the following pairs are equivalent ratios?

   a) 2:5 and 4:25
   b) 4:20 and 1:5
   c) $\frac{64}{16}$ and $\frac{4}{1}$

2. Apply the following questions to your own last name.

   a) Using a ratio, compare the number of vowels in your last name to the number of consonants in your last name.
   b) Using a ratio, compare the number of consonants in your last name to the number of vowels in your last name.
   c) Explain the difference between your answers in a) and b).

3. Find the following ratios as they apply to school days.
   a) the hours in school to the hours not in school
   b) the hours in school to the hours spent watching television
   c) the hours spent watching television to the hours not in school
   d) the hours doing homework to the hours in school
   e) the hours doing homework to the hours not in school

4. To make orange juice, 1 can of concentrate is mixed with 3 cans of water.

   a) Find the ratio of cans of concentrate to cans of water.
   b) Find the ratio of cans of concentrate to the total cans of orange juice prepared.

5. A bakery estimates that the ratio of loaves of white bread sold compared to loaves of whole wheat bread sold is 3:1.

   a) Explain what this means in your own words.
   b) If the bakery sold 100 loaves of whole wheat bread in a day, how many loaves of white bread would they expect to sell?

6. Dan has a part-time job working 12 hours a week. His gross pay is $79.20 a week. Cecelia has a part-time job working 8 hours a week. Her gross pay is $70.40 a week.

   a) Find the ratio of the number of hours Dan works to the number of hours Cecelia works during a week.
   b) Find Dan's gross hourly rate of pay.
   c) Find Cecelia's gross hourly rate of pay.
   d) Find the ratio of Dan's gross hourly rate of pay to Cecelia's gross hourly rate of pay.

7. The ingredients for a recipe that makes 6 waffles are the following:

    $1\frac{3}{4}$ cups flour
    3 teaspoons baking powder
    $\frac{1}{2}$ teaspoon salt
    1 tbsp sugar
    3 eggs
    4 tbsp melted butter
    $1\frac{1}{2}$ cups milk

    a) List the quantities of ingredients required to make 12 waffles.
    b) List the quantities of ingredients required to make 3 waffles.

8. Bonnie is drawing her room to scale. The dimensions of the room are 3 m x 3.5 m. Her scale drawing is 6 cm x 7 cm.

    a) What is the ratio of the length of the scale drawing to the length of the actual room?
    b) What is the ratio of the area of the scale drawing to the area of the actual room?

Extension

9. Sandeep wants to construct a model of a structure that is 275 m high. The model has to be no more than 1.5 m high.

    a) If Sandeep uses a scale of 1:200 to build his model, will it be less than 1.5 m high?
    b) If Sandeep uses a scale of 1:150 to build his model, will it be less than 1.5 m high?
    c) If Sandeep wants his model to be exactly 1.5 m high, what scale should he use? (Round to the nearest whole number.)

Chapter Review

1. Calculate the unit price for each of the following.

   a) $2.60 for 12 pencils
   b) $3.69 for 3 kg of apples
   c) $5.00 for 12 bagels
   d) $7.88 for 10 disks
   e) $3.49 for 225 g of cereal

2. A store sells salt in three different sizes: 250 g for $0.89, 500 g for $1.59, and 2.5 kg for $2.99.

   a) Find the unit price of each size.
   b) Which of these has the lowest unit price?

3. A grocery store sells a 5 lb. bag of potatoes for $1.49 and a 20 lb. bag of potatoes for $3.99.

   a) Find the unit price of each size.
   b) Which of these has the lowest unit price?
   c) Name two things other than unit price you should consider when you are buying potatoes.

4. **a)** What does GST stand for?
   b) What is the percent rate of the GST?
   c) List 5 goods and/or services on which you pay GST.
   d) What does PST stand for?
   e) If there is PST where you live, list 5 goods and/or services subject to this tax.

5. During a Boxing Day promotion, one store is selling its video game cartridges at 3 for $28.99. A second store is selling its cartridges at 4 for $34.99. The stores are in British Columbia.

   a) Calculate the unit price of a cartridge at each store.
   b) Calculate the total cost of 12 cartridges at each store.

6. The regular price of a particular brand of jeans in a Manitoba department store is $29.95. During a sale, the jeans are reduced by 25%.

   a) Calculate the amount of the discount.
   b) Calculate the sale price.
   c) Calculate the total cost of these jeans during the sale.

7. Calculate the unit rate for each of the following. Include correct units in all your answers.

   a) 30 metres in 4 seconds
   b) net pay of $24.00 for 3 hours' work
   c) $1.80 for 12 eggs
   d) 75 students in 3 buses
   e) $10.00 for 4 pairs of socks
   f) 300 kilometres in 6 hours

8. Karl works 30 hours during a week and his net pay is $225.20. Dominique works 35 hours during that same week and her net pay is $280.75.

   a) Find Karl's hourly rate of pay.
   b) Find Dominique's hourly rate of pay.
   c) Both students are saving for an overseas trip that costs $1400.00. How many hours will each of them have to work to earn the $1400.00 for the trip?

9. A recipe calls for $2\frac{2}{3}$ cups of flour to $\frac{1}{2}$ cups of sugar.

    a) Calculate the number of cups of flour you would use with 1 cup of sugar.

    b) Calculate the number of cups of sugar you would use with $3\frac{1}{2}$ cups of flour.

10. During a sale at an electronics store, a calculator sells for $19.95. The regular price of the calculator is $22.98. Calculate the amount of the discount.

11. A jewellery store sells a watch for $39.95. During a promotion, the manager of the store reduces the price to $32.98. The store is in Yukon. Calculate the total cost of the watch if it is bought on sale.

12. A clothing store in British Columbia is having an end of season promotion, a "2-for-1" sale. During the promotion, you pay the regular price on the more expensive item and receive the second item "for free." Tannis buys 2 sweatshirts. One sweatshirt has a regular price of $29.98 and the other sweatshirt has a regular price of $24.95.

    a) Calculate the total cost using the regular prices of the two sweatshirts, including taxes.

    b) Calculate the total cost using the sale prices of the two sweatshirts, including taxes.

Project Presentation

• •

If you have not completed the six charts and/or spreadsheets, complete them now. You will need to refer to them to answer the following questions.

1. **a)** Calculate the cost per person of each meal. Enter the cost of each meal into a chart like the following:

Day	Cost of Breakfast	Cost of Snack	Cost of Lunch	Cost of Snack	Cost of Supper	Cost of Snack
Day 1						
Day 2						
Day 3						

   b) Which of the meals is the most expensive?
   c) Which of the meals is the least expensive?

2. **a)** Calculate the total cost of the 2 breakfasts.
    b) Calculate the total cost of the 3 lunches.
    c) Calculate the total cost of the 2 suppers.
    d) Calculate the total cost of the 8 snacks.

3. Calculate the total cost of food per person for the camping trip.

4. If you had to reduce the cost of the food by 10%, what adjustments would you make to your menu?

5. Compare your menu and costs to those of another group in your class.

Case Study

• •

A student council in British Columbia wants to raise $1000.00 for its school charity. The council decides to sell T-shirts as a fundraiser. The T-shirts will be navy with a one-colour logo on the front of the shirt.

Members of the council volunteer to contact five sportswear companies. They decide to buy the T-shirts from one of two companies, the A & B Sportswear Company or the Specialty T-shirt Company.

Both companies list the cost of the T-shirts in terms of the number of T-shirts purchased. The more T-shirts the council buys, the less each T-shirt will cost.

1. The A & B Sportswear Company lists the prices of its T-shirts and printing separately. The prices of the T-shirts at the A & B Sportswear Company are organized in the following categories.

A & B Sportswear

Number of T-shirts	Cost per T-shirt	Cost of Printing per T-shirt	Cost per Printed T-shirt	Total Tax (GST and PST)	Final Cost per Printed T-Shirt
1–24	$6.75	$1.95			
25–49	$6.50	$1.60			
50–120	$6.25	$1.35			
121–180	$6.00	$1.15			
181–240	$5.75	$1.00			
241–300	$5.50	$0.85			

Find the total cost per printed T-shirt in each category for the A & B Sportswear Company by completing the chart above. Students have to pay the GST and PST for the T-shirts. Round the GST and PST to the nearest cent.

2. The Specialty T-Shirt Company lists just one cost per T-shirt. This cost includes the cost of the T-shirt and the printing. The Specialty T-Shirt Company reduces the cost per T-shirt in each category by 5%. The cost of ordering between 1–24 T-shirts is $8.40 per T-shirt. The cost per T-shirt for 25–49 T-shirts is 5% lower than $8.40. The cost per T-shirt for 50–120 T-shirts is 5% lower than that of the previous category. The categories of the T-shirts are the same as the categories at the A & B Sportswear Company.

Specialty T-Shirt Company

Number of T-shirts	Cost per Printed T-shirt	Total Tax (GST and PST)	Total Cost per Printed T-Shirt
1–24	$8.40		
25–49			
50–120			
121–180			
181–240			
241–300			

Find the total cost per printed T-shirt in each category for the Specialty T-Shirt Company by completing the chart above. Round all answers to the nearest cent.

3. The following chart lists the number of students at the school. It also lists the ratio of students in each grade that the student council estimates will buy T-shirts.

Grade	Number of Students	Estimated Sales Ratio	Estimated T-shirt Sales
9	135	1:6	
10	142	1:4	
11	138	2:5	
12	127	2:3	

Complete the chart above to calculate the number of T-shirts the student council estimates it will sell.

4. **a)** Based on the number of T-shirts the student council plans to sell, which company offers the better price?

    b) What are some other things the student council should consider in deciding where to buy their T-shirts?

5. **a)** If the student council charges $12.00 a T-shirt, calculate the profit if they sell all of the T-shirts. The student council does not collect sales tax.

    b) The student council hopes to raise $1000.00. Will they raise that amount?

6. If the student council increases the selling price of each T-shirt to $15.00, they estimate they will sell 20% fewer T-shirts.

    a) How many T-shirts do they estimate they will sell at $15.00?

    b) What will their profit be if they sell all the T-shirts at $15.00?

    c) The student council hopes to raise $1000.00. Will they raise that amount?

7. If the student council decreases the selling price of a T-shirt to $10.00, they estimate they will sell 20% more T-shirts.

    a) How many T-shirts do they estimate they will sell at $10.00?

    b) What will their profit be if they sell all the T-shirts at $10.00?

8. Suppose you were a member of the student council.

    a) How many T-shirts would you order?

    b) How much would you charge per T-shirt?

    c) How many T-shirts do you believe you would sell?

    d) What would be your profit?

Chapter 5

Geometry Project

Designing in Three Dimensions

Playground equipment design, creating images for video games, fashion design, furniture making, planning a new office space: all require spatial geometry, measurement, and careful planning. One of the ways to tell what objects look like without actually building the whole thing is to create a scale model.

Designers use measurements, estimates, sketches, two-dimensional plans and three-dimensional models as a part of their creative process. This chapter deals with systems of measurement, spatial geometry representations, and trigonometry.

Chapter Goals

In this chapter you will learn to measure using both imperial and metric units as well as to estimate volume and mass. You will draw in two and three dimensions. You will explore scale modelling and solve related problems using mathematical tools such as trigonometry. Finally, in this chapter you will design and build a three-dimensional model.

Chapter Project

In this project, you will act as a designer of recreational spaces. Fast food restaurants, parks, ferries, and school playgrounds often have places where children can climb, slide, swing, or crawl as they play and get exercise. Your company is planning to expand its line of recreational spaces. In this project, you will plan, design, and build a three-dimensional model of a new recreational space.

The space may be for any age group. It could be an indoor climbing area, a skateboard park, or another recreational area that would appeal to teens or others. The recreational space must be no larger than 25 m x 25 m x 10 m, and it must be an enclosed indoor space.

When your project is completed, you will display your three-dimensional model as if it were being presented to potential customers.

At the end of this chapter, your project file will contain:

- sketches of the model
- scale diagrams of parts of the model
- a creative presentation outlining the features of your recreational space
- a labelled three-dimensional model of your recreational space

Career Connection

Name: Sam Derrick

Job: computer assisted design (CAD) technician in Trail, B.C.

Current wages: $20.67 an hour

Education: grade 12; computer-assisted design course at Kwantlen College, BC

Career goal: computer-assisted designer

Keyword search: CAD college Canada

This CAD technician has been working on developing a truck model. The design begins with a sketch.

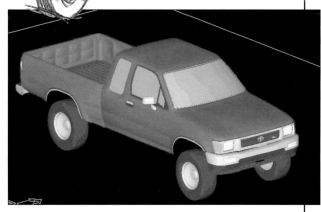

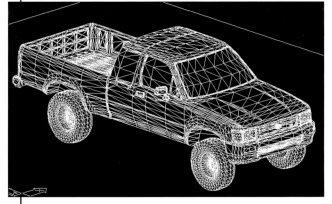

Next, the technician uses CAD software to develop a wire model of the truck. Then he fills in the model visually to create a computerized picture. If the design is workable, it is eventually used to manufacture a real truck.

Designing, Modelling, and Constructing a Building

These pages show the process of creating a building from the initial design stage, through making a two-dimensional plan and a three-dimensional model, to constructing the building itself. Almost all design of buildings, vehicles, and industrial products follows a similar process from idea to real object.

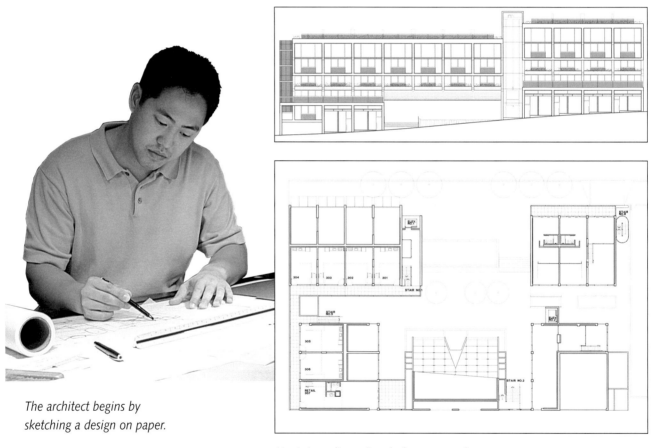

The architect begins by sketching a design on paper.

Next, two-dimensional plans are made. Shown here is both a two-dimensional plan of the building's front and a floor plan for one of the floors.

Once the two-dimensional plans have been completed, they are used to build a three-dimensional model.

The finished building has commercial space on the street level and residential lofts on the upper floors.

When all the design and planning is complete, construction begins.

Exploration 1

Setting Design Parameters

Suppose you are working for a company that makes recreational spaces. The company specializes in indoor environments that are sold to malls, schools, daycares, and restaurants.

The company wants to expand their business to include other age groups. They have looked at climbing walls and laser tag centres for ideas. They are considering making indoor spaces for those interested in skateboarding, mountain biking, or other traditional outdoor sports. The company has decided the spaces need to be enclosed and the dimensions are not to exceed 25 m by 25 m by 10 m.

Small Group Activity

In small groups, brainstorm answers to the following questions. Have someone in your group record the ideas.

What could your company create that would serve as recreational spaces for:

- **a)** older children?
- **b)** teenagers?
- **c)** handicapped individuals?
- **d)** adults?

What would be included in the recreational space to provide activities for these groups? What criteria could be used to evaluate a space designed for one of these groups? Record the criteria in your notebook for future use.

Goals

In this exploration, you will determine the initial design parameters for a recreational space.

Project Activity

Think about the age group for which you prefer to build a recreational space. Keep safety considerations in mind. Make sure your recreational space is not overly complicated. As you generate ideas, write or draw them in your project file.

Answering the following questions will help you to choose the recreational space you will design and model:

a) For what age group will you design your space?
b) What are the physical sizes of members of that age group?
c) For what type of recreational activity will your space be designed?
d) What will be the components of your recreational space?
e) What will be the dimensions of your space? (Remember it cannot exceed 25 m x 25 m x 10 m.)
f) What could you name your recreational space?

Once you have decided on a recreational space, draw a rough sketch of the layout.

Research Activity

Research and collect pictures or images in which scale models or plans are being used. For example, aircraft are often tested using models. New buildings are often displayed in the form of a model.

This model for a Boeing aircraft is being tested before it is manufactured.

Exploration 2

Measurement in the Metric System

The system of measurement used extensively in most countries of the world is a version of the *Système Internationale* (SI), more commonly called the metric system. This system is based on the metre, which is defined as the distance light travels in 1/299792458 of a second. Smaller and larger lengths are based on divisions and multiples of the metre. For example, a centimetre is one-hundredth of a metre and a kilometre is one thousand metres.

Metric rulers are often marked in centimetres on one side of the ruler and millimetres on the other.

Goals

In this exploration, you will learn about measurement in the metric system.

Hint

1 km	=	1000 m
1 m	=	100 cm
1 m	=	1000 mm
1 cm	=	10 mm

Example 1

Look at the metric ruler shown above. How many millimetres are there in one centimetre? How many centimetres are there in 90 millimetres? How many millimetres are there in 8.5 centimetres?

Solution

There are 10 millimetres in 1 centimetre. To calculate how many centimetres are represented by 90 millimetres, divide 90 by 10:

90 mm ÷ 10 = 9 cm

Therefore, there are 9 cm in 90 mm.

To find out how many millimetres there are in 8.5 centimetres, multiply 8.5 by 10:

8.5 cm x 10 = 85 mm

There are 85 millimetres in 8.5 centimetres.

Hint

Below is a list of prefixes used in the metric system and their meaning.

Prefix	Quantity
tera	trillion
giga	billion
mega	million
kilo	thousand
hecto	hundred
deca	ten
basic unit	one
deci	one-tenth
centi	one-hundredth
milli	one-thousandth
micro	one-millionth
nano	one-billionth
pico	one-trillionth

Example 2—Perimeter

The perimeter of a geometric figure is the distance around it. To find the perimeter of a geometric figure, add the lengths of all its sides. Find the perimeter of Figures A and B.

Figure A

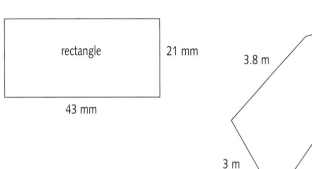

Figure B

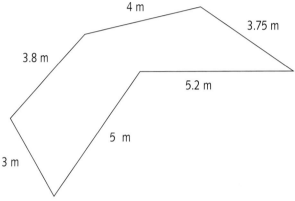

Solution

Figure A. One property of a rectangle is that opposite sides are equal. The perimeter of the rectangle is found by adding the lengths of its 4 sides as follows:

P = 21 + 43 + 21 + 43
P = 128 mm

The perimeter of the rectangle is 128 mm.

Figure B. The perimeter of this shape is found by adding the lengths of all its sides as follows:

P = 3 + 3.8 + 4 + 3.75 + 5.2 + 5 = 24.75

The perimeter of the shape is 24.75 m.

Example 3—Circumference of a Circle

The perimeter or distance around a circle is known as its circumference. The circumference (C) of a circle is about 3 times its diameter (d), which is the distance across the circle measured through its centre. The formula for the circumference of a circle is $C = \pi d$ or $C = 2\pi r$, when r is the radius. The value π (pronounced pi) is an irrational number, and can be approximated by 3.14. Find the circumference of the following circle:

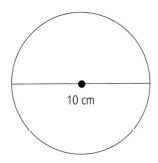

10 cm

Solution

The circumference of the circle can be found as follows:

$$C = \pi d$$
$$= \pi(10) \text{ cm}$$
$$= 31.4 \text{ (rounded to the nearest tenth)}$$

The circumference of the circle is 31.4 cm.

Hint

To find the circumference, you can use the π key on your calculator or approximate its value using 3.14.

Example 4—Area

When the word "area" is used in geometry, it refers to the measure of a region. The area of a geometric figure is the number of square units needed to cover the interior region of that figure. Find the area of each of the following figures:

Figure A

10 mm

3 mm

Figure B

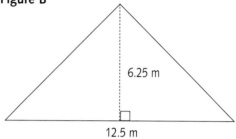

6.25 m

12.5 m

Solution

Figure A. Find the formula for the area of a parallelogram in the Area Formulas chart and substitute in the given values for the base and height.

$A = bh$

$\quad = (10)(3)$

$\quad = 30$

The area of the parallelogram is 30 mm^2.

Figure B. Using the formula for the area of a triangle (see Area Formulas chart), substitute in the given values for the base and height.

$A = (\frac{1}{2})bh$

$\quad = (\frac{1}{2})(12.5)(6.25)$

$\quad = (\frac{1}{2})(78.125)$

$\quad = 39.1$ (rounded to the nearest tenth)

The area of the triangle is 39.1 m^2.

Hint

Area is always expressed in square units.

Area Formulas		
Figure	**Diagram**	**Area (in square units)**
square		s^2
rectangle		bh
parallelogram		bh
trapezoid		$(\frac{1}{2})(a+b)h$
triangle		$(\frac{1}{2})bh$
circle		πr^2

Example 5—Surface Area

The area of the entire surface of a three-dimensional object is known as its surface area. Find the surface area of the following objects.

Figure A

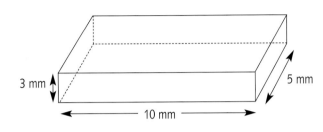

3 mm

5 mm

10 mm

Figure B

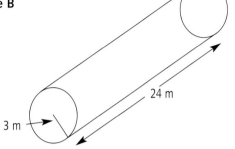

24 m

3 m

Solution

Figure A. Find the formula for the entire surface area of a rectangular solid (see Surface Area and Volume Formulas chart) and substitute in the given values for the length, width, and height.

$$SA = 2lw + 2lh + 2wh$$
$$= 2(10)(5) + 2(10)(3) + 2(5)(3)$$
$$= 100 + 60 + 30$$
$$= 190$$

The surface area of the rectangular solid is 190 mm^2.

Figure B. Find the formula for the surface area of a cylinder (see Surface Area and Volume Formulas chart) and substitute in the given values for the radius and height.

$$SA = 2\pi rh + 2\pi r^2$$
$$= 2\pi(3)(24) + 2\pi(3)^2$$
$$= 2\pi(72) + 2\pi(9)$$
$$= 452.16 + 56.52$$
$$= 508.68$$

The surface area of the cylinder is approximately 508.7 m^2 (rounded to the nearest tenth).

Hint

Surface area is two-dimensional and is always expressed in square units.

Surface Area and Volume Formulas			
Object		**Surface Area Formulas (in square units)**	**Volume Formulas (in cubic units)**
Rectangular Solid		Top or bottom = lw Front or back = lh Either end = wh Entire rectangular solid = $2lw + 2lh + 2wh$	lwh
Sphere		$4\pi r^2$	$\frac{4}{3}\pi r^3$
Cone		Side = πrs Bottom = πr^2 Entire cone = $\pi rs + \pi r^2$	$\frac{1}{3}\pi r^2 h$
Cylinder		Side = $2\pi rh$ Bottom = πr^2 Top = πr^2 Entire cylinder = $2\pi rh + 2\pi r^2$	$\pi r^2 h$
Pyramid		Each side = $\frac{1}{2}bs$ Bottom = b^2 Entire pyramid = $2bs + b^2$	$\frac{1}{3}b^2 h$

Example 6—Volume

The volume of an object is the amount of space occupied by the object.
Formulas for the volume of some geometric objects were given in the
same chart as formulas for surface area.

Find the volume of the following objects.

Figure A

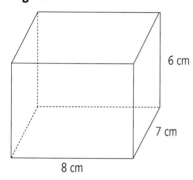

6 cm

7 cm

8 cm

Figure B

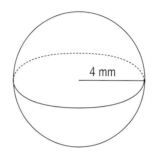

4 mm

Solution

Figure A. Find the formula for the volume of a rectangular solid and
substitute in the given values for the length, width and height.

$$V = lwh$$
$$= (6)(7)(8)$$
$$= 336$$

The volume of the rectangular solid is 336 cm³.

Figure B. Find the formula for the volume of a sphere, and substitute in the
given value for the radius.

$$V = \frac{4}{3}\pi r^3$$
$$= \frac{4}{3}\pi(4)^3$$
$$= \frac{4}{3}\pi(64)$$

$$= 268 \text{ (rounded to the nearest whole number)}$$

The volume of the sphere is 268 mm³.

Hint

Since volume is three-dimensional, it is always expressed in units
cubed or cubic units.

Project Activity

Consider the dimensions of your recreational space. Add metric measurements to the rough sketch from Exploration 1. What is the approximate area of the walls? What is the volume of the enclosure? Ensure that your dimensions do not exceed the available space.

Notebook Assignment

1. Find the lengths of the objects below.

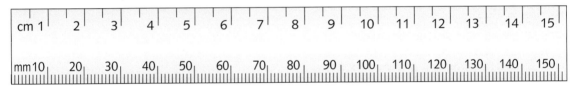

2. Which metric unit would you use?

   a) the length of a sheet of paper is 27.5 ____.
   b) the distance from Winnipeg to Kenora is 216 ____.
   c) the thickness of a shirt button is about 2 ____.
   d) the height of a telephone pole is about 9 ____.

3. Convert the following measures as indicated:

   a) 2.57 m   =   _____ cm
   b) 450 mm   =   _____ m
   c) 0.517 km   =   _____ m
   d) 0.5 m   =   _____ mm
   e) 315 mm   =   _____ cm
   f) 6027 cm   =   _____ m
   g) 2500 m   =   _____ km
   h) 6.3 m   =   _____ cm
   i) 2460 mm   =   _____ cm
   j) 1.6 m   =   _____ km

4. Estimate and measure each of the following using metric units.

   a) the length of a new pencil
   b) the length of a shoe
   c) the thickness of your mathematics textbook
   d) the diameter of a pop can
   e) the height of a bookcase

5. Find your height in metres and centimetres.

Mental Math

1. How many centimetres are there in 250 millimetres?

2. If there are 1000 g in 1 kg, how many grams are in 5 kg?

3. If there are 1000 m in 1 km, how many metres are in 2.4 km?

Hint

1 cubic centimetre equals 1 millilitre.

6. Find the perimeters of the following figures:

Figure A

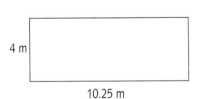

2 cm

3 cm

4 cm

2 cm

3 cm

Figure B

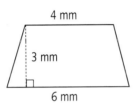

4 cm

2 cm

3.5 cm

Figure C

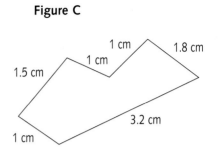

1 cm

1.8 cm

1 cm

1.5 cm

1 cm

3.2 cm

7. Find the area of the following figures:

Figure A

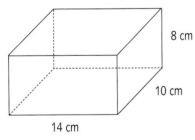

4 m

10.25 m

Figure B

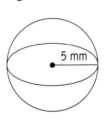

4 mm

3 mm

6 mm

Figure C

8.5 cm

8. Find the surface area of the following objects:

Figure A

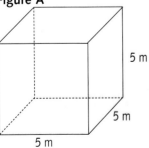

8 cm

10 cm

14 cm

Figure B

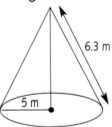

5 mm

Figure C

6.3 m

5 m

9. Find the volume of the following objects:

Figure A

5 m

5 m

5 m

Figure B

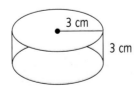

3 cm

3 cm

10. The floor of a school stage needs to be painted. The floor is shaped like a trapezoid. The floor measures 8.5 m front to back. The bases measure 12 m and 14 m. Find the area of the stage.

11. A cone-shaped funnel has a radius of 21 cm and a slant height of 33 cm. Find the surface area of the funnel.

12. The floor of a square pyramid tent is 3.4 m on each side. The height of the tent is 3.2 m. Find the volume of the tent.

13. The diameter of a pizza is 25.4 cm. Find the area of the pizza.

Extension

14. Find the volumes of a basketball and a softball in both cubic centimetres and litres.

Exploration 3

Imperial Measurement

Because of the influence of the British Empire, many Commonwealth and other English-speaking countries did not change to the metric system until recently. In fact, the United States has still not done so. While some technical work in the United States is carried out in the metric system, most daily work uses the imperial system. For measurements of length, the imperial system uses inches, feet, yards, and miles. It is important to be familiar with imperial measurements because they are used in construction and because the United States is Canada's largest trading partner.

An imperial ruler is divided into feet, inches, and fractions of an inch. Look at the rulers below and see how the fractions of an inch are marked.

Each inch on the ruler is marked with a long line and is labelled 1, 2, 3, 4, and so on. The next longest line, midway between the inch marks, indicates half inches. Point A is at $1\frac{1}{2}$ inches. Point B is at $3\frac{1}{2}$ inches.

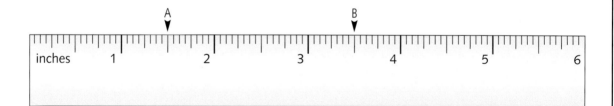

Goals

In this exploration, you will learn to measure in the imperial system.

Example 1

Find the lengths of the objects pictured below.

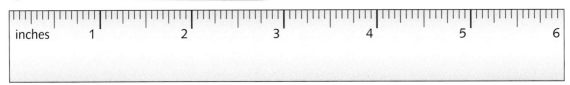

Solution

The paper clip is 2 inches long. The leaf is $3\frac{5}{8}$ inches long. The pencil is $5\frac{1}{2}$ inches long. The nail is 3 inches long.

Mental Math

If there are 12 inches in a foot, how many inches are there in 5 feet?

Career Connection

Name: Ron McGregor

Job: carpenter's apprentice at Lynn Lake, Manitoba

Current wages: $13.50 an hour

Education: grade 12; 8-month carpentry program at Northwest Community College

Career goal: journeyman carpenter

Keyword search: Canada college carpentry

Hint

Lumber is sold using imperial sizes. One common size is called a "two by four" because it is 2 inches by 4 inches when it is rough cut. However, once it has gone through a planer to make it smooth a "two by four" measures $1^1/2$ inches by $3^1/2$ inches.

Table of Conversion

1 inch	=	2.54 centimetres
1 inch	=	25.4 millimetres
1 foot	=	30.5 centimetres
1 foot	=	305 millimetres
1 foot	=	0.305 metres
1 yard	=	3 feet
1 yard	=	0.915 metres
1 mile	=	1760 yards
1 mile	=	1.6 kilometres
1 kilogram	=	2.2 pounds
1 litre	=	1.06 US quarts

Inputting data on the size of a grain crop.

Technology

Some calculators are able to convert imperial to metric measurements or from metric to imperial.

Notebook Assignment

1. Consider the imperial ruler shown in Figure 1. Half-way between the
   $1/2$-inch marks and the inch-marks are marks slightly shorter than
   the $1/2$-inch mark. Point C marks such a point.

   Figure 1

   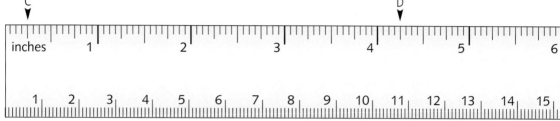

   a) What fraction of an inch does Point C designate? How far is
       point C from the left end of the ruler?
   b) What distance is Point D from the left end?

2. Use a ruler or tape measure marked in inches to measure the
   following objects to the nearest $1/4$ inch:

   a) a sheet of paper (width and length)
   b) your desk top
   c) the width and length of your teacher's desk

3. For points A to E on the ruler in Figure 2 shown below, state the
   length of the measure.

   Figure 2

   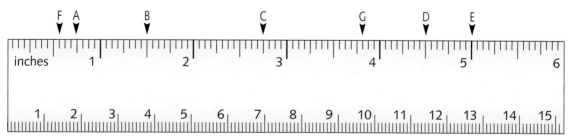

4. The smallest indicators on the ruler in Figure 2 are sixteenths of an
   inch. What length is measured by F?

5. In Figure 2, what length is marked by G?

6. Measure the following items:

   a) the width of the classroom door to the nearest one-eighth of an inch

   b) the width of a shelf in your classroom to the nearest sixteenth of an inch

   c) the length of your pencil or pen to the nearest sixteenth of an inch

   d) your height to the nearest half inch

7. For longer measurements, feet are commonly used. One foot is equal to 12 inches. In framing a house with "dimensional" lumber, carpenters use studs that are 2" x 4" x 8' (read this as "two by four by eight") for the walls. These are finished to $1^1/2$ inches by $3^1/2$ inches by 8 feet long. How many inches long is an 8' board bought at the lumber yard? What is the surface area of one of these boards?

8. A doorway may be 7' 6" high; we can also say that it is $7^1/2$ feet high. Make the following measurements using a measuring tape marked in inches and feet.

   a) Measure the height of your classroom door in feet and inches.

   b) Have someone measure your height in feet and inches.

   c) Measure the length and width of your classroom or the hall in feet and inches to the nearest inch.

9. Calculate the surface area of each cube. Why is only one dimension given?

A

B

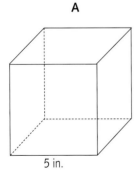

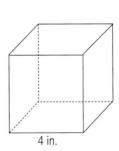

5 in.   4 in.

Hint

The symbol for inch is ".
The symbol for foot is '.

10. For the pair of boxes shown below:

    a) Estimate which has the greater volume. Estimate which uses less material.

    b) Calculate the volume and surface area of each box.

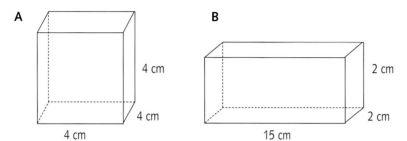

11. a) Calculate the amount of glass needed to construct the aquarium shown.

    b) What is the volume of the aquarium?

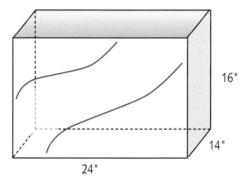

12. Calculate perimeter and area for each of the following figures:

a)

b)

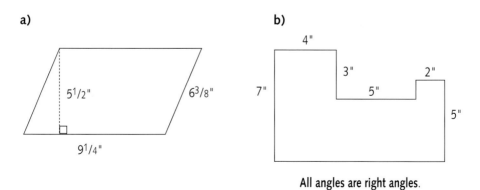

All angles are right angles.

13. Find the surface area of the following wedge.

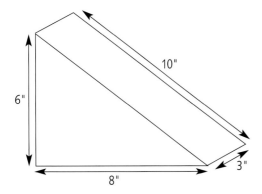

14. The following diagram is an illustration of a family room.

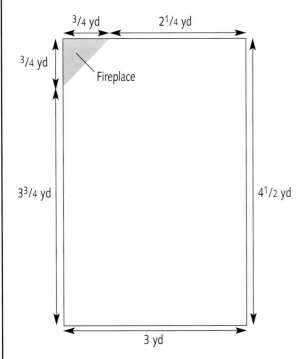

    a)   If the family room is carpeted, except for the fireplace, what area is carpeted?

    b)   If the carpeting costs $14.98 a square yard, find the cost of carpeting the room. Do not include taxes.

15. The following diagram illustrates a podium. The entire podium is painted, except for the bottom. What area is painted?

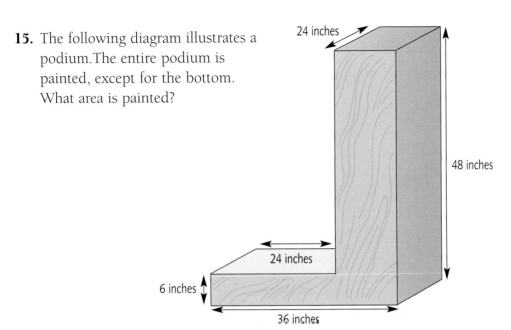

16. The following diagram is an illustration of stonework around a rectangular garden.

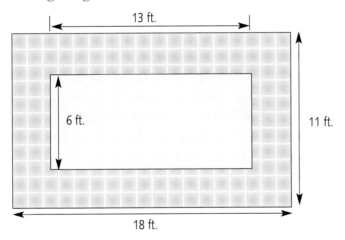

a) What is the area of the stonework that surrounds the garden?
b) If the stonework costs $29.98 a square yard, what is the cost of the stonework including taxes? Assume no waste of materials.

17. Use a measuring device to find the length and width of your desk or the table you work on in both metric and imperial units. Find the area of your work space using the imperial system and then using the metric system. Which did you find easier to calculate? Why?

Problem Analysis

Sandbag Dikes

In the spring of 1997, Manitoba experienced the "Flood of the Century" as the Red River overflowed its banks. Residents affected by the rising waters combatted the flood by building sandbag dikes. An engineer at the University of Manitoba predicted that many of the dikes would fail. He suggested that dikes would be most effective if they were built in a certain fashion, according to certain specifications. The Works and Operations Division in Winnipeg's Water and Waste Department reminded homeowners that the base of any dike must be two feet wider than the dike's intended height. This means that if a dike is meant to be three feet high, the base must be five feet wide. If it is to be six feet high, the base must be eight feet wide. The diagram shows a typical sandbag dike cross-section.

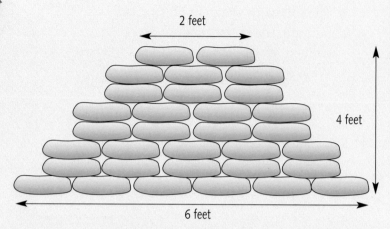

Base width = height plus 2 feet

1. Assuming that the diagram is drawn to scale, how many bags would you expect to find in the cross-section of a dike that is four feet high?

2. Complete the following table:

3. Look for a pattern in the table. What pattern(s) do you notice?

4. Use the pattern to determine the number of bags in the cross-section of a dike that is 8 feet high.

Height of Dike (in feet)	Number of Bags in Cross-Section
0	
1	
2	
3	
4	
5	
6	

5. Construct a graph using the information in the table.

6. Using the graph you constructed, describe the relationship between the height of a dike and the number of bags in the cross-section of the dike.

7. Do you think that the rule "Base width = height plus 2 feet" applies to all sandbag dikes, no matter how high? Why or why not?

8. If each bag measures 18 inches long, how many bags are needed to construct a dike five feet high and 240 feet in length?

9. If a sandbag line consisting of 18 people can deliver bags to the dike site at the rate of 20 bags a minute, how long would it take to build the dike in question 8?

10. If the rate at which the dike can be built is equal to the rate at which it can be removed, how long would it take one person working alone to remove the dike?

Games

Dots and Dashes

Materials Needed

- dot paper

Rules of the Game

A game for two people.

Taking turns, each player joins two vertically or horizontally adjacent points. These lines form the sides of a square. The player who completes the fourth side of a square claims the square (writing his or her initial in the square).

A player who completes a square gets another turn. This second turn may lead to completing another claimable square, which would result in another turn, and so on.

The objective is to construct as many squares as you can and to block your opponent from making squares.

The game itself is trivial. The objective is to develop a winning strategy for a limited number of rectangular dots.

There is a limit to the number of squares which can be used. Otherwise, the strategy, if there is one, is too complex.

Exploration 4

Metric and Imperial Estimation

"The fish was *this* big!"

"I got at least 10 feet of air off that jump."

"I need about 1 kilogram of potatoes to feed the family."

Have you heard estimations like these? Sometimes estimates are guesses, and other times they are more precise. For example, a person shooting a gun will often estimate how high to aim based on their sense of the distance of the target. A courier will look at their route and estimate when they will finish. An airline pilot carries enough fuel in the plane to ensure safety based on estimates of distances, winds, and load.

Goals

In this exploration, you will learn to estimate and calculate in metric and imperial units.

Example 1

Identify an appropriate unit of measurement in the metric and imperial systems.

Item	Metric	Imperial
Distance from Winnipeg to Brandon		
Length of a pencil		
Volume of a basketball		
Height of a school gymnasium		

Solution

Item	Metric	Imperial
Distance from Winnipeg to Brandon	kilometres	miles
Length of a pencil	centimetres	inches
Volume of a basketball	cm^3	$inches^3$
Height of a school gymnasium	metres	feet

Example 2

Use the information below to estimate as indicated.

Item	Metric	Imperial
Length of a pencil		
Volume of a basketball		
Height of a school gymnasium		

Solution

Item	Metric	Imperial
Length of a pencil	15 centimetres	6 inches
Volume of a basketball	14000 cm^3	900 in^3
Height of a school gymnasium	10 metres	30 feet

Project Activity

Include measurements on the rough sketch of your recreational space. Show both imperial and metric units so that the plans for your recreational space can be used in both Canada and the United States.

Notebook Assignment

1. Give appropriate metric and imperial units of measurement for the following:

Item	Metric	Imperial
Length of a school bus		
Length of a $10.00 bill		
Volume of a garbage can		
Height of a 1-storey school		
Area of a hockey rink		

2. Estimate the following:

Item	Metric	Imperial
Diameter of a soccer ball		
Volume of a bath tub		
Height of a flagpole		
Area of a soccer field		

3. We often measure mass and weight of items such as hamburger meat. While the two are different, we often treat them the same. For our purposes, 1 kilogram is about the same as 2.2 pounds. Estimate the mass of a well known NHL hockey player. Give your estimate in both imperial and metric units. Check your estimates.

4. Calculate the volume for each suitcase shown below. How many bricks of size 10 cm by 2 cm by 5 cm could fit into the smallest suitcase?

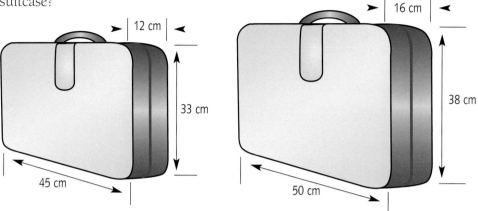

5. Which of the following containers of ice cream has the largest volume? Which has the largest surface area?

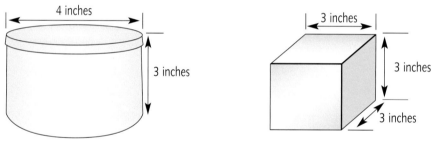

6. Estimate the length of the track of a snowmobile.

7. Estimate the perimeter of your home.

Extension

8. Suppose an electric car is developed to reduce pollution in cities. The car is meant to carry four adults but very little luggage. What would be an estimate of the minimum dimensions of a rectangular prism similar in shape to the interior of an electric car? What would be the volume of the interior? Use metric and imperial measurements.

Mental Math

What is the volume of a gift box measuring 5 centimetres by 5 centimetres by 10 centimetres?

Exploration 5

Working to Scale

How big should you make your model of the recreational space? What factors are important in deciding what the dimensions of the model should be? What is the smallest the model could be to show significant details?

In this exploration, you will choose an appropriate scale for your recreational space model. You will explore how changing the dimensions of an object changes other aspects such as volume and perimeter.

Small Group Activity

1. In a small group, make a list of places where scale is used. What scales are common? How is scale shown on maps?
2. Estimate the dimensions of your classroom.
3. What is an appropriate scale for building a model of the classroom if the model must sit on one of your tables or desktops?
4. Estimate the height of the tallest person in the room. Suppose the model classroom contained a figure representing the tallest person in the class. How tall would the figure be?
5. What measurement in your model would represent 1 foot in the classroom? How would 1 metre in the classroom be represented in your model?

Goals

In this exploration, you will determine the relationships among linear measurements, area, surface area, and volume of similar objects.

New Terms

scale drawing: a drawing in which the dimensions are proportional to the actual object.

floor plan: a top-down view of a floor area that shows the placement of furniture or other structural features superimposed on the floor area.

A scale factor can be presented in several ways. If 1 cm on a model represents 50 cm on the actual object, the scale can be given as:

1 cm represents 50 cm or $\frac{1}{50}$ or 1:50

Normally, a scale factor of 1:50 means 1 unit on the model represents 50 of the same units on the actual object.

Example 1

Represent each of the following scales in two additional ways.

a)   1:25

b)   1 cm represents 6 km

Solution

a) This scale factor can also be represented by $^1/25$ or 1 unit represents 25 units.

b) 6 km = 6 x 10 x 10 x 10 x 10 x 10 = 600000 cm.

This scale can also be represented by 1/600000 or 1:600000.

Example 2

A window that is 2 feet wide is drawn to $^1/12$ scale. How wide is the drawing of the window in inches?

Solution

2 feet = 2 x 12 = 24 inches
24" x $^1/12$ = 2"
The window is 2 inches wide in the drawing.

Example 3

A deck on a model boat measures 2 cm x 2 cm. If the scale of the model is 1:100, what are the dimensions of the full-size deck? What is the area of the deck on both the model and full-size? How do they compare?

Solution

The scale is 1:100 so 2 cm equals 200 cm. The deck is 200 cm by 200 cm, which can also be expressed as 2 metres by 2 metres. The area of the model deck is 4 square cm and on the full-size deck it is 40000 square centimetres, or 4 square metres.

$$40000 \text{ cm}^2 \div 4 = 10000 \text{ cm}^2$$

The area of the full-size deck is 10000 times greater than that of the model deck.

Example 4

Measure the life-size drawing of a climbing wall grip shown below. Make a scale drawing that is half-size that could be used by a builder.

Solution

If the drawing is half-size, the scale factor is 1:2.

Example 5

Create a floor plan of a classroom. Represent student and teacher desks, and other objects that occupy the classroom. Draw your floor plan to scale.

Solution

Scale: 1 to 40

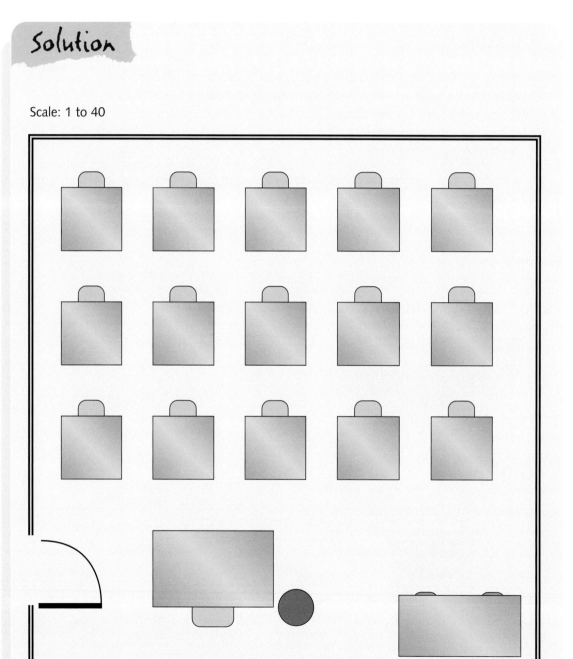

Project Activity

Draw a floor plan of your recreational space. Select a scale and use it to make an accurate drawing.

Notebook Assignment

1. The following line represents a scale drawing on a map. If the scale for this line is 1:20, measure the line, and then calculate the actual distance. _____

2. The actual distance to a beach resort is 240 km. What would you suggest as a reasonable scale for a map of the route to the beach? Why?

3. You have a rectangular back yard and wish to do some landscaping. The yard measures 30 m by 20 m.
    a) Find an appropriate scale to draw a diagram of the yard.
    b) If you wanted to plant bushes every 4 m across the width of the yard, how far apart would they be on your diagram?
    c) How many bushes would be shown on your diagram? What are your assumptions?

4. If the scale is 1:300, fill in the following.

Drawing	Actual
5 cm	
3 cm	
	2400 cm
	120 m

5. A scale drawing shows a play wheel twice as big as its actual size. If the drawing is 4 cm across, what is the actual diameter?

6. A rectangle has dimensions of 3 cm x 4 cm. If the width is doubled, how much bigger is the area?

7. A box measures 4" x 4" x 8". Draw a top view of the box. Use a 1:2 scale representation. Find the volume and outside surface area of the full-sized box.

Hint

Graph paper is helpful when drawing to scale.

8. A model of a box measures 2 cm x 2 cm x 3 cm. If the scale is 1:20, what is the volume of the actual box?

9. **a)** Complete the following table which lists the dimensions of various rectangular prisms. All measurements are in inches.

Width	Length	Height	Outside Surface Area	Volume
2	2	2		
4	4	4		
5	5			100
2	10		112	

b) Consider the table above. How did doubling the width, length, and height affect the volume? Was the volume doubled? Why or why not?

10. **a)** Complete the following table, which lists the dimensions of various rectangular prisms. All measurements are in centimetres.

Width	Length	Height	Volume
1	1	1	
1	1	2	
1	2	2	
2	2	2	

b) Use the data from Part a). Describe how the volume of a rectangular prism is affected by changing the dimensions.

Hints

A rectangular prism is a solid whose six faces are rectangles.

11. Raul is an interior designer for The Brick. He makes a scale drawing for a customer using the scale 1 cm = 0.25 m. Find the scale dimensions for the bedroom and for each piece of furniture.

bedroom	3.6 m by 3.5 m
bed	1.95 m by 1.4 m
night table	0.6 m by 0.4 m

12. A photograph shows a computer chip magnified by a factor of 15.

a) Write the scale factor.

b) What length on the chip is shown by a length of 5 mm on the photograph?

c) What length on the photo shows a length of 0.5 mm on the chip?

13. The following floor plan of a house is drawn using a scale factor of 1 cm:2.5 m.

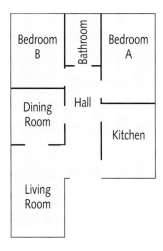

   a) Find the actual dimensions of each room in the house.
   b) Find the perimeter of the house.

Extension

14. Determine what happens to the area and perimeter of a rectangle when the dimensions are doubled. Make a chart to show your results. Predict the effect of doubling the dimensions on the area and perimeter of any size of rectangle.

Exploration 6

Representing Three-Dimensional Objects

In this exploration you will learn some methods of drawing images in both two and three dimensions. This will be necessary to create customer requested drawings of your recreational space.In the activities you will be using simple boxes, rods, or interlocking cubes to help you create your images. It will be helpful to have pencil crayons for these activities.

You will consider front, side, and top views. These are from the perspective (point of view) of someone looking at the object. Think about what the front view, the top view and the side view of an airplane would look like.

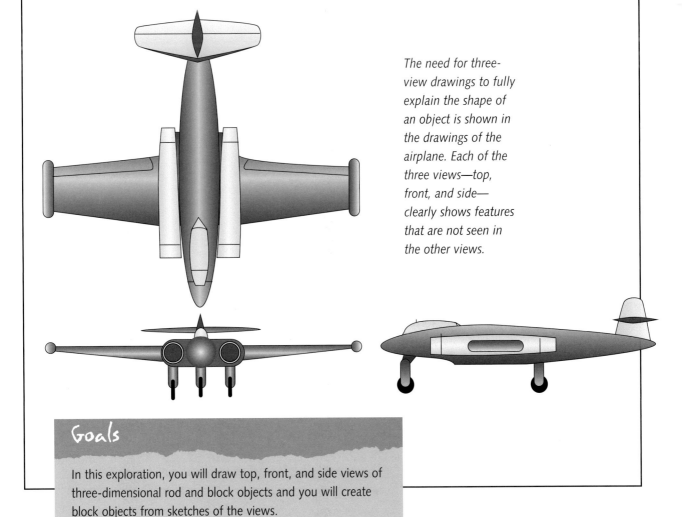

The need for three-view drawings to fully explain the shape of an object is shown in the drawings of the airplane. Each of the three views—top, front, and side— clearly shows features that are not seen in the other views.

Goals

In this exploration, you will draw top, front, and side views of three-dimensional rod and block objects and you will create block objects from sketches of the views.

Consider the following block object. Its three-view drawings are:

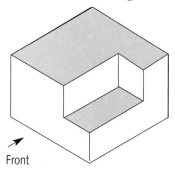

Top View

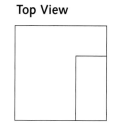

Front View

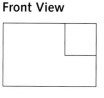

Side View

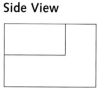

Front

Example 1—Using Cuisenaire Rods

Build the three-dimensional rod design shown using one yellow, one light green, one red, and one white rod. This design can also be built using interlocking cubes: 5 yellow, 3 light green, 2 red, and 1 white.

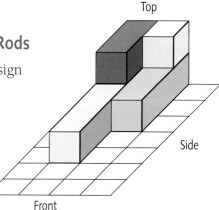

Top

Side

Front

Solution

Pictured below are the top, front, and side views of the rod design. Examine these views carefully.

Top View

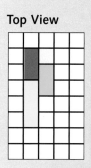

Front View

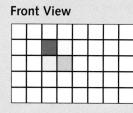

Side View

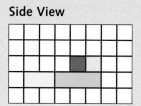

Hint

The side view of an object is normally the view of its right side. The right side of the object is determined when you are facing the front of the object.

Example 2

Build the rod design shown below using 1 purple, 1 light green, 2 red, and 2 white rods.

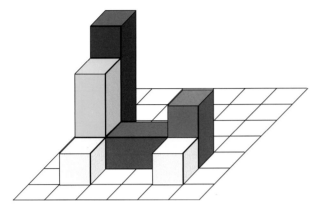

Draw the top, front, and side views. Try this on your own before looking at the solution.

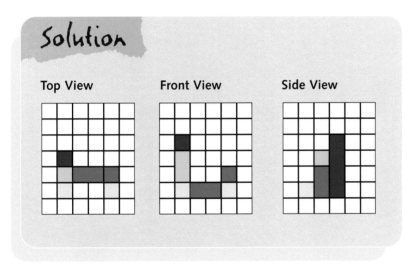

Example 3

Below are the top, front, and side views of a rod design. Build the three-dimensional rod design that goes with these views. Use 3 white, 2 light green, and 2 red rods.

Top View

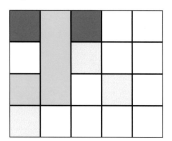

Front View

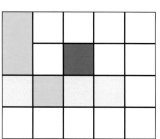

Side View

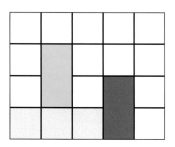

Solution

Your three-dimensional rod design should look like the following.

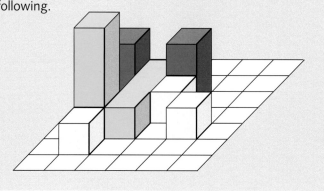

Example 4

Draw the top, side, and front views of a tube slide that could be used in a recreational space.

Solution

Top View   **Front View**   **Side View**

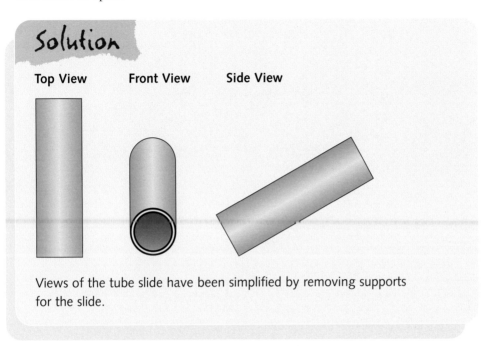

Views of the tube slide have been simplified by removing supports for the slide.

Project Activity

Imagine your recreational space as a box. Think of looking at it from the outside with the walls removed. What would your space look like? What would a person see if they looked at your space from the top? What would a front view look like? Think about your space from the right side. Draw these views to scale. Include as much detail as possible.

Notebook Assignment

1. Match each of the three-dimensional drawings of an object with its views. The front is shown by an arrow.

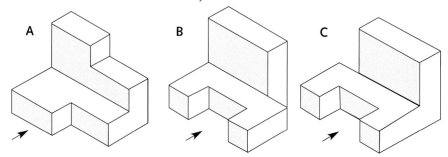

A   B   C

Views are simplified to show what is visible.

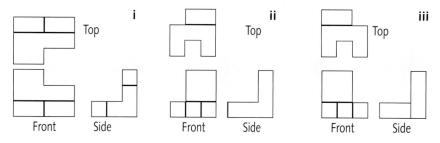

2. Match the three views of an object with the drawing of that object. The following views are simplified to show only what is visible.

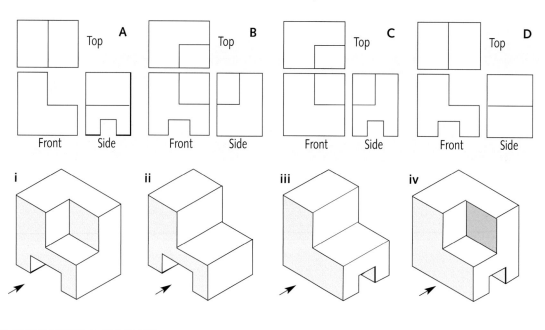

3. Build the three-dimensional rod designs shown below. For each one draw the top, front, and side views. Use graph paper.

a)

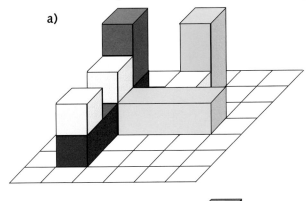

a) Use 3 white rods, 1 red rod, 2 light green rods, and 1 purple rod.

b) Use 3 white, 2 red, and 2 light green rods.

c) Use 3 white rods, 3 red rods, and 1 yellow rod.

b)

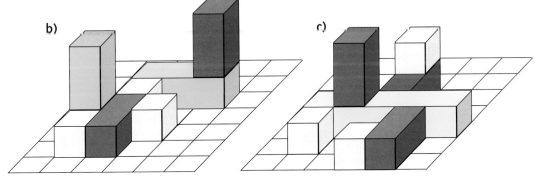

c)

4. Consider the top, front, and side views of a rod design. Build the three-dimensional rod design that goes with these views. Use 2 white rods, 2 red rods, 1 light green rod, and 1 purple rod.

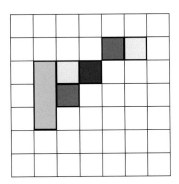

Top View

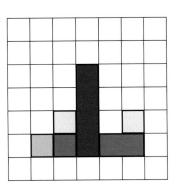

Front View

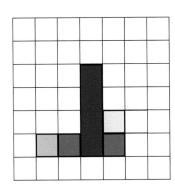

Side View

5. Draw the three views for each of the objects shown below. The dotted lines are not to be included in your views. These are provided to show sizes for your graph paper drawings of the views.

A

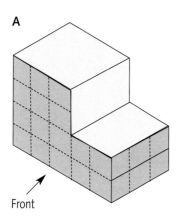

Front

B

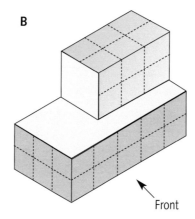

Front

6. Place two boxes, rods, or cubes together and draw their top, side, and front views.

7. Select a structure that could be built using 3–5 blocks or rods. Make drawings showing the top, front, and side views. Ensure that someone looking at the drawings could build the structure.

8. Work in pairs. Each partner will build the structure that his or her partner designed in question 7. As you build the structure, answer the following questions. Is the drawing easy to follow? If so, what makes it easy? If not, what makes it difficult? What could be improved?

9. Draw top, side, and front views of a toy car or another model to a scale you select.

Extension

10. Use construction materials such as interlocking cubes or Lego to create a model of an object that is identifiable in your community. Draw top, side, and front views of the model. Have a partner build the structure from the drawings you created.

Exploration 7

Isometric Dot Paper

You have learned to draw three-dimensional objects in two dimensions by using top, side, and front views. In real life, however, you do not see objects only in two dimensions. Imagine that you are looking straight on at a large cube. It looks like a square. You may not be able to see the sides, top, bottom or back. Now, picture the same cube from a corner view, one in which you can see only the front and side of the cube. Notice how the faces of the cube appear to be at an angle and heading off into the distance.

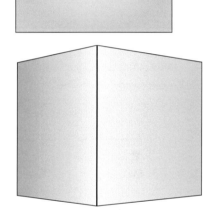

One tool that can help you draw two-dimensional images that represent three dimensions is isometric dot paper. This paper is printed with a pattern of dots that you can use to draw images. Look at the diagram below. It illustrates how a cube can be drawn using isometric dot paper. Notice that the cube or rod can be drawn from various perspectives.

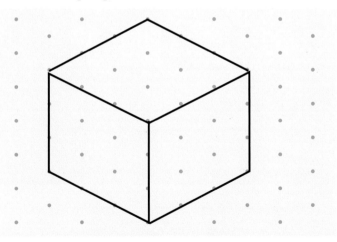

Career Connection

Name: Josh Schmike

Job: Volunteer tour guide at Science World in Vancouver, BC

Current wages: unpaid volunteer

Education: Bachelor of Fine Arts, University of British Columbia

Career goal: director of acquisitions, provincial art gallery

Keyword search: Canada university fine arts

Science World is a geodesic dome. Such domes are constructed using repeating triangles that give strength to the structure.

Mental Math

Find the missing measurements in the table.

Scale used	Length of object in drawing	Actual measurement
1:10	7 inches	
1:50	10 centimetres	
1:30		60 metres

Example 1

Draw a box using isometric dot paper. Show all six representations.

Solution

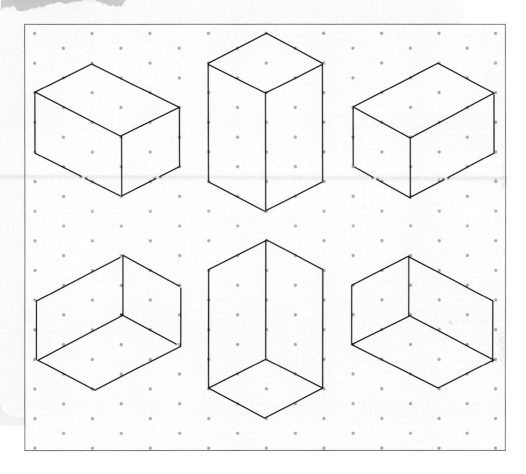

Example 2

Draw the following figure on isometric dot paper. Be sure to draw the figure and not just look at the solution.

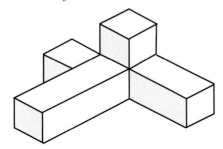

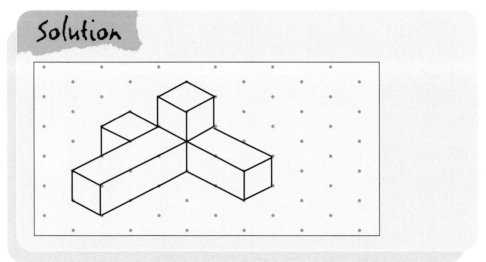

Project Activity

Create line drawings of 2 recreational space objects. Use isometric dot paper to create a three-dimensional image of each object. Add these to your project file as they could be used to help the graphic artists in the company create sales brochure images.

Notebook Assignment

1. Draw the following figures on isometric dot paper.

    A 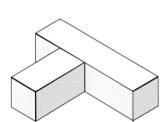   B 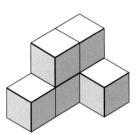   C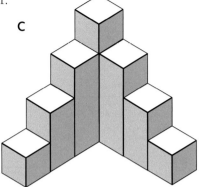

2. Consider the top, front, and side views of the rod design shown below. Build the three-dimensional object which has these views. Using isometric dot paper draw the three-dimensional object.

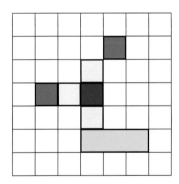
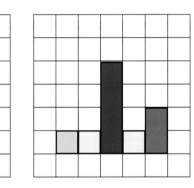

   Top View   **Front View**   **Side View**

3. Create a company logo using lines on isometric dot paper. Add additional lines to give your logo a three-dimensional effect. Colour the images to enhance the three-dimensional effect.

4. Draw the image of a recreational space staircase. Use isometric dot paper to make the image appear three-dimensional.

5. Use isometric dot paper to create a front view of a wedge-shaped object such as a slice of layer cake. Is it possible to create a drawing that shows both sides of the slice and the top using isometric dot paper? Why or why not?

Extension

6. Arrange 3 identical cubes in as many different ways as possible. The side of each cube must always be in contact with at least one side of another cube. Create images of your arrangements using isometric dot paper. Arrangements are considered different if their views are different.

7. Suppose plywood was used to construct the staircase in question 4. Use a diagram to show how you would cut plywood sheets (4 feet by 8 feet) to make the stairs. Use the plywood as efficiently as possible. Could left over pieces be used to construct parts of other sets of the same stairs? Show how you would use the plywood in a factory setting where many sets of stairs are being produced. In the factory setting, if plywood costs $40.00 a sheet, what would be the plywood costs for 10 sets of the stairs?

Hint

To find the total cost of materials required to build an object such as furniture, break down the object into smaller sections and find the costs one at a time. Add up the costs of the pieces to find the total cost of the object.

Exploration 8

Using Similar Triangles

Many structures are based on triangles. One reason to use triangles is that they help create strong, stable structures. Can you think of any structures that are made with triangles? What features of triangles would be helpful in creating different-sized triangle components?

Your recreational space may include triangles. In order to complete a model of your recreational space, you need to understand certain properties of triangles.

Example 1

Examine the triangles below. Measure the angles and the lengths of their sides. What do you notice?

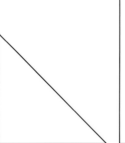
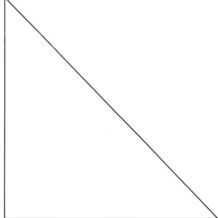

Solution

The angles in each triangle are the same. The length of each side on the large triangle is twice the length of the corresponding side on the small triangle.

Goals

In this exploration, you will investigate properties of similar triangles and use these properties to solve problems.

New Terms

similar triangles: triangles that have the same size of angles but whose sides are not necessarily the same size.

Example 2

Draw two different-sized similar triangles. The interior angles of the triangles should measure 20°, 70°, and 90°. Measure the length of the sides. Find the ratio of the length of the sides opposite the smallest angles. Repeat for the sides opposite the 70° and the 90° angles. How do they compare? How would you express this as a rule?

Solution

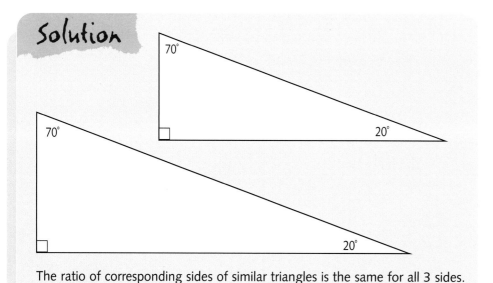

The ratio of corresponding sides of similar triangles is the same for all 3 sides.

Hint

The angles of a triangle are labelled with upper case letters, for example ∠A. The sides of a triangle are labelled with lower case letters. The side opposite ∠A is labelled side *a*, the side opposite ∠B is labelled side *b*, and the side opposite ∠C is labelled side *c*.

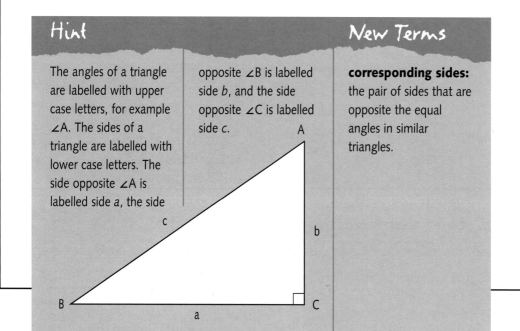

New Terms

corresponding sides: the pair of sides that are opposite the equal angles in similar triangles.

Project Activity

A model-maker is producing a scaled-down version of a recreational space. The space contains triangular shapes. The model-maker knows the model triangles and the corresponding recreational space triangles will be similar. How could the model-maker use the sizes in the recreational space to find the measures of angles and the lengths of sides for the triangles in the model? Describe, using examples.

Notebook Assignment

1. Complete this activity in small groups.

    a) Draw a triangle where two of the angles are between 10° and 60°. Label the base *a*. Label the other two sides *b* and *c* in a clockwise direction from side *a*. Label angles with capitals. An example is shown below.

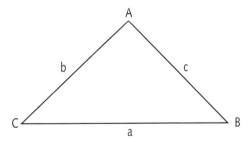

    b) Draw a second triangle, larger than the first one, where the three angles of the triangle are the same as the three angles of the previous triangle. Label it using D, E, and F, where ∠D = ∠A, ∠E = ∠B, and ∠F = ∠C.

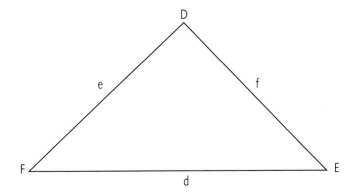

c) On the first triangle, draw a line AM that is perpendicular to BC.
On the second triangle, draw a line DN that is perpendicular to
EF (as shown below).

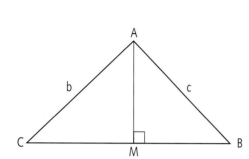

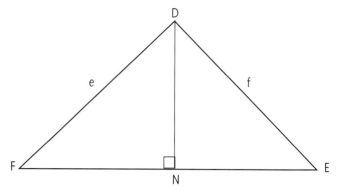

d) Fill in a data table such as the one shown on the facing page.

e) Compare the angle ratios. What pattern do you see?

f) Compare the lengths of sides ratios. What patterns do you see?

g) What is the ratio of the two triangles' areas? How is this ratio
related to the other ratios in the data table?

Data Table

∠A	
∠B	
∠C	
∠D	
∠E	
∠F	
∠A/∠D	
∠B/∠E	
∠C/∠F	
length of side a	
length of side b	
length of side c	
length of side d	
length of side e	
length of side f	
a/d	
b/e	
c/f	
a/b	
d/e	
a/c	
d/f	
b/c	
e/f	
length of AM (cm)	
length of DN (cm)	
area of ΔABC	
area of ΔDEF	
area of ΔABC/area of ΔDEF	

2. Find the missing sides of the following triangles using equivalent ratios.

a)

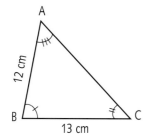

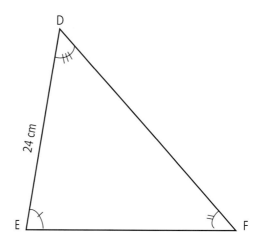

b)

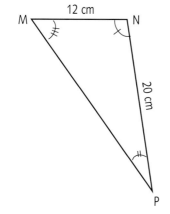

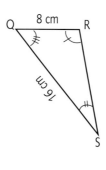

c)

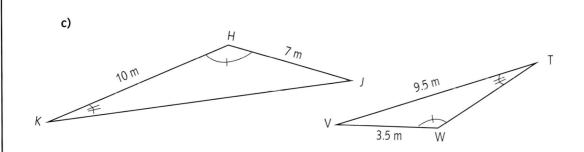

d)

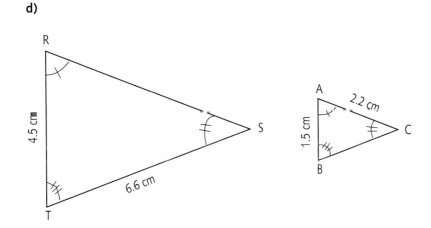

3. Find the length of the missing side of each of the following triangles by using equivalent ratios.

   a) In ΔHJK and ΔUVW, ∠H = ∠U, ∠J = ∠V, and ∠K = ∠W. If j = 17 mm, k = 20 mm, and v = 30 mm, find UV or w.

   b) In ΔABC and ΔDEF, ∠A = 32°, ∠B = 90°, ∠E = 90°, and ∠F = 58°. If a = 1.2 m, b = 2.4 m, and e = 1.8 m, find EF.

   c) In ΔMNP and ΔTVW, ∠M = 90°, ∠P = 39°, ∠T = 90°, and ∠V = 51°. If NP = 86 cm, MN = 64 cm, and TV = 118 cm, find VW.

4. The length of the shadow cast by a tree is 6.8 m. At the same time the length of the shadow cast by a 40-cm plant is 65 cm. How tall is the tree?

5. In triangles LMN and XYZ, ∠M is 90°, *n* is 4.8 cm long, *l* is 8.5 cm long, ∠Y is 90°, and *z* is 12 cm long. ∠L equals∠X. Calculate the length of side *x*.

6. In triangles ABC and DEF, ∠B equals ∠E and both are 90°, ∠A equals 60°, ∠F equals 30°, AC is 22 cm long, BC is 12 cm long, and DF is 18 cm long. Calculate the length of EF.

7. The length of a shadow cast by a telephone pole is 21 m. At the same time of day, the length of a shadow cast by a 90 cm post is 190 cm. How tall is the pole?

Extension

8. Jane places a mirror flat on the ground 35 m from a building. When she stands 0.5 m beyond the mirror, she can see the top of the building in the mirror. If her eyes are 1.2 m above the ground, how tall is the building?

Exploration 9

Using Trigonometry

There is a consistent pattern in similar triangles. Previously, you used similar triangles and ratios to find the lengths of sides. You can also use trigonometry to find angles and the lengths of sides of right triangles. Right triangles have one 90° angle. In this exploration, you will use a scientific calculator to solve problems involving trigonometric ratios.

Pairs Activity

Complete the following activity in pairs.

1. Draw and label a right triangle with the following angles:

    ∠A is 30°
    ∠C is 90°
    Label each angle and side of the triangle

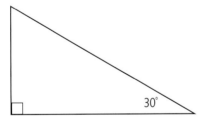

2. What is the measurement of ∠B? How can you determine this?

3. Measure each side of the triangle you drew in centimetres and label your measurements on the diagram.

Goals

In this exploration, you will use trigonometry to find angles and lengths of sides in right triangles.

4. Calculate the following ratios using the side measurements of your
    triangle.

    a/b =   **b/c =**
    a/c =   **b/a =**

5. Begin with ∠A = 30°. Determine the sine of ∠A using your
    calculator.

    To find the sine of 30° (sin30°) with a calculator, enter:
    SIN 30 = 0.5 or 30 SIN = 0.5, depending on your calculator.

    Which of the four ratios in question 4 matches this number? Write
    the ratio down.

6. Determine the cosine of ∠A using your calculator.

    To find the cosine of 30° (cos30°) with a calculator, enter:
    **COS 30 = 0.8660 or 30 COS = 0.8660, depending on your
    calculator.**

    Which of the four ratios in question 4 matches this number? Write
    the ratio down.

7. Determine the tangent of ∠A using your calculator.

    To find the tangent of 30° (tan30°) with a calculator, enter:
    **TAN 30 = 0.5774 or 30 TAN = 0.5774, depending on your
    calculator.**

    Which of the four ratios in question 4 matches this number? Write
    the ratio down.

8. Repeat steps 5 to 7, finding the sine, cosine, and tangent of ∠B, and
    matching the ratio value. Write the ratios out.

Hint

In this exploration, you will be using a scientific calculator to
determine trigonometric ratios. Make sure your calculator is set
to degrees. You can test it by finding the sine of 30. If the
answer is 0.5, your calculator is set properly.

The three basic trigonometric ratios from steps 5 to 7 for ∠B are:

sine B = opposite/hypotenuse
cosine B = adjacent/hypotenuse
tangent B = opposite/adjacent

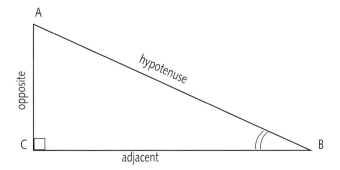

Notice that sinB – b/c but that sinA – a/c. The trigonometric ratios can also be used to find angle measurements.

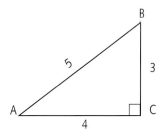

For example, find the measure of ∠B.
sinB = opposite/hypotenuse
sinB = 4/5
sinB = 0.8

| INV | | SIN | | 0.8 | | = | 53.13° or you may need to enter
| 0.8 | | INV | | SIN | | = | 53.13°

Hint

1. Depending on the calculator, the INV button may be replaced by ARC, 2nd, or SHIFT.

2. When solving a problem involving a trigonometric ratio, first label the sides of the right triangle using the words opposite, adjacent, and hypotenuse.

Project Activity

Work with a partner. Each partner needs to sketch two different right triangles. The first triangle should have values for two sides and an unknown angle labelled. The second triangle should have a value for one side, a value for one angle (not 90°), and an unknown side labelled. On a separate page, find the value of the unknowns for your triangles.

Suppose these triangles represent support brackets for your recreational space. The builders need to know the missing lengths or angles in order to build the parts. Switch drawings with your partner and calculate the unknowns in your partner's drawings. Compare your results.

Notebook Assignment

1. State whether you would use the sine, cosine, or tangent ratio to find x for each figure below.

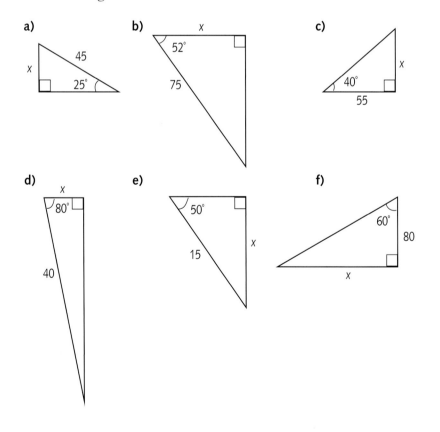

2. Calculate how long the guy wire (*x*) must be for the tent, given the information on the diagram.

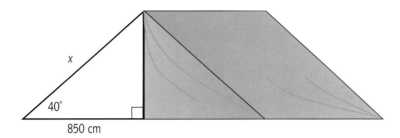

3. The sign at the local pizza place hangs 190 cm out from the store front and is supported by a cable. If the angle between the cable and the sign is 40°, find the length of the cable that supports the sign.

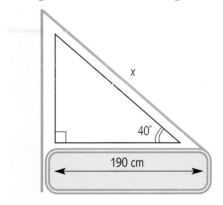

4. A ramp reaches a height of 2.1 m above the ground and forms an angle of 14° with the ground at the other end. How long is the ramp?

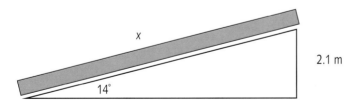

5. A kite string is extended 26.4 m and is held by a person at a height of 1.4 m above the ground. The angle the kite string makes with the horizontal is 57°. What is the height of the kite above the ground?

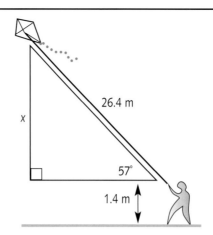

6. A rope 6.2 m long is attached to a tree 2.7 m above the ground. At what angle will the rope meet the tree?

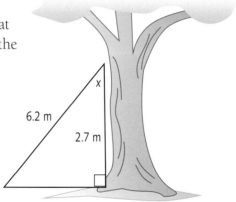

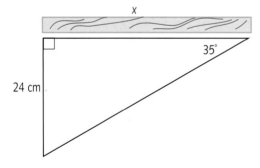

7. A shelf is held up by a triangular brace with a vertical length of 24 cm. If the outer edge of the shelf meets the brace and forms an angle of 35°, what is the length of the horizontal part of the brace?

Extension

8. A staircase is 12 m in length with a 35° incline. How high is the staircase? Illustrate and show all your calculations.

Exploration 10

Indirect Measurement

What is the tallest structure within walking distance of your school? Is it a flagpole, a building, a satellite tower, or a tree? Do you know how high it is? What strategies could you use to measure it indirectly? You could use the trigonometric ratios you have just learned to do this.

In this exploration, you will learn how to use trigonometry to find hard-to-measure distances such as the height of a tall structure, the width of a river, or the height of a pole. You will learn how to construct a clinometer, an instrument for measuring angles. Using your clinometer, and the trigonometric ratios, you will be able to find the height of the various structures.

Goals

In this exploration, you will find indirect measurements using trigonometric ratios.

New Term

clinometer: a device used to determine the measure of an angle from the horizontal.

Pairs Activity
Part A: Build a Clinometer

In order to find the measurement of an unknown side in a right-angled triangle, you have to know the measure of one of the acute angles. A clinometer is an instrument that measures angles. In order to construct a clinometer you will need the following:

wooden ruler (30 cm)   thumbtack
photocopy of a protractor   a piece of thread
a drinking straw   a small weight, for example, a nut or bolt

Choose a partner and build a clinometer together. The following diagram shows you what your clinometer should look like.

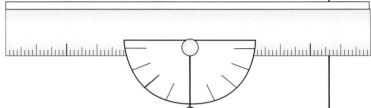

a) Using tape, attach the drinking straw to the top of the ruler. It is best if you align it so that one of its ends is at the end of the ruler.

b) Using tape, attach the protractor in the middle of the ruler.

c) Put a thumbtack through the ruler at the 90° line of the protractor.

d) Wind thread around the thumbtack.

e) Attach the small weight to the end of the thread. The weight should extend just below the edge of the protractor.

Hold the clinometer level. Note that the thread falls on the line marked 90°. Have one partner hold the clinometer and view an object by placing one end of the clinometer near the eye and point the other end at the top of the object. While one partner is viewing the object, the other partner should read the number of degrees the thread is from its starting position.

If the thread is now at 80° according to the protractor, it means that the angle of inclination of the object is 10°. The angle of inclination is the angle of an object measured from the horizontal. Note that to find the angle of inclination, you have to find the difference between the angle indicated on the protractor and 90°. Experiment with the clinometer. Are your results consistent?

Part B: Taking Measurements

In this activity, you will measure the height of three objects in your classroom. Choose three objects you wish to measure. Complete a chart like the one below to record your measurements of the three objects.

   Note: In this activity, you need to know the vertical distance your eyes are from the floor.

Object	Distance from Object	Angle of Elevation	Diagram of Triangle	Trigonometric Ratio Needed	Indirect Height of Object	Actual Height of Object	Difference between Indirect and Actual Measure

a) Have your partner stand a distance away from your first object. Measure the distance your partner is from the object using a metre stick. Record this distance on the chart.

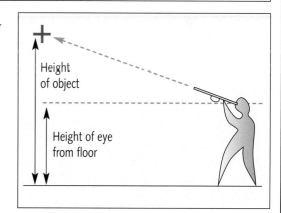

b) Have your partner view the top of the object with your clinometer. Determine the angle of inclination of the object by finding the number of degrees the thread is from its starting position.

c) Trade places with your partner. Now you hold the clinometer and view the same object. Have your partner find the number of degrees the thread is from its starting position. What is the angle of inclination this time? Are the two angles the same? If not, why would they be different? Record the angle of inclination in the chart.

d) After you have found the angle of inclination, draw a representative right triangle. Label the right triangle in terms of the distance you are from the object and the angle of inclination.

e) Using this diagram, determine the trigonometric ratio needed to find the height of the object. Remember to add the vertical distance your eyes are from the floor. Record the total height in the chart.

f) Now use a metre stick to find the actual height of the objects. Record this height on the chart.

g) Compare the two heights. How close are they? Did you expect the difference to be greater or less than what you found?

h) Do the same procedure for the other two objects in the classroom.

Trigonometry has many practical applications. Consider the following example.

Example 1

A 7.5 m flagpole is supported by two guy wires. The two guy wires are attached on opposite sides of the flagpole. Each guy wire makes an angle of 50° with the ground. Determine the total length of guy wire needed to support the flagpole. Round the length to the nearest tenth of a metre.

Solution

First draw a diagram.

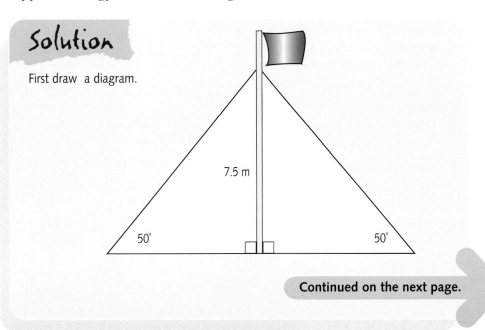

7.5 m

50° 50°

Continued on the next page.

Mental Math

Round the following values to 4 decimal places.

a) 0.882947292

b) 1.732050808

c) 0.698864072

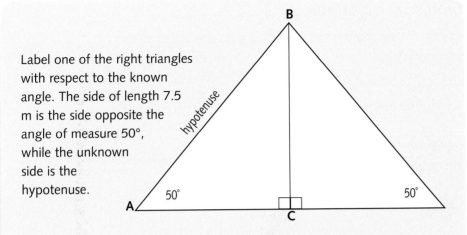

Label one of the right triangles with respect to the known angle. The side of length 7.5 m is the side opposite the angle of measure 50°, while the unknown side is the hypotenuse.

Because the sine of an angle is the ratio of the side opposite and the hypotenuse, choose the sine ratio to solve this problem.

$$\sin A = \frac{\overline{opp}}{hyp}$$

$$\sin 50° = \frac{\overline{7.5}}{x}$$

$$(\sin 50°)(x) = (7.5)$$

$$\frac{(\sin 50°)\,x}{\sin 50°} = \frac{7.5}{\sin 50°}$$

$$x = 9.8 \qquad \text{(rounded to the nearest tenth)}$$

The length of each guy wire is 9.8 m. The length of both guy wires needed to support the flagpole is:

$$2 \times 9.8 \text{ m} = 19.6 \text{ m}$$

Since the length of the guy wire is the hypotenuse of the right triangle, and the hypotenuse is the longest side, an answer of 9.8 m is reasonable.

You can also check your answer as follows:

$$\sin 50° = 0.77 \qquad \text{(rounded to two decimal places)}$$

$$\frac{\overline{7.5}}{9.8} = 0.77 \qquad \text{(rounded to two decimal places)}$$

Solving Problems in Trigonometry

To solve problems involving trigonometric ratios, you can use the
following six-step procedure:

1. Read the problem.
2. Check what information is given and what information is to be
   found.
3. Draw a diagram and label it appropriately.
4. Set up the appropriate trigonometric ratio.
5. Solve for the unknown.
6. Check your answer.

Example 2

Petra skis down a slope that is inclined at a 15° angle to the horizontal. If
she reaches ground level after travelling a distance of 128 m, how high is
the practice ski slope?

Solution

First draw a diagram. Label the given side and the unknown side with
respect to the angle of 15°. The unknown side is the side opposite angle
D, while the given side is the hypotenuse.

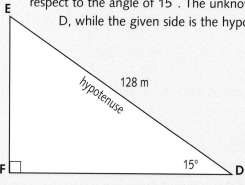

Continued on the next page.

Hints

When labelling a right-angled triangle
with respect to an angle, first find the
side opposite the 90° angle. This side is
the hypotenuse. Next, find the side
opposite the angle you are considering.
This is the side opposite. The third side
is the side adjacent.

New Terms

adjacent: means beside; the side
adjacent to the angle is beside the
angle.

Because the sine of an angle is the ratio of the length of the side opposite and the length of the hypotenuse, choose the sine ratio to solve this problem.

$$\sin D = \frac{opp}{hyp}$$

$$\sin 15° = \frac{x}{128}$$

$$(\sin 15°)(128) = x$$

$$x = 33.1 \qquad \text{(rounded to the nearest tenth)}$$

The practice ski slope has a height of 33.1 m.

You should always check that your answer is reasonable. Is an answer of 33.1 m reasonable? It is. The hypotenuse of the triangle is 128 m and it is the longest side of the triangle. Therefore, an answer of 33.1 m is reasonable.

You can also check your answer as follows:
$$\sin 15° = 0.26$$
$$\frac{33.1}{128} = 0.26$$

Pairs Activity

Calculate the height of the tallest structure within walking distance of your school. To do this you will need to use your clinometer. You will also have to measure the distance you are from the structure using a metre stick, tape measure, or trundle wheel.

To complete this activity, use the same procedure used previously in this exploration.

Notebook Assignment

1. **a)** If a rocket flies 2° off course for 5000 km, *estimate* how far from the correct path it will be.

   b) If a rocket flies 2° off course for 5000 km, *calculate* how far from the correct path it will be.

   c) If a rocket flies 45° off course for 5000 km, *estimate* how far from the correct path it will be.

   d) If a rocket flies 45° off course for 5000 km, *calculate* how far from the correct path it will be.

2. A 6-metre ladder is leaning against a wall. The angle formed by the ladder and the wall is 25°.

   a) How far is the base of the ladder from the wall? Round the answer to the nearest tenth of a metre.

   b) How far up the wall does the ladder reach? Round the answer to the nearest tenth of a metre.

   c) If the wall is 7 m high, will a person 2 m tall standing on the top of the ladder be able to see over the wall? Explain.

3. An airplane is flying at an altitude of 10 km. You spot the airplane at an angle of 55° to the horizontal.

   a) Determine the distance the airplane is from you. Round your answer to the nearest tenth of a kilometre.

   b) How far away from you is a point on the ground directly underneath the airplane? Round your answer to the nearest tenth of a kilometre.

   c) Are these measurements exact? What did you assume as you solved this problem?

4. A lighthouse is at the top of a steep cliff. The top of the lighthouse is 30 metres above sea level. A small boat is sighted from the lighthouse at an angle of 28° from the horizon (angle of depression). Determine how far the base of the cliff is from the fishing boat. Round the answer to the nearest metre.

5. The rafters of a roof form a 24° angle with the horizontal. The height of the roof support is 2.5 m. Find the width of the house to the nearest tenth of a metre.

6. A forester is doing a survey of the heights of trees.
   a) He walks a distance of 15 metres from a tree. The angle of inclination is 74°. Find the height of the tree.
   b) He walks a distance of 20 metres from a tree. The angle of inclination is 69°. Find the height of the tree.
   c) Are the answers close? Explain.

7. A fire ranger is looking at the ground from the top of a 30 m fire tower. He notices a fire at an angle of 3° to the horizon. Calculate the distance the fire ranger is from the fire.

8. A fire ranger is looking upwards from a platform at the top of a 20-metre fire tower. The ranger spots a water bomber above a fire at an angle of inclination of 12° to the horizontal. If the distance from the tower to the fire is 250 m, find the height of the water bomber.

9. In measuring the height of clouds at night, an airport controller shines a light vertically. An observer measures the angle of inclination of the light to the clouds to be 56°. If the horizontal distance from the light to the observer is 200 m, find the height of the clouds.

Hints

Navigation 1 to 60 Rule: for every 1° off course over a 60 km distance, the pilot is roughly 1 km off course

Extension

10. Design a ski hill with four levels of difficulty: a bunny trail, a beginner trail, an intermediate trail, and an expert trail. Suppose the entire horizontal distance is 1200 m. Suppose the bunny trail takes up $1/3$ of the horizontal distance, each of the beginner and intermediate trails are of equal horizontal distance, and the expert trail takes up $1/6$ of the horizontal distance. Suppose the angle of inclination of the bunny trail is 3°, the beginner trail is 7°, the intermediate trail is 26°, and the expert trail is 40°.

a) Sketch the ski hill.
b) Find the length of each of the trails.

Chapter Review

1. Use a tape measure to find the diagonal length of your desk or table top. Record your answer in both inches and centimetres.

2. Estimate the height of your classroom in feet, the area of a whiteboard in square centimetres, the volume of a coffee mug in cubic centimetres, and the mass of a scientific calculator in grams. Then, measure each item to see how close your estimate is to the actual measurement.

3. Complete each of the following:

   a) 1 m   = _____ cm
   b) 47 cm   = _____ feet
   c) 3 yards   = _____ cm
   d) _____ yds = 3.7 miles
   e) 71 km   = _____ miles

4. Consider the following ruler with the points A, B, C, and D marked on it.
   a) What measurement is shown by A?
   b) What measurement is shown by D?
   c) What is the difference in the measurements shown by A and B?
   d) Point C represents the length of a rectangle. Point D represents the width of the rectangle. Find the perimeter of the rectangle.

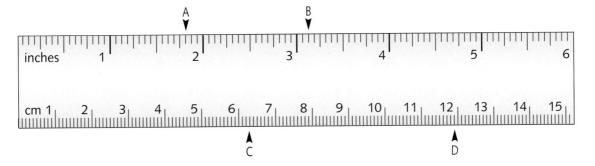

5. A small pizza has a diameter of 10 inches. A large pizza has a diameter of 15 inches. Find the ratio of the areas of the pizzas (leave your answer in the form 1:x.

6. A photograph 25 centimetres long and 20 centimetres wide must be enlarged to fit in a frame 30 centimetres long. Find the width of the enlarged photograph.

7. Remove the shaded Cuisenaire rod from the figure and draw the new figure on isometric dot paper.

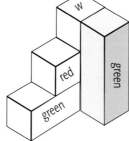

8. The following is an illustration of a yogurt container. The yogurt container is in the form of a truncated cone. Explain how to find the volume of the yogurt container.

9. The logo of a design company is a plus sign. The company builds a model of their logo using a 5 cm by 1 cm by 1 cm rod with 2 cm by 1 cm by 1 cm rods attached to the middle. Draw an arrangement of the three rods used to make the plus sign. Show a top, side, and front view.

10. Use isometric dot paper to show a three-dimensional image of a television set.

11. a) A model sandbox is made of cardboard. Its dimensions are 15 cm x 5 cm x 2 cm. If the depth of the box is increased from 2 to 4 centimetres, how many times greater is the volume? Explain your reasoning.

    b) Draw a half-size representation of the model sandbox. Use isometric dot paper.

12. Draw the top, front, and side views for the object shown below. Do not include the dotted lines in your graph paper drawings.

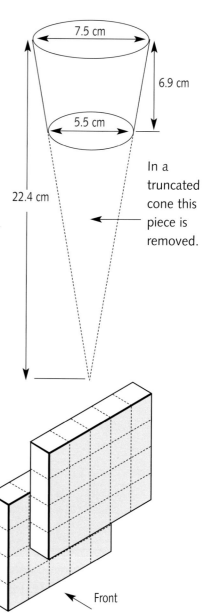

In a truncated cone this piece is removed.

Front

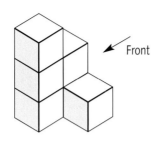

13. Build the object shown on the left using 6 small cubes. Draw the top, front and side (right) views for the object.

14. A diagram of a park is shown on the right. A groundskeeper must apply grass seed to the unpaved areas, taking care not to get any on the paved areas. The directions on the grass seed recommend sowing 3.75 kg/100 m².

   a) Calculate how much grass seed the groundskeeper will need if there is to be grass under the bleachers.

   b) Calculate how much grass seed would be saved if the area under the bleachers was gravel.

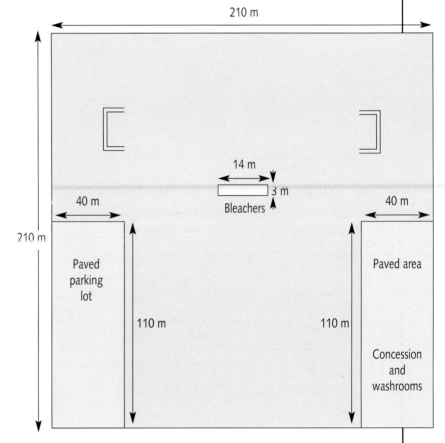

15. a) Sketch a plan for a simple peaked-roof dog house. Identify all the necessary dimensions on your sketch. Use either metric or imperial measurement units. Show the top, front, and side views. Estimate the amount of plywood it would take to cover the entire doghouse.

   b) Use stiff cardboard to make a simple scale model of the doghouse.

16. Find the area of the following
    figure.

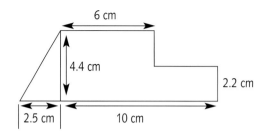

17. Find the volume of the
    following object.

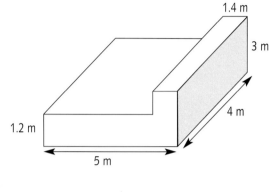

18. Find the surface area of the
    following object.

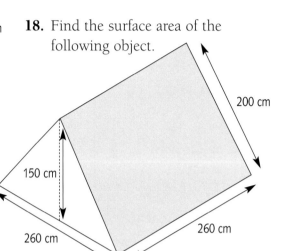

19. The following chart shows ratios from similar solids. Complete the chart.

Ratio of Side Length	Ratio of Surface Areas	Ratio of Volumes
1:5		
1:8.5		
	1:36	
	1:144	
		1:1000
		1:3375

20. A trapezoid has an area of 82 cm². Find the area of a trapezoid with
    dimensions 2 times as large.

21. A cone has a volume of 20.8 cm³. Find the volume of a cone with
    dimensions 3 times as large.

22. Each side of a square room is 3 m long. Each side is increased by 1
    m. Compare the areas of the rooms before and after the sides are
    lengthened. Express this comparison as a ratio in the form 1:x.

23. A sphere has a radius of 8 cm. The radius is increased by 1 cm. Compare the volumes of the spheres before and after the length of the radius is increased. Express this comparison as a ratio in the form 1:x.

24. A basketball has a diameter of 23.5 cm, a volleyball has a diameter of 21.3 cm, and a tennis ball has a diameter of 6.25 cm. Find the following ratios of their volumes in the form 1:x.

   a) tennis:volleyball
   b) volleyball:basketball

25. Use your calculator to find each value to 3 decimal places.

   a) $\dfrac{36}{\cos 10^\circ}$ **b)** $\dfrac{0.034}{\sin 13^\circ}$ **c)** $16 \sin 28^\circ$ **d)** $\dfrac{5.1}{\tan 38^\circ}$

26. Find the value of x. Give answers to 3 decimal places.

a)

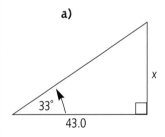

b)

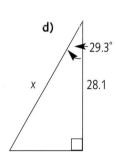

c)

d)

27. Calculate the height of the tree in the following diagram. Give your answer to 1 decimal place.

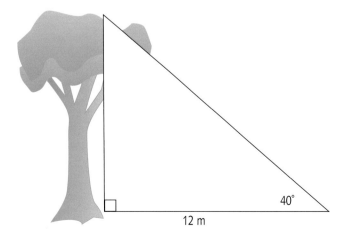

28. To find the distance AB across a marsh, a surveyor made the measurements shown in the diagram below. Calculate AB.

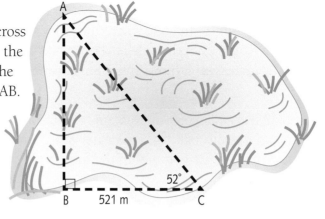

29. Mr. Kerko installs a TV antenna on his flat roof. Each supporting wire is attached to the antenna 5.0 m above the roof. The wires make angles of 30° with the antenna. How long is each wire?

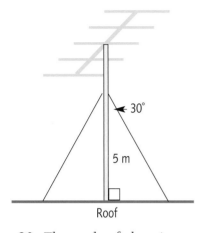

30. The angle of elevation to the top of a flagpole, from a point 10 m from the base of the flagpole and 1 m above the ground, is 70°. Find the height of the flagpole.

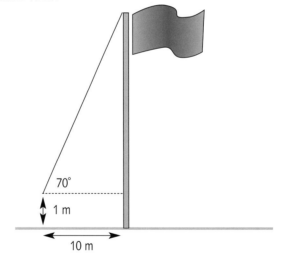

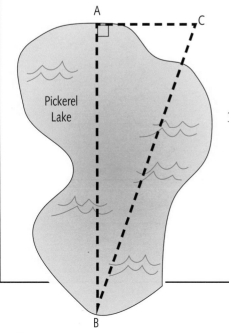

31. To calculate the width of Pickerel Lake, Susan took sightings with her transit at the points marked A and C. Then she measured the distance between them. She found that AC = 260 m, ∠ACB = 64°, ∠CAB = 90°. Calculate the width, AB, of the lake.

Project Presentation

Creating something in three dimensions is a challenge. Your challenge is to finalize a three-dimensional model of your recreational space. You may use ideas and drawings from your project file.

Your project presentation must display the model of your recreational space plus a creative way of presenting your ideas. You could use a sales brochure, booklet, create a television advertisement, or a Power Point presentation that explains the features of your recreational space.

Remember to include an explanation of what it is about the design that will suit the target group. Highlight portions of the space by including scaled floor plans and three-dimensional isometric diagrams of some of the features.

This castle is part of a children's recreational area on Blackcomb Mountain.

Case Study

Design a floor plan of a 1000 square foot house or apartment. You must include a kitchen, living room, bedroom, and bathroom. Show all doorways, hallways, and closets.

Provide the following information with your plan: the scale of your model, metric dimensions for all rooms, the area of the floor space in metric units, and the volume of the second largest room.

Chapter 6
Sampling and Probability

Publishing an E-zine for Teens

In this chapter, you will act as a researcher working for an electronic publishing company. In this role, you will explore the mathematics of sampling and probability.

A sample is part of a population. A sample can be used to predict the size of the population, or it can be used to represent the population in a research study. Sampling is used to collect data. The collected data is then analyzed and used to make predictions about what the total population might be, do, or think.

Chapter Goals

In this chapter, you will learn to collect and analyze data. You will become familiar with sampling methods and learn how sample data can be used to make predictions. You will learn to present data effectively and to examine and interpret data presented by others. You will develop a plan to collect, display, and analyze data.

New Terms

data: information gathered from a study

population: the total collection of items or individuals being studied

probability: the likelihood of an event happening expressed on a scale from 0 to 1

sample: 1. to sample means to select a number of items or individuals from a total population **2.** a sample is the group selected to represent a total population

Career Connection

Name: Taylor Quinton

Job: production assistant at a magazine

Current wages: $12.50 an hour

Education: grade 12; creative writing student at University of Victoria

Career goal: magazine journalist

Keyword search: journalism Canada college

Chapter Project

In this project, you will play the role of a researcher working for an electronic publishing company. Your research will help the publisher develop a new school-based electronic magazine for teens. To test market the new magazine, a front cover design and a proposed table of contents are needed. As part of the research team, you will gather data necessary to predict the most effective cover and contents.

During the project, you will

- estimate the total population of grade 10 students that will read the magazine
- select a sample from that population
- collect data
- analyze and present the data graphically to the publisher
- use the data to predict the most interesting table of contents and cover design

Your project presentation will consist of a cover design proposal and a table of contents for one issue of the e-zine.

Exploration 1

Determining Total Population

It is often necessary to determine the size of a population of people, plants, or animals. For example, nature enthusiasts, biologists, park officials, hunters, fishers, guides, businesses, and government officials often want to know the size of specific populations. Exact numbers may be difficult to count so sampling is often used to estimate a total population.

In wildlife studies, one method is called capture-mark-recapture. For example, a biologist may want to know how many trout there are in a lake. He captures and marks 36 trout and releases them back into the lake. He waits a certain length of time so that the marked trout can mix into the general population. A month later, he captures 30 trout and finds that 4 of them are marked. He can use ratios to estimate the total number of trout in the lake. There are about 270 trout in the lake.

A second way to determine total population is to count the number of individuals in a small area and then multiply the number counted by the total area. This is called the quadrat method. This method is used to estimate the population of herd animals, such as caribou or elk. An aerial photograph of a herd can be sectioned into smaller areas and the number of animals in the sections counted.

Trout tagged in a capture-mark-recapture project.

A related method of counting animal populations can help us find out whether the population is increasing, decreasing, or migrating. Bird counts are often used to evaluate changing populations. Counts are done annually at the same place so that the study animals can be tracked from year to year.

Goals

In this exploration, you will learn about sampling methods and how samples can be used to estimate total population size.

Career Connection

Name: David George

Job: fisheries worker

Current wages: $10.50 an hour

Education: grade 12

Career goal: fisheries technician

Keyword search: courses fisheries Canada

A Sto:lo fisheries officer from the First Nations Fishing Authority.

Example 1—Capture-Mark-Recapture Method

David Maitland captures and marks 50 salmon fingerlings from a small pool. A week later, he captures 112 fingerlings and finds that 17 of them have been marked. How many fingerlings are there in the pool?

Solution

David's calculation can be expressed as a ratio:

$$\frac{\text{number captured and marked } (N)}{\text{total } (T)} = \frac{\text{marked number recaptured } (M)}{\text{number recaptured } (R)}$$

$$\frac{50}{T} = \frac{17}{112}$$

David knows the number marked in the first place, the number he recaptured, and the number of those that were marked. To solve for the total number in the pool, he cross-multiplies:

$$(50)(112) = (17)(T)$$

$$\frac{(50)(112)}{(17)} = T$$

$$T \approx 329 \text{ (rounded to a whole number)}$$

There are 329 fingerlings in the pool.

Fingerlings are baby fish about the size of a person's little finger.

Hints

1. When calculating a total population, round to the nearest whole number.

2. $\approx$ is the symbol for "approximately equal to."

Example 2—Count Method

Jeff has counted bald eagles gathered at the mouth of a river on the same day of the year for the last ten years. His counts were: 25, 21, 18, 22, 25, 28, 30, 32, 25, and 34. Over a five-year period, has the number of eagles increased, decreased, or stayed the same? Could you conclude from the data that the total number of eagles has changed? Why or why not?

Each year bald eagles are counted at Brackendale on the Squamish River.

Solution

The average number of eagles for the first 5 years was 22.2 eagles. In the last 5 years it was 29.8. The number of eagles in Jeff's study area has increased. You could not be certain that the total number of eagles has increased because he was only counting eagles in one small area. That area might not represent the whole population.

Example 3—Quadrat Method

Fishers are concerned about the number of salmon accidentally caught in the nets of large trawling ships out at sea. They obtain permission to study the catch in three ships from a fifteen-ship fleet. They count the salmon accidentally caught by the three ships in one day. The counts are 15, 56, and 27. How many salmon are caught by the whole fleet in a day?

Solution

The daily salmon catch of the fleet can be calculated by adding the number of salmon caught by the 3 ships and dividing by 3 to find the average number each ship caught:
(15 + 56 + 27) ÷ 3 = 32.666 or 32.67

Then multiply the average number per ship by the number of ships:
32.67 x 15 = 490.05

About 490 salmon are accidentally caught each day by the fleet.

Counting Sharks Activity

In the ocean off Canada's Pacific coast live several varieties of sharks. One of these is the dogfish, also known as the mudshark. Marine biologists are studying these sharks to find out how they live. One thing they want to determine is the number of mudsharks. How might marine biologists estimate the number of sharks?

In this activity, you will work with a partner to simulate a capture-mark-recapture project to estimate the size of a population of mudsharks. You will need one container of 400-500 white beads and another container of about 100 red beads to complete the activity.

Mudsharks are commonly known as dogfish.

1. Begin by considering how marine biologists might estimate the number of mudsharks. It would be impossible to count each individual shark swimming in the ocean. What other ways can you use to determine the size of the population?

2. Estimate the number of beads in your container. Describe how you arrived at your estimate.

3. Remove a handful of white beads from the container and count them. This is your first sample, representing the number of mudsharks you have captured. There should be between 15 and 40 beads. Record the sample size.

4. Replace the white beads that have been removed from the container with the same number of red beads. The red beads represent the marked sharks you have released back into the population. Mix the beads thoroughly to represent the natural mixing process of fish in the ocean. With your partner, discuss the effect inadequate mixing could have on future sampling.

5. Now take a second sample. Without looking in the container, remove about the same number of beads that you removed in step 3.

6. Count the number of red beads in your sample. These represent the marked sharks that have been caught in the second sample.

7. Now calculate the number of mudsharks in the total population. Call the total number of white beads in the container T. Call the number of white beads in the first sample N. Call the number of red beads in the second sample M. Call the number of beads in the second sample R.

8. Use the proportion N/T = M/R to find T, the total number of beads in the container. Count the actual number of beads to find out how close your estimate is. Explain why you would not expect the estimate to equal the exact amount.

    Discuss whether the capture-mark-recapture method makes common sense. What are some things that must be true for this method to work? Give another example where this method could be used.

MEMORANDUM

From: Editor-in-Chief
To: Research Team

Our company is planning to publish a new e-zine for grade 10 students. Your first task is to estimate the population of grade 10 students. Your school's grade 10 students will serve as the total population for your research study. It will provide you with the data used to develop our e-zine. Your research will help us determine the interests of grade 10 students, and what they would like to read in a magazine.

Project Activity

In this activity, you will count grade 10 students in the lunch room or another limited area of your school on consecutive days. Use the capture-mark-recapture method to predict the total population of grade 10 students. Follow the steps below:

a) Count and record the names of grade 10 students in the specified area during a 5-minute stretch of time.

b) Count the grade 10 students in the same area for the same length of time the next day. Record their names.

c) Identify the number of students on the second day who were also counted on the first day.

d) Find the total population using the appropriate ratios.

e) How could you improve your sampling method to get more reliable results?

Notebook Assignment

1. For this activity, you will need a package of popcorn kernels or dried beans and a partner. Select 25 of the kernels and mark them with a coloured marking pen. Return the marked kernels to the bag and mix them well. Remove 50 kernels from the bag and count the number of marked kernels. Using your count data, estimate the total number of kernels in the whole bag. Next, do an actual count of the total number of kernels and compare the count with your estimate. If your estimate is very different from the count, describe how your method could be improved.

2. A wildlife biologist is studying perch that have been introduced into a lake where they do not naturally live. He captures and marks 46 fish. He returns in a week's time and catches 90 fish and finds that 7 of them are marked. How many perch are in the lake? Is this an exact number? Why or why not?

3. A research team is trying to estimate the number of marmots that live on a mountain. The team captures, marks, and releases 43 marmots from various spots on the mountain. Three weeks later they capture 115 marmots and find that 17 of them are marked. How many marmots are there on the mountain? Is this an exact number?

4. A ranch in the Rocky Mountains is located in an area that elk migrate through every year. For the last eight years, the rancher has recorded the number of elk he sees during the week they migrate. He counts the following number of elk: 22, 23, 20, 15, 25, 13, 11, 14. Based on his results, would you judge that the population of elk is increasing, decreasing, or staying the same? Explain your reasoning. State two reasons why the rancher's counts may not be a fair representation of the total elk population.

5. A tourist information centre kept track of the number of people stopping by for information. In 1997, the town began promoting itself as a tourist destination on the internet. The average number of people stopping at the information centre each day is recorded in the table below.

Before Internet Advertising	After Internet Advertising
1992 100	1997 135
1993 115	1998 150
1994 123	1999 201
1995 102	2000 185
1996 117	2001 122

Do you think the internet advertising was effective? What might have happened in 2001? What would you predict next year's average to be? Why?

6. A researcher is studying prairie dog towns. She selects a small town with an area of 112 m². She fences off the area and captures all the animals over a period of a week, finding a total of 35 animals. Nearby she finds another town with an area of 200 m². Estimate the number of animals that live in the larger town, based on the researcher's data.

Extension

7. A timber cruiser must estimate the number of trees in an area 80 km². The cruiser selects nine 10 m x 10 m locations evenly distributed throughout the area. He counts the number of trees in each location and records the number of trees as follows: 8, 12, 11, 7, 4, 5, 13, 11, 10. Estimate the number of trees in the 80 km² area.

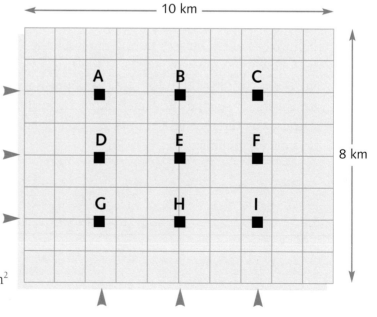

Exploration 2

●●●●●●●●●●●●●●●●●●●●

What Type of Sample?

Just as sometimes you need to estimate the total population from a sample, you sometimes want information that would be difficult to collect from the total population, even if you know its size. In this case, you need a sample that represents the whole population. For example, the owners of a new restaurant want to find the food preferences of potential customers in their community. They decide to survey possible customers to find which foods they prefer. How could they select a group of people to survey?

There are four main ways to select samples to represent a larger population.

1. In a simple random sample, the individuals who become part of the sample are randomly selected. Every member of the total population has an equal chance of being selected for the sample. The selection of one individual does not influence whether or not another individual is selected. Drawing names from a hat, using a spinner to pick student numbers, or picking people from a list by using dice or a random number table are methods of selecting a simple random sample.

2. In a systematic sample, one person represents a certain number of people. For example, selecting every twentieth person from an alphabetical list is an example of systematic sample selection. If every tenth item on an assembly line is doubled-checked, the manufacturer is using systematic sampling to control the quality of its products.

3. In a cluster sample, certain segments of the total population are randomly selected and then each member of that segment is surveyed. For example, if you wanted to measure how well students are doing in grade 10 mathematics, you might randomly select a certain number of schools and then test each grade 10 mathematics student in those schools.

Goals

In this exploration, you will learn to select and defend a sampling method.

4. A stratified random sample can be the fairest form of representation if a large population is to be studied. For example, suppose a survey on the health care requirements of the western provinces and the northern territories is needed. Each province and territory would be assigned a number of survey participants based on their total population, and that number would be randomly selected to take part in the survey. The total survey would then represent each region proportionally.

Example 1

How many students prefer hamburgers to pizza? To find a sample of students, a surveyor obtains an alphabetical student list and throws dice to determine who is asked. If he throws a 6, the sixth student on the list is selected. If he then throws a 3, the third student after that student is selected, and so on. What kind of sample has the surveyor selected? Is it appropriate in this situation? Why or why not?

Solution

This is a simple random sample. It is appropriate as long as the total population being studied is the group of students on the original alphabetical list.

Example 2

Your class is making apple tarts to sell as a fundraiser. You are in charge of quality control. You agree to taste-test every fifth tart. What kind of sample is that? Is it appropriate in this situation? Why?

Solution

This sample method is a systematic sample. It is not appropriate because you eat too many of the tarts. Testing 20% of your production would reduce your profit significantly.

Example 3

You are asked to find how students in a school district feel about separating their homerooms into grade groups. Currently, their homerooms are mixed grade groups. You select three schools in the district randomly and then survey each student in those schools. What kind of sample is this? Is it appropriate in this situation? Why?

Solution

This is a cluster sample. It is appropriate as long as the three schools are randomly selected.

Example 4

You are surveying students in order to pick new school colours. Your school has 60 grade 8 students, 70 grade 9 students, and 50 grade 10 students. You randomly select 6 grade 8, 7 grade 9, and 5 grade 10 students. What kind of sample is this? Is it appropriate in this situation? Why?

Solution

This is a stratified random sample. It is appropriate because each grade is represented proportionally.

MEMORANDUM

From: Editor-in-Chief
To: Research Team

Your second assignment is to explore four types of sampling to find out which one will give us the best information about our target audience. Are they workable in the school? Will they supply the kind of information we are looking for? Write a comment about each type of sampling method that describes its advantages and disadvantages. Recommend the method you prefer.

Project Activity

In this activity, consider the four types of sampling that could be used to determine the type of e-zine that would appeal to grade 10 students. What are the advantages and disadvantages of each of the four sampling methods? Make a recommendation for the type of sampling you prefer to use.

Notebook Assignment

1. Describe how you would select a sample in the following situations:

   a) a simple random sample of the people attending a hockey game;
   b) a systematic sample of chocolates made at a chocolate factory;
   c) a cluster sample of the residents of a large neighbourhood;
   d) a stratified random sample from members of the Canadian Curling Association.

2. Select a sampling method that will allow you to determine the favourite type of restaurant among your classmates. Justify your choice of sampling method.

3. The school store would like to sell basic school supplies to students. How should the school population be sampled to find the three most important items to stock in the store? Justify your answer.

4. A school has 80 grade 8 students, 95 grade 9 students, and 112 grade 10 students. The school council wants to find out how many hours students spend on sports or hobbies. How would you sample the population? Describe your method in detail and defend your choice.

5. As a member of the student council, you wish to determine the number of students who will attend a school dance. Explain how you could collect this information. Justify your decision.

6. A city council is trying to determine if a major road in your district needs to be widened. Explain a procedure that could be used to help city council make this decision.

7. Bill surveyed people entering a theatre and asked them if they would support building a new sports arena in the community. Discuss the appropriateness of this method of collecting data.

Extension

8. Explain what the most appropriate methods for collecting data would be for each of the following questions:

   a) Does smoking cause lung cancer?
   b) Does pet ownership enhance the quality of life for senior citizens?

   Identify potential ethical problems, the need for sensitivity to personal and cultural beliefs, and the cost when designing questions and collecting data.

Exploration 3

Random Numbers

There are a number of ways to generate and use random numbers in selecting a study sample. On a list of random numbers, every number within the range of the list has an equal chance of being selected.

Random numbers can be useful for collecting unbiased data. For example, a list of random numbers can be used to select students to participate in a survey. If the students participating in the survey are selected using random numbers, the results should be unbiased.

Some ways to make a random list are to use dice, the random number feature of some calculators or spreadsheet software, a spinner, or a table of random numbers.

Example 1—A Table of Random Numbers

The mascot for the school rugby team is a rhinoceros. Select six sample students from a grade 10 class to pick a name for the mascot.

Solution

Use a random number table to determine a sample of six students from a class of 30.

22	16	1	15
2	29	18	7
1	24	9	3
3	11	16	1

The students in the class are assigned numbers from 1 to 30. A table of random numbers that ranges from a minimum of 1 to a maximum of 30 is used. The first six numbers (22, 16, 1, 15, 2, 29) indicate which students make up the sample.

Goals

In this exploration, you will learn how random numbers can be used to select a sample.

New Terms

bias: inaccurate representation; if a sample is biased, it is an inaccurate representation of the population.

Example 2—A Spinner or Die

Use a spinner or a die to select a student to lead the discussion about mascot names.

Solution

Rolling a 3 on a single die means that student #3 is selected to lead the discussion.

Example 3—A Calculator or Spreadsheet

Use a graphing calculator or spreadsheet software to select a sample from the entire population of grade 10 students to see if the mascot name is liked by the students as a whole. There are 120 students. Refer to the user's manual to obtain the steps required.

Solution

List the students alphabetically and then number them from 1 to 120. Use the random number generator on a graphing calculator and set the minimum number to 1 and the maximum to 120. Pick the first 20 random numbers and match them to the students' names. These students will become the sample.

Group Activity

Work in a group of four students to complete the following activity, which will show you a way to estimate the area of hard-to-measure shapes.

1. Make two sets of cards from white and one other colour of cardboard. Make 20 white cards and label them 1 to 20. Mix these cards and place them in a container labelled "X". Make 40 coloured cards, label them 1 to 40, mix them, and place them in a container labelled "Y".

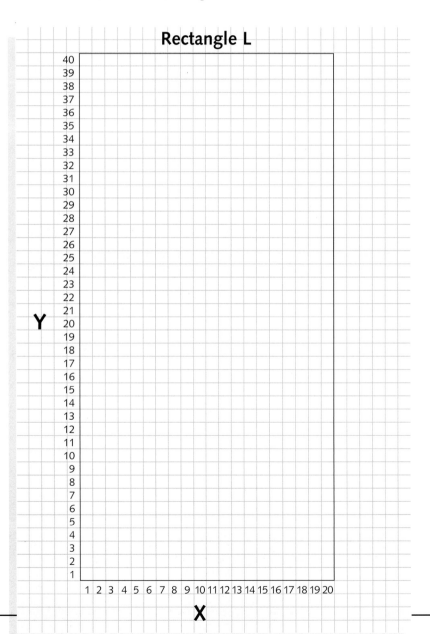

2. Use a piece of grid paper at least 21 squares wide and 41 squares long. Label the outside squares on the X-axis 1 to 20 and the outside squares on the Y-axis 1 to 40. Label the rectangle formed by the X and Y axes "L," for large. What is the area of the portion of the grid paper you have numbered in square units?

3. The first person in your group will select cards from the X container and the second person will select cards from the Y container. The third person will record the X and Y numbers on a chart like the one shown below. The last person will draw a diagonal line through the square that has the pairs of X and Y values. (See example on the next page.)

   Begin by selecting a card from each of the containers. Replace the cards and mix.

Number Pair		Number Pair		Number Pair		Number Pair	
X	Y	X	Y	X	Y	X	Y

4. Continue this process until 50 squares are marked. If you select the same pair again, mark a diagonal line in the square running the opposite direction. The 50 marked squares are a representative sample of the whole grid. The population in this case is the whole group of squares.

5. Why is it important that the marked squares are picked randomly? Are the marked squares randomly distributed?

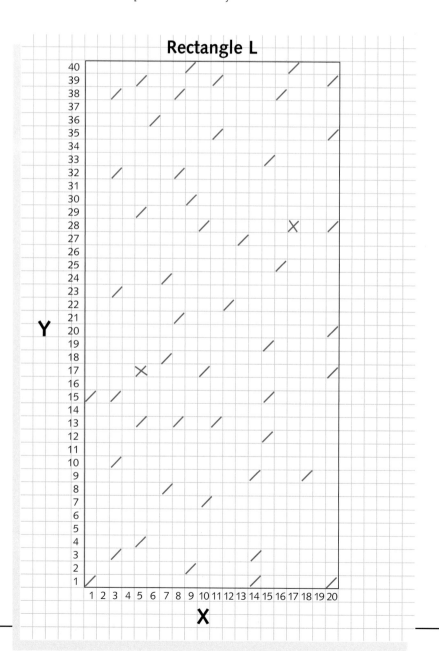

Rectangle L

6. Test this method for calculating area by cutting out a 10-square by 10-square piece from a separate sheet of grid paper. Label it "S" for small. Place the square anywhere on the Large rectangle, trace its shape, and then count the number of marked squares that are inside the Small square.

7. The ratio below can be used to estimate the area of the Small square. Use the ratio and the equation to find the estimated area of the Small square. How does it compare to the actual value? Would you expect the estimate to be the same as the actual value? Why? Would you describe this method as being an effective way of estimating area? Why or why not?

$$\frac{\text{Number of marked squares in "S"}}{\text{Total number of marks inside "L"}} - \frac{\text{Area of "S"}}{\text{Area of "L"}}$$

$$\text{Area of "S"} = \frac{(\text{Area of "L"}) \times (\text{Number of marked squares in "S"})}{\text{Total number of marks inside "L"}}$$

8. Place the Small square on another location in the Large rectangle and repeat the process from step 6. Is the result different? Overall, how close are the estimates? Would the average of the two estimates be closer to the actual value?

9. On the Large rectangle, draw an odd-shaped "lake" with an area of about 150 squares. Count the number of marked squares the lake encloses and use the ratio in step 7 to estimate its size. Would this method work for odd-shaped lakes? Why might the method be better suited to odd-shaped lakes than for rectangular reservoirs?

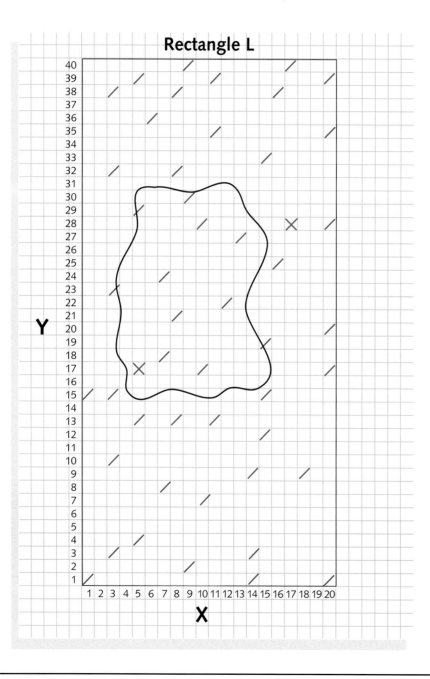

Rectangle L

10. Cut out a variety of rectangular shapes, repeat step 6, and compare the results. Is a 5 x 5-square area estimate as accurate as the 10 x 10-square or a 20 x 20-square? How does changing the sample size affect the accuracy of the area estimates?

Notebook Assignment

1. A baseball team is divided into small groups. Explain how a spinner could be used to select randomly which group would have batting practice first.

2. Explain why a pair of dice cannot be used to randomly select numbers from 1 to 12.

3. Use a computer and Microsoft Excel to create a list of random numbers. Insert the following formula into a cell on an Excel spreadsheet and use the fill command to create a list of random numbers with a range of 1 to 10.

   = ROUND(RAND()*10,0)

4. Describe how the government could use a spreadsheet such as the one in question 3 to select participants in a census.

5. A telemarketing company wants to phone 100 people in Vancouver to determine whether they go to the movies. How could they determine whom to telephone?

Extension

6. One group of students created a list of numbers by writing down the first numbers that came to mind. They did not intentionally pick any one number over any other. Would this list be random? Why or why not?

Exploration 4

Representative Samples

A representative sample is a sample that has the same characteristics as the total population you are studying. Depending upon your particular survey, you should include similar numbers of males and females, a variety of ages, people from various geographic regions, a variety of educational backgrounds, and so on.

A representative sample is unbiased. If a sample is biased, some factor is causing one category of individual to have a greater chance of being selected than another. For example, picking your friends to represent the population of grade 10 students in your school is biased. One of the best ways to increase the probability of finding a representative sample is to select the participants randomly.

Class Discussion

Discuss ways to find out whether your class would be a representative sample of your school's population. Is your school a representative sample of Canada's grade 10 population? Discuss why or why not.

Small Group Discussion

Discuss how dice, a random number table, or a telephone book and a list of students could be used to find a representative sample of students for a survey.

Goals

In this exploration, you will learn about representative samples.

Example 1

How could you select grade 10 students randomly to participate in a survey? How could you find out whether the group you selected was representative of grade 10 students?

Solution

You could use a student list and a random number generator to select the students from the list. To find out if the group is representative, you could test your results by collecting and comparing them against another randomly selected group of grade 10 students.

Example 2

Lucy is a camp counsellor. She is assigning 80 female campers to 8 cabins at summer camp. She wants the campers assigned as randomly as possible. Select a method for assigning the campers to the cabins.

Solution

Lucy could create a spinner by dividing a stiff 10-centimetre paper circle into 8 equal, numbered sections. Each section would represent a specific cabin. She places a pencil through a paper clip and into the middle of the chart. Lucy gets a list of the campers and spins the paper clip to determine which cabin number the camper goes into. If a cabin is filled, she will need to spin again to select a cabin with space available.

MEMORANDUM

From: Editor-in-Chief
To: Research Team

It is time to select a sample of grade 10 students for our research. Use a random sampling method to pick a representative sample from the grade 10 students in your school. These students will provide data to help us plan our e-zine.

Project Activity

In this activity, you will create a list of grade 10 students from your school who will become your research sample. Your sample students should be selected randomly and should be representative of the total population. Some or all of your classmates may form your sample. Do you think their opinions are similar to those held by the population of grade 10 students in your school?

Notebook Assignment

1. Edward wants to survey a grade 9 class of 90 students to find out if they would buy a yearbook at the end of the year. He can only ask 20 of them. Describe a way he could select the students randomly for his sample to ensure that it is representative. Justify your answer.

2. Jean wants to predict the five most popular menu items for a new school lunch program. Explain how she could obtain the participants for a survey. Justify your answer.

3. Susie wants to make a list of the "top ten" favourite songs of the students in her school to play at a school dance. Describe how she could select the participants for a survey.

4. Michelle's group is doing a survey on whether the school should have mandatory school uniforms. She asks a variety of students in all grades, but they are all her friends. Is this a fair survey? If not, how could it be made fair?

5. Richard's group is doing a survey to find out which model of car most sixteen-year-olds would like to own. He asks all the members of his hockey team. Is this a fair survey? If not, what changes would make it fair?

Extension

6. Describe how you would select a representative sample for the grade 10 population of Canada. Explain your method and your reasoning. How does your method prevent bias?

Exploration 5

• • • • • • • • • • • • • • • • •

Collecting Data: Surveys and Experiments

Once a representative sample has been selected, researchers collect data from the sample. There are several ways to collect data. One of the most important is the survey. Surveys may be conducted through questionnaires or interviews.

A questionnaire is a list of questions. The questions may have simple yes or no answers. Often, people being questioned are presented with a list of alternative answers and they are able to choose the answer they most prefer.

Some surveys are presented as a series of statements. The person interviewed responds to the statements by rating them on a value scale such as: strongly agree, agree, disagree, or strongly disagree. Other surveys ask interviewees to rate statements on a numerical scale, perhaps 1 to 10.

Interviews can be used where extended questioning is required, such as on complex issues. It is a challenge for an interviewer to convert the information he or she gets from interviews into statistical data because each interview is different. Often, an interviewer will ask only pre-selected questions, and is unable to deal with casual comments.

Goals

In this exploration, you will learn about surveys and experiments used to collect data, and how that data must be fair, accurate, and respectful of the rights of the members of sample populations.

Experiments are designed to give reproducible results. In other words, another researcher should be able to repeat the experiment and get the same data. Experiments are often used to gather scientific data. Many studies that investigate the occurrence of diseases or the impact of nutrition choices are designed as experiments.

Researchers must design their research so that it is accurate. If a survey is used, questions must be clearly stated and cover the topic fairly. Surveyors must consider the rights of the individuals in the sample and design their research to respect those rights.

Example 1

A researcher was trying to evaluate student performance in mathematics at St. Matthew School. How could he collect the data and, at the same time, respect the students' right to privacy?

Solution

The researcher could ask the school to supply the marks list with the student identities removed.

Example 2

A researcher was interviewing people visiting a tourist information booth to see if they received the information they wanted. Describe how the researcher could select the interviewees randomly. How could the researcher ensure that data was collected accurately?

Solution

The interviewer could interview every third person to ensure a random selection, ask the same pre-determined questions to each tourist, and record the answers using a tape recorder.

Example 3

A questionnaire on responses to impolite behaviour is being prepared. Suggest a clearly stated and fair question to include.

Solution

Question: Suppose you were standing in line at the bank and someone stepped into line in front of you. Would you:

a. ignore them?
b. mutter something just loud enough for them to hear?
c. tap them on the shoulder and ask them to move to the back of the line?
d. demand that they move to the back of the line?

Project Activity

Prepare a survey that will provide the information requested in questions 1 to 5 below from each member of your sample group. Can the results be recorded as numbers? How would you have to ask the questions in order to get a number for the results? Give an example of a question for which it is difficult to get a number for a response. Why is it difficult?

1. What age in months are most students in grade 10?

2. How many students are male? How many are female?

3. What are the five favourite leisure-time activities of grade 10 students?

MEMORANDUM

From: Editor-in-Chief
To: Research Team

The advertising department wants to gather some details about the students who will read our new e-zine. They specifically want answers to the following questions.

1. What age are most students in grade 10?
2. How many students are male? How many are female?
3. What are the five favourite leisure-time activities of grade 10 students?
4. What are their five favourite story or article topics?
5. What are their top three favourite foods? Top three drinks?

4. What are students' five favourite story or article topics?

5. What are the top three favourite foods of grade 10 students? Top three drinks?

After the survey is developed, conduct the survey using your sample population.

Notebook Assignment

1. Select and describe an appropriate way to collect sample data on soft drink preferences.

2. Describe a way to use telephone numbers to select survey participants randomly. Explain why such a selection is random.

3. A social researcher wants to find the most common countries of birth for a city of 50,000 households. Select a method for conducting this survey and describe it. State how you would respect the rights of individuals while gathering and reporting the data.

4. A new clothing store wants to find the percent of students that wears black tops to school. Describe a study that could find the answer to this question.

5. A scientist wants to discover whether vitamin C helps prevent colds. Describe how the scientist could select a sample of university students for her study. Discuss possible problems with the sample and how she could better collect results.

6. Science Fair participants were studying the effect of changing the shape of the nose cones on model rockets. Describe how to conduct an experiment using several nose cone samples and to draw conclusions that would be fair. Assume that experimenters are able to use a large number of rockets and motors.

Extension

7. Create a fair and appropriate survey to find the number of students your age who expect to look for full- or part-time jobs within the next year. Conduct the study and report the results to your class.

Problem Analysis

Pizza Party

In your town, there are three pizza restaurants. You are having a party for 25 friends where pizza will be served. Costs for the pizzas are as follows:

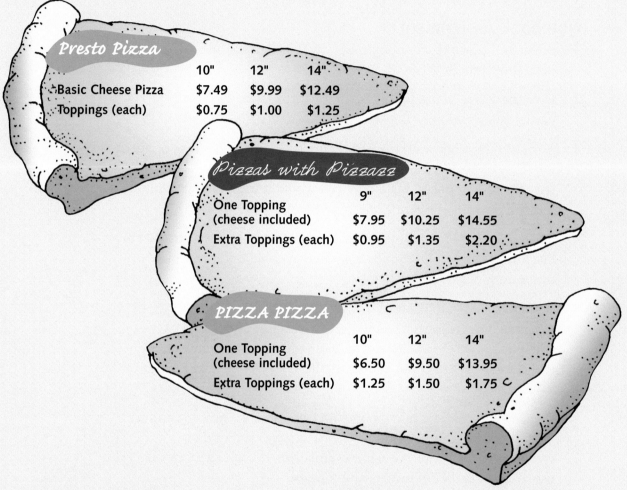

Presto Pizza

	10"	12"	14"
Basic Cheese Pizza	$7.49	$9.99	$12.49
Toppings (each)	$0.75	$1.00	$1.25

Pizzas with Pizzazz

	9"	12"	14"
One Topping (cheese included)	$7.95	$10.25	$14.55
Extra Toppings (each)	$0.95	$1.35	$2.20

PIZZA PIZZA

	10"	12"	14"
One Topping (cheese included)	$6.50	$9.50	$13.95
Extra Toppings (each)	$1.25	$1.50	$1.75

You decide to buy pizzas with three toppings for your guests.

Which size pizza and from which company would give you the best buy? Explain your decision.

How many pizzas would you buy? What factors might affect your decision? In order to improve your decision-making, what other information would be useful to know?

Games

The Game of Nim

Materials Needed

- bingo chips

Rules of the Game

This is a game for two people.

Arrange the bingo chips in rows. One sample arrangement is shown.

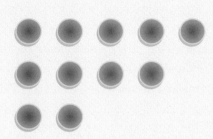

Players take turns removing chips. A player can remove one chip, or as many chips as he or she wishes from a row.

The objective of the game is to make your opponent remove the last bingo chip.

Sample Game

Player A
removes three chips from row 1
leaving:

removes one chip from row 1
leaving:

Player B
removes all chips from row 2
leaving

removes two chips from row 2
leaving

Player B wins because Player A is forced to remove the last chip.
Can you find a winning strategy? In this game, is it better to go first or second? Explain your strategy.

Exploration 6

Survey Results

Surveys are conducted to gather information about people. Some surveys poll people about political or community issues. Other surveys test public response to commercial products or businesses. Surveys are often held to test the effectiveness of recent advertising campaigns.

To understand what survey results are saying, you need information about the survey itself. Who was surveyed? How were participants selected? How many people were surveyed? Which questions were asked? Answers to these questions will help you determine whether the results reported from a survey are accurate.

If a survey is fair, accurate, and valid, it may be a useful decision-making tool.

Classroom Discussion

List factors that make a survey fair. Think about who participates, how they are selected, and how the survey items are worded.

Goals

In this exploration, you will develop a survey that is fair and that gathers accurate data. You will learn how to determine whether a survey is fair, accurate, and valid.

Example 1

What are five statements Gerald could present to see if someone is knowledgeable about and enjoys hockey?

Solution

Gerald could select the following statements to use in his survey.

1. I follow hockey statistics in the newspaper or on TV.
2. I know the rules of hockey.
3. Hockey is my favourite sport to watch.
4. I have been to an NHL game.
5. I play hockey.

Example 2

How could Gerald give a numerical rating to the responses to the statements above?

Solution

Gerald could use a 4-point scale to rate the responses he receives. Beside each question he could include a scale. The individuals being surveyed would receive 1 point if they strongly disagree, 2 points if they disagree, 3 points if they agree, and 4 points if they strongly agree. Gerald could add the points and record the result as a total score. If an individual received a score of 17 or more, Gerald might say that person loves the game.

Example 3

Your school newspaper reports on a survey showing that the school store should only sell health food. Create a list of questions that will help you judge whether the survey was fair and accurate. Explain why you would ask the questions or give an example of how the survey could have been unfair.

Solution

I would need to ask:

1. Who was surveyed? This reveals the population; perhaps only vegetarians were asked their opinion.
2. How were the people selected? Maybe the surveyor only asked his/her friends.
3. What questions were asked? Perhaps people were asked a question such as, "If there was nothing else in the school store, would it be good to have healthy food?"
4. Was data collected from all the people who were surveyed? Perhaps only those who said they felt strongly about the issue returned the survey; perhaps only a few people returned their surveys.
5. Were the calculations done accurately and reported fairly? Maybe only 50.1% of those surveyed felt that the store should only sell health food. This means that just about the same number did not agree.

Notebook Assignment

1. Form a small group. Select a topic category such as sports, fashion, or environmental issues. Base your selection on the ability of your class to collect data or opinions about a topic within the category.

   a) Create a list of three survey questions that could be used to test the opinions of grade 10 students on the topic. Describe how you would obtain numerical data from the survey.

b) Test the questions in the survey by having each member of your group complete the survey. Modify the questions if necessary.

c) Randomly select five members of your class and ask them to complete the survey. Indicate how you randomly selected them. Each member of your group should record the results. Find the average point score for the 5 students surveyed.

d) Randomly select another five students to complete the same survey. Find their average point score.

e) Compare the results of the surveys. Were the scores close to each other or were they very different? Explain.

2. Suppose a magazine was doing an article on student use of computers. List several survey questions that could fall under that category.

3. Analyze the following survey results and state what you would need to know before you declared them fair and accurate. Explain your reasoning.

a) Three out of four dentists recommend sugarless gum.
b) Most people want school dances cancelled.
c) Adults watch an average of 21 hours of TV a week.
d) The minimum driving age should be raised to 18.

Extension

4. What are the advantages and disadvantages of using the internet to gather responses to a survey?

5. A survey was conducted on the use of bicycle helmets. Over 1000 people were surveyed by telephone. A computer program that randomly called numbers selected those to be surveyed. The program selected numbers in such a way that all geographic areas were represented fairly. The calls were placed between the hours of 3:00 pm and 8:00 pm and whoever answered the phone was asked the question "Are you in favour of making the wearing of bicycle helmets mandatory?" Only "yes" or "no" votes were recorded.

The survey results indicated that over 60% of the people surveyed were in favour of a bicycle helmet law.

Extension continued

Your assignment is to write a letter that either supports the conclusion of the survey or disagrees with it. You must not use only your opinion, but must use the survey facts to support your ideas. Remember to ask all the necessary questions.

Exploration 7

Presenting Data

Data are often presented visually in the form of graphs. Each type of graph can best present certain kinds of information. You need to choose the type of graph carefully so that it presents your data persuasively but is not misleading. There are 4 basic types of graphs: bar, circle, broken line, and histogram. Each type is shown in example 1.

Data can be understood better by averaging. Averages are often called "measures of central tendency." There are three measures of central tendency. The first is the mean. The mean is calculated by adding the numbers in a list and dividing by the number of entries. The second measure is the mode. The mode is the number that occurs most often in a list. The third measure is the median. The median is found by listing the numbers in order of size and identifying the middle number. If the list has an even number of entries, the mean of the two middle numbers is considered the median.

Example 1

Select the best type of graph to display the information described below. Explain why you chose each type of graph.

   a) the favourite sport of grade 10 students in your class
   b) the percent of students in grades 10, 11, or 12 at Central High
   c) the height of students in your grade 10 mathematics class
   d) the temperature at a ski hill during skiing season

Goals

In this exploration, you will examine ways to show data in graphs. You will use mean, median, and mode to help with your presentation of data.

New Terms

mean: measure of central tendency sometimes referred to as the average or arithmetic mean. It is found by adding the numbers in the list and dividing by the number of entries.

median: middle number when a series of numbers is arranged in either ascending or descending order.

mode: most frequently occurring number in a list of numbers.

Solution

a) I picked a bar graph to show the favourite sports in our class because each sport is discrete and bar graphs show it clearly.

b) I picked a circle graph to show the percentage of students by grade at Central High because a circle graph is a good way to show percent comparisons.

c) A histogram makes sense to show the heights of students because everyone's height falls within a specific range.

d) A broken line graph shows temperature changes well because temperature changes are continuous.

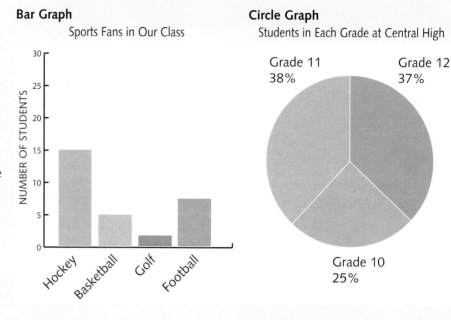

Bar Graph

Sports Fans in Our Class

Circle Graph

Students in Each Grade at Central High

Grade 11 38% Grade 12 37% Grade 10 25%

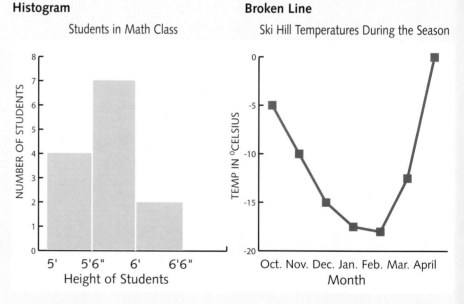

Histogram

Students in Math Class

Broken Line

Ski Hill Temperatures During the Season

Technology

Spreadsheet software provides an easy way to create graphs. Enter your data and select a graph type and then the software generates a graph.

Example 2

Travis's class created models of inline skate helmets they had designed. They measured the circumference of the heads of class members to learn what sizes would be needed by students their age. The measurements in centimetres were as follows:

53, 55, 57, 53, 54, 54, 58, 53, 56, 55, 55, 55, 58, 55, 57

Use this data to find the mean and median size as well as the class mode.

Solution

$$\text{Mean} = \frac{53 + 55 + 57 + 53 + 54 + 54 + 58 + 53 + 56 + 55 + 55 + 55 + 58 + 55 + 57}{15}$$

$$= \frac{828}{15}$$

$$= 55.2$$

The median is 55 which is the eighth number when the numbers are arranged in ascending order. The mode is 55 since there are more "55's" than any other number.

Mental Math

1. What is the mode of 10, 20, 20, and 30?

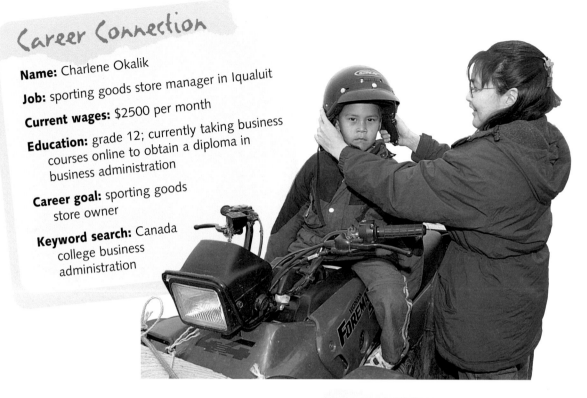

Career Connection

Name: Charlene Okalik

Job: sporting goods store manager in Iqualuit

Current wages: $2500 per month

Education: grade 12; currently taking business courses online to obtain a diploma in business administration

Career goal: sporting goods store owner

Keyword search: Canada college business administration

Project Activity

Use your survey data to compile a table of contents for an issue of your e-zine. List at least 5 article/story ideas that will interest readers according to your survey data. Present the supporting documentation in graph form. Examine the data you collected in Exploration 5. How many students in grade 10 are old enough to have their driver's licences? This information could be used in an article on teenage drivers. Use your data to find the mean age, the modal age, and the median age of grade 10 students. Give answers in months. Display your data using appropriate graphs.

MEMORANDUM

From: Editor-in-Chief
To: Research Team

On Friday, the publisher would like you to present your recommendations for the table of contents. Use your survey data to develop a list of 5 article/story ideas. Present your table of contents with support for your choices displayed in graph form.

Notebook Assignment

Use the data shown in the following tables to answer questions 1 to 5.

Forest Fires 1997

	Total[1] Number	Intensive Protection Zone[2] Causes		
		Human Activities	Lightning	Unknown Causes
Canada[3]	6002	3101	2326	189
Newfoundland	110	75	14	—
Prince Edward Island	x	x	x	x
Nova Scotia	371	308	24	39
New Brunswick	368	290	33	45
Quebec	876	502	317	—
Ontario	1636	856	548	36
Manitoba	373	185	147	—
Saskatchewan	491	219	201	—
Alberta	456	204	242	10
British Columbia	1161	432	675	54
Yukon	x	x	x	x
Northwest Territories	105	13	90	2
National Parks	55	17	35	3

x Data unavailable, inapplicable, or confidential
— No incidences

[1] The total combines intensive protection zone and limited protection zone (zones of special intervention where people, property, or forest reserves are threatened by fire).

[2] An intensive protection zone is where there is a system that provides forest fire prevention and systematic control.

[3] Prince Edward Island and Yukon are not included in the Canada total.

Source: Natural Resources Canada, Compendium of Canadian Forestry Statistics, 1998.

Forest Land Burned 1997

| | | Intensive Protection Zone[2] | | |
| | | Causes | | |
	Total[1] Hectares	Human Activities	Lightning	Unknown Causes
Canada[3]	620 471	14 567	244 153	648
Newfoundland	8981	480	227	—
Prince Edward Island	x	x	x	x
Nova Scotia	564	502	24	38
New Brunswick	172	137	17	18
Quebec	393 078	527	93 226	—
Ontario	38 524	2177	15 183	34
Manitoba	41 796	3605	7437	—
Saskatchewan	3885	1570	695	—
Alberta	4725	4384	322	19
British Columbia	1876	1050	287	539
Yukon	x	x	x	x
Northwest Territories	126 531	10	126 521	x
National Parks	339	125	214	x

x Data unavailable, inapplicable, or confidential
— No incidences

[1] The total combines intensive protection zone and limited protection zone (zones of special intervention where people, property, or forest reserves are threatened by fire).

[2] An intensive protection zone is where there is a system that provides forest fire prevention and systematic control.

[3] Prince Edward Island and Yukon are not included in the Canada total.

Source: Natural Resources Canada, Compendium of Canadian Forestry Statistics, 1998.

1. What was the greatest cause of forest fires in Canada in 1997?

2. Draw a pie graph showing the causes of forest fires. Use the data in the chart Forest Fires 1997.

3. What are possible reasons that the causes of forest fires and the amount burned by the fires seem so unrelated?

4. In 1997, Nova Scotia had 308 fires caused by human activities and 24 started by lightning. In the same year Quebec had 502 human fire starts and 317 started by lightning. Suggest why Nova Scotia might have had so few fires started by lightning compared to Quebec.

Hints

A tally sheet is a convenient way to record data as it is collected. To make a tally sheet, list the items you are counting. For each item counted, mark a vertical slash. Every fifth item is marked with a horizontal slash through the preceding four. This makes it easy to count by fives.

For example: ✚✚✚

5. A newspaper article states that Prince Edward Island residents and visitors are the worst in Canada at protecting their forests because they have 14 times as many fires started by human activity as started by lightning. Write a letter to the editor that argues against the newspaper article. Include several possible explanations for the data.

6. Travis's class created models of inline skate helmets they had designed. They measured the circumference of the heads of class members to learn what sizes would be needed by students their age. The measurements in centimetres were as follows:

    54, 53, 55, 57, 53, 54, 58, 53, 56, 55, 55, 55, 58, 55, 57

    Use this data to create a bar graph and a circle graph.

Hints

To create a circle graph, convert percent values to degrees by multiplying by 360.

7. Mean annual precipitation in the various regions of Canada is shown below:

Coastal regions	120 cm
Ontario and Quebec	78 cm
Prairie region	48 cm
Northlands	27 cm

Display the data shown above using a suitable graph. Briefly describe why you chose that type of graph.

8. The following data were collected with a telephone survey of 1000 people. Each was asked to name his or her favourite spectator sport.

Favourite Sport	Number	Percent	Degrees
Hockey	450	45.0	162
Football	240		
Baseball	120		
Soccer	58		
Volleyball	24		
Other	108		
Total	1000		

Complete the table and construct a circle graph to display the data.

Extension

9. A magazine wants to print an article which proposes that use of computers be made mandatory in schools. What data might be used to support such a proposal? Find data to support or reject this proposal. Draw a graph that could be used to display your findings.

Exploration 8

Probability Statements

The likelihood of events happening is called probability. The probability of something happening can be expressed in a mathematical statement. You may remember that the probability of getting heads when you flip a coin is 1 in 2. This can be expressed as the following probability statement:

$$P(\text{heads}) = \frac{1}{2} \text{ or } P(H) = \frac{1}{2}$$

Example 1

A multi-coloured wheel is spun. Out of 15 spins, the colour red is selected 5 times. What is the probability statement that describes this? What is the probability of a colour other than red being selected? Which would you select as being most likely, red or another colour?

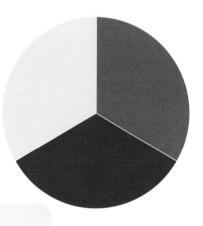

Solution

$$P(\text{red}) = \frac{5}{15} \qquad P(\text{not red}) = \frac{10}{15}$$

$$\text{or} \quad P(R) = \frac{5}{15} \quad \text{or} \quad P(\text{not R}) = \frac{10}{15}$$

The probability of a colour other than red being selected is 10/15. A colour other than red is most likely to be selected.

Goals

In this exploration, you will learn how probability statements can help make your decisions.

Mental Math

What is the probability of rolling a six-sided die and getting a four?

MEMORANDUM

From: Editor-in-Chief
To: Research Team

We are looking for a title for our new e-zine. Please create a short list of possibilities. Use the information you gathered previously to suggest ideas that will appeal to the target audience. Test your title ideas by creating a survey that has a sample of students in grade 10 rate your short list of titles from best to worst.

Project Activity

In a small group, brainstorm ideas for the title of the e-zine. The title must appeal to both males and females. Use the data you have gathered to narrow the list to the 3 best choices. For example, if nine out of ten students prefer to read about sports, sports could be reflected in the title. If entertainment is a top priority, that too may be reflected in the title.

Survey a sample of students from your grade 10 class to test your ideas. Also, survey five people outside your class to assess whether they like the proposed title. Record your results. As a class, select a title for the e-zine from the most popular suggestions made by the small groups.

Notebook Assignment

1. Complete this assignment with a partner. Obtain two coins. First, discuss the probability of getting either both heads or both tails when you flip two coins. Which is most likely, pairs of heads/tails or one of each?

   One partner could record the number of times the coins were either both heads or both tails. The other partner could record the number of times the coins were one heads and one tails.

   a) Flip the two coins twenty times.
   b) Write your results as a probability statement.
   c) Are your results the same as those obtained by the other students? If they are different, describe why you think they are different.

d) What would the probability statement be if the class results were grouped together?

2. In this activity, you will first count out 100 popcorn kernels or dried beans. One partner will use a coloured marker to secretly mark a number of kernels. (Remember this number and don't reveal it to your partner!) This number should be a multiple of 10 no higher than 50 (that is, exactly 10, 20, 30, 40, or 50 kernels). Once marked, place all the kernels in a paper bag and shake the bag to mix the kernels.

   The other partner will reach into the bag and remove kernels one at a time, keeping track of the number of marked and unmarked kernels. Both partners should record the results in their notebooks. After selecting 10 kernels, the partner reaching into the bag should estimate the original number of marked kernels. If he or she is correct, the activity ends. If incorrect, continue removing 10 kernels at a time until the number of marked and unmarked kernels is predicted accurately.

3. In the activity above, what is the probability statement that gives the likelihood of selecting a marked kernel? If 20 kernels are selected, how many would you expect to be marked?

Extension

4. Return the kernels to the bag. If one partner removes 1 kernel, what are the chances of it being marked? Explain your answer. If you keep this kernel out of the bag and remove another one, would the kernel you kept out have any impact on the probability statement? Why?

5. A magazine is running a contest in which entrants mail in an entry form taken from the magazine. The winning entry will be drawn from a barrel. The rules state that photocopies of entry forms will not be accepted, but hand-drawn copies will be. Explain why the magazine might have this rule. How would the probability statement that expresses the likelihood of winning change if someone sent in a large number of photocopied entries?

Chapter Review

1. It is common practice to band birds such as Canada geese. These birds migrate but return to their nesting grounds in the spring. Describe how banding birds from a certain nesting area could provide information about the changing bird population over a period of years. Discuss how wildlife officials could collect and use the information gained from the banding program.

2. Select a sampling method that determines how many passengers using the SkyTrain in Vancouver do not purchase tickets. Tickets are not always checked on the train.

3. Describe how a large department store could randomly select 10 shoppers for a prize draw. Identify the best selection method.

4. A survey of listeners to a radio station in one of the prairie provinces found a high number of students enjoyed country music. Would this sample be representative of Canada's student population? Why or why not?

5. A scientist examined the stomach contents of coyotes trapped near the city of Vancouver in order to study their diet. Discuss whether the coyotes trapped are likely to be representative of the coyote population of B.C. What type of interesting information could the scientist discover using this sample? Explain your reasoning.

6. A school committee wants to find out whether students attending a school are being bullied. The committee received permission to survey a sample of 30 students. Describe the steps the committee could take to survey the sample students and give an example of one possible survey question.

7. Suppose a school orders school sweatshirts. The sizes needed are: 56 size small, 80 size medium, 85 size large, and 72 extra large. Graph this data.

8. Give a probability statement for the chances of rolling a seven using two six-sided dice.

9. Find the mean, median, and mode for the following sets of test scores:

   a) 42, 62, 68, 73, 75, 75, 86, 89, 92
   b) 10, 20, 20, 30, 50, 70

10. Explain why each of the following people might select the mean, median, or mode in a set of data.

    a) a store owner deciding what sizes of shoes to order
    b) someone moving to a new city and looking at house prices
    c) a teacher reporting scores on a test

11. The number of passengers in different buses was recorded. The mean was 46 and the median was 47. If 20 extra passengers rode on each bus, what would the new mean and median be? If all passengers paid $1.25 to ride the bus, what would be the mean and median amount of money collected?

12. The graph below shows the results of a survey of 60 students. What do you think the survey is about? Approximately how many students are in each category?

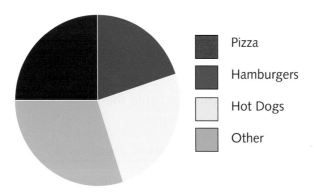

■ Pizza

■ Hamburgers

□ Hot Dogs

■ Other

Project Presentation

Part A: Presenting a Mock-up

For your project presentation, you will create a sample front cover and table of contents for one issue of the teen e-zine you have been developing. Such samples are known in publishing as "mock-ups." A mock-up is a visual and text proposal.

Your samples will be examined by the editorial committee of the publishing company to see whether to proceed with a real publication. The committee will expect you to explain your choices, and to indicate how you used the research data you obtained to create your presentation.

Your presentation will use the data you have collected. If necessary, use information and ideas from other sources. Your presentation will include:

- a description of the readership and their interests based on your survey data; include supporting text and graphics
- a mock-up of a cover; include the magazine title, a picture, and the titles of the top three articles
- a table of contents page with the titles of 5 articles and any other special features of the e-zine

Part B: Editorial Committee Evaluation

As a member of the editorial committee, you will participate in the
evaluation of the presentations. Working in a small group, your task is to
develop a list of 8 criteria that you will use to evaluate the presentations.
These criteria will be expressed in the form of statements.

To express your evaluation numerically, use the following scale:

4.   strongly agree

3.   agree

2.   disagree

1.   strongly disagree

The final task is to graph your results to determine which proposal the
publisher should select.

Case Study

Part A: Designing a Recreational Facilities Survey

The local government wants to study recreation areas in your community. They want to conduct a survey to find out who uses these areas, what activities they use them for, and what facilities are important to local people. In this case study, you will design a survey to answer the government's questions.

1. Name the type of population sampling that you think would be the best way to collect this data. Explain your choice.

2. Describe how bias could be avoided while survey participants are selected.

3. Give examples of three questions that the participants could be asked. Develop a way to record the answers numerically.

4. Describe how the data collected could be presented.

Part B: Analyzing Data from a Recreational Survey

The following data was collected by a company studying the recreational use of ski hills. The company surveyed the first 100 people who went up a chair lift. Here are the data they obtained.

QUESTION 1:
How many days do you ski during the ski season?

Number of Days	Number Selecting this Option
Under 10 days	20
10 to 25 days	35
26 to 50 days	20
over 50 days	25

QUESTION 2:

On this ski trip, do you plan to stay overnight in the ski village? If yes, how many nights will you stay?

Number of day skiers	50
Number who planned to stay overnight	30
Number who planned to stay 2–3 nights	15
Number who planned to stay more than 3 nights	5

QUESTION 3:

Select the most important feature of a ski hill from the following list.

a) quality of ski runs	35
b) restaurant facilities	15
c) day care or activities for young children	15
d) overnight accommodation	10
e) rental equipment	5
f) cost of passes	20

1. Graph the responses to each of the questions.

2. Describe how the survey could have been improved.

Answer Key

Chapter 1

• • • • • • • • • • • • • • •

WAGES, SALARIES, AND EXPENSES

Exploration 1
Investigating Career Options

Notebook Assignment

1. Five benefits that would be important for a job in northern Canada might include: isolation pay, an extra clothing allowance for winter wear, reduced rent, transportation to and from home, and extended vacation time to allow for travel to and from work to major centres.

2. Self-employed refers to someone who works for their own business and does not work for someone else as a regular employee. A regular employee usually does not control what work they do and when it is done. A self-employed person usually determines what work they do and how they go about doing it.

3. Naomi might want to find out if there are jobs for the careers in carpentry or electrical work. She might want to know what education is needed, and what the working conditions are like for each trade.

Exploration 2
Beginning a Budget: Income and Expenses

Notebook Assignment

1. Your estimates should reflect the current cost in your own community. An example might be:

Rent	$400 per month
Telephone	$50
Utilities	$50
Food	$100
Clothing	$50
Recreation	$70
Personal Care	$45
Magazines, Books, CDs	$50
Savings	$90
Other Expenses	$100

(Your budget may vary.)

2. Annual take-home pay: $18,300
   Monthly take-home pay: $1525

A possible budget:

Rent	$400 per month
Telephone	$50
Utilities	$50
Food	$100
Clothing	$50
Recreation	$70
Personal Care	$45
Magazines, Books, CDs	$50
Savings	$153
Car expenses	$427
Other Expenses	$130

(Other budgets are possible.)

3. Five expenses of owning a vehicle include: gas, maintenance, loan payments, tires, and repairs. These can be kept to a minimum by saving money before buying a vehicle to save on or remove loan payments, using a vehicle that has low gas consumption, and using the vehicle as little as possible. (Other answers are possible.)

Extension

4. Weekly salary: $240.00
   Monthly salary: $960.00
   Money available for saving each month:
   $260.00
   Number of months required: 7 months

Exploration 3

Gross Pay

Notebook Assignment

1. a) **regular time:** time that is not overtime or
      not over the regular length of a shift
   b) **overtime:** time that is beyond the regular
      shift amount
   c) **wage:** the amount earned for a specific
      time, such as an hour
   d) **time and a half:** a wage often given for
      overtime; to find the overtime wage,
      multiply the regular wage by 1.5
   e) **gross pay:** the amount of earnings before
      deductions such as income tax are
      subtracted
   f) **double time:** a wage that is sometimes
      paid for work done in unusual
      circumstances, such as working on a
      statutory holiday; the wage is found by
      multiplying the regular wage rate by 2.0

2. a) $560.00
   b) $524.40
   c) $309.38
   d) $375.25
   e) $594.00

3. a) $334.69
   b) $400.35
   c) $359.74
   d) $334.09
   e) $434.77

4. a) $545.56
   b) $522.75
   c) $621.77
   d) $542.43
   e) $648.21
   f) $925.59

5. $685.13.

6.
Regular Time	Time and a Half	Double Time
$6.90	$10.35	$13.80
$7.50	$11.25	$15.00
$6.50	$9.75	$13.00
$9.40	$14.10	$18.80
$6.00	$9.00	$12.00

7. a) $81.60
   b) $134.14
   c) $124.43
   d) $168.54
   e) $288.23

8. $121.63

9. $189.50

10. $387.60

11. a) $760.75
    b) $731.00
    c) Daily time and a half pays more.

12. $1450.77

13. $1271.88

Extension

14. If Arnold wants to earn the most money, he
    should work the Saturday shifts. If he wants to
    spend more time off work, he should work
    the Sunday shifts.

15. It is difficult to tell which is better because we
    cannot tell who needs the benefits more, or
    how much the benefits would cost to buy
    privately. For example, a person with a family
    might find the benefits to be very valuable,
    and a single person with no children might
    find it cheaper to pay the cost of the benefits
    themselves.

Exploration 4
Keeping Track of Time

Notebook Assignment

1. 5.75 h

2. 36 h 35 m

3. 23 h 25 m

4. 29 h 7 m

5. 7 h 10 m

6. 13.05 h

7. 16 h 9 m

8. 26 h 59 m

9. 16 h 22 m

10. 11:00 to 15:00

11. 06:30

12. Ways to keep track of time include using a paper or electronic journal and a watch. If a company overcharges for the time spent on a job, they can be charged with fraud or at the least the customer might find a better company to do their work. (Other answers are possible.)

Extension

13. An advantage of the job where you work straight through is that once you are finished work for the day, you are finished. An advantage for the split shift job is that you have time in the middle of the afternoon to do things that you might not be able to do in the evening. (Other answers are possible.)

Exploration 5
Time Cards

Notebook Assignment

1.
Ameralik	4 h	or	4.00 h
Bancroft	3 h 45 m	or	3.75 h
Boulanger	3 h 45 m	or	3.75 h
Combhoaua	3 h 45 m	or	3.75 h
Gauthier	3 h 30 m	or	3.50 h
Krivan	4 h	or	4.00 h
McIvor	3 h 45 m	or	3.75 h
Orsi	3 h 30 m	or	3.50 h
Peart	2 h 45 m	or	2.75 h
Romanko	3 h 45 m	or	3.75 h

2.
Heft	4 h	or	4.00 h
McKee	3 h 45 m	or	3.75 h
Sandahl	3 h 45 m	or	3.75 h
Singh	3 h 15 m	or	3.25 h
Teese	2 h 45 m	or	2.75 h
Worsley	2 h	or	2.00 h

3. a) Monday: 7:32 am
Thursday: 7:35 am
b) Monday and Thursday
c) Tuesday: 12:02 pm
Friday: 11:58 am
d) 30 minutes

4. a) Wednesday
b) Tuesday
c) Wednesday and Friday
d) one hour
e) Wednesday and Friday
f) Tuesday
g) 8 hours

5. 75.75 h

6. Employee 1 $610.00
Employee 2 $842.51
Employee 3 $352.54
Employee 4 $447.23

7. Assumption: paid for every minute worked
   23.75 h $289.75
   Assumption: round weekly hours to the
   nearest 15 minutes
   23.75 h $289.75
   Assumption: quarter-hour penalty
   22.75 h $275.55
   Assumption: half-hour penalty
   22.50 h $274.50
   (Other assumptions may produce different
   answers.)

8. Ellen worked 27 h and 37 m. She will be paid
   for 27.5 hours. Her gross pay will be $404.25.

9. $154.05

10. $190.13

11. $122.40

12. $216.20

13. Answers will vary by community. For
    example, the sawmill and the muffler shop use
    time cards.

Extension

14. An employee might have to sign a time card to
    indicate that the times are correct and that
    they recorded them.

15. An employer might use a time card machine
    to track employees who arrive late and/or
    leave early.

16. Military services use a 24-hour clock to avoid
    the confusion of there being two 7 o'clocks.

Exploration 6
Payroll Deductions

Notebook Assignment

All answers in this exploration are based on B.C.'s
deduction tables as of July 1, 2001. Amounts were
taken from the Tables on Diskette feature of the
Revenue Canada web site.

1.

	CPP	EI	Federal Tax	Provincial Tax	Net Pay
a)	$10.01	$6.75	$45.15	$17.50	$220.59
b)	$11.15	$7.35	$18.95	$6.35	$282.70
c)	$14.74	$9.23	$39.10	$14.45	$332.48
d)	$10.43	$6.97	$6.45	$1.15	$284.76
e)	$18.86	$11.38	$30.40	$10.45	$434.80
f)	$10.92	$7.23	$13.30	$4.00	$285.87
g)	$15.84	$9.80	$40.15	$14.75	$355.21
h)	$13.14	$8.39	$33.15	$12.15	$306.13

2. Gross Pay $395.00
   CPP $14.09
   EI $8.89
   Federal Tax $34.20
   Provincial Tax $12.45
   Net Pay $325.37

3. Gross Pay $540.50
   CPP $20.35
   EI $12.16
   Federal Tax $57.95
   Provincial Tax $22.00
   Net Pay $428.04

4. Gross Pay $396.00
   CPP $14.13
   EI $8.91
   Federal Tax $34.20
   Provincial Tax $12.45
   Net Pay $326.31

5. Gross Pay $385.00
   Taxable Income $381.20
   CP $13.66
   EI $8.66
   Federal Tax $7.10
   Provincial Tax $1.05
   Dental Plan $1.85
   Union Dues $3.80
   Net Pay $348.88

6.

	Gross Pay	Taxable Income	CPP	EI	Federal Tax	Provincial Tax	Union Dues	Group Insurance	Dental Plan	Net Pay
a)	$1254.90	$1246.95	$48.17	$28.24	$146.25	$55.25	$6.95	$1.76	$3.85	$964.43
b)	$1128.00	$1121.05	$42.72	$25.38	$107.90	$39.40	$6.95	$2.09	$3.85	$899.71
c)	$700.00	$700.00	$24.31	$15.75	$55.20	$19.80	$0.00	$0.00	$0.00	$584.94
d)	$1149.16	$1142.21	$43.63	$25.86	$120.40	$45.55	$6.95	$1.76	$3.85	$901.16
e)	$1212.60	$1205.65	$46.35	$27.28	$110.90	$41.75	$6.95	$1.76	$0.00	$977.61

Since all employees are paid bi-weekly, the gross pay is calculated for the week and then doubled. The assumption is that the employees work the same number of hours for both weeks of the pay period.

7. Gross pay: $484.00
Take-home pay: $290.40

8. Six examples of deductions include CPP, EI, income tax, dental plan, union dues, and group insurance. An employee would be happy to have paid into Employment Insurance if he or she were laid off and needed replacement income. (Other answers are possible, especially for the examples of payroll deductions.)

9. A pension plan is a "good" deduction because it pays benefits once a person retires.

10. Deductions: $125.00
Take-home pay: $375.00

11. Michelle:
Monthly income tax deducted:
    Federal: $816.20
    Provincial: $328.00
    Total: $1144.20
Annual income tax paid: $13,730.40

Virginia:
Bi-weekly income tax deducted:
    Federal: $375.25
    Provincial: $150.75
    Total: $526.00
Annual income tax paid: $13,676.00

Although they earn almost the same annual salary, Virginia pays slightly less income tax over the period of a year. Virginia, however, pays her taxes earlier and more frequently.

Exploration 7
Making Career Choices

Notebook Assignment

1. Weekly salary:
Library Aide: $385.80
Custodian: $423.60

Category	Aide	Custodian
Pay		+1
Hours	+1 (daytime job)	
Job Satisfaction	+3	+1
Clean or dirty		-1
Total	+4	+1

The aide job seems the best. (Other answers are possible and other conclusions may be drawn.)

2. **One possible answer is:**

Questions: How long would it take to become a full-time pilot? What is the pay scale for a full-time pilot? Describe the working conditions of the job. Are there benefit programs? Are there opportunities for advancement in the company?

Category	Manitoba	Yukon
Pay	$1000 (4 points)	$600
Pilot Hours	20	20
Other hours	20 (1 point—keep busy)	0 (2 points—free time)
Total	5 points	2 points

Using these criteria, it looks as if the job in Manitoba would be better.

3. The sports clothing store pays more if a bonus can be earned once a month. A person could earn more at this job if they worked hard and earned the bonus more than once a month. (Possible reasons for choosing the other job might be only having to work for one day and not having to worry about how much is sold to determine wages.)

4. Possible answers include:
    job satisfaction: you feel that what you do is important
    enjoyment: your job is fun
    distance from home: if the job is far away from home or school, you may need transportation and you need to factor in travel time when considering the hours you are at work.
    clothes or uniform needed: do you need to buy clothes for work or is a uniform provided?
    hours: will the number of hours interfere with other activities?
    From most important to least important: job satisfaction, distance from home, and hours worked. If the job is not enjoyable, the amount of money made may not be worth the aggravation. If you have to travel a long way, the expenses of travel may interfere with the plans you have for the money. If you can only work a few hours a week, it may not allow you to make enough money. If, however, you work too many hours, the job may interfere with other activities you've planned (such as school work, sports activities, or social obligations).

5. Assume each worker works 40 hours a week for 8 weeks.

    Construction: $3840.00
    Grocery: $2720.00

    Therefore, the grocery store worker would have to work 132 hours to catch up to the construction worker. Students might choose the grocery clerk job because they would have earnings during the school year. (Other answers and reasons are possible.)

6. Pierre could establish some criteria and weigh the advantages and disadvantages of each job. After assigning points, Pierre can make a decision about which job he prefers.

Category	Camera Shop	Sawmill
Money		+1
Type of Work (along career lines)	+2	
Available Times	+1 (can work during school and use information from courses)	
TOTAL	+3	+1

Pierre might choose the camera shop because it relates to his career goal. (Other criteria and other conclusions are possible.)

Exploration 8
Changing Earnings

Notebook Assignment

1.

	Present Salary	Percent Rate of Increase	Increase (Dollars)	New Salary
a)	$7.65 an hour	2%	$0.15	$7.80
b)	$310.00 a week	11%	$34.10	$344.10
c)	$1087.25 a month	3.5%	$38.05	$1125.30
d)	$14.95 an hour	1.5%	$0.22	$15.17
e)	$20,800.00	2.75%	$572.00	$21,372.00
f)	$15,000 annually	18.3%	$2750.00	$17,750.00

2. $13.82

3. $22,907.40

4. $8.93

5. $354.20

6. $13,693.68

7. $1297.92

8.

Present Salary	Rate of Increase	Percent Amount of Increase
a) $6.00 an hour	$0.30	5%
b) $6.75 an hour	$0.52	7.7%
c) $280.00 a week	$19.80	7.1%
d) $320.00 a week	$40.00	12.5%
e) $1700.00 a month	$350.00	20.6%
f) $2100.00 a month	$50.40	2.4%
g) $13,480.00 a year	$600.00	4.5%
h) $22,800 annually	$1003.20	4.4%

9. 5.9%

10. 26.3% over the two years

11. 19.6%

12. 10%

13. 23.3%

14. 22.2%

15. 18.8%

16. **One possible answer:**

Save for college, buy golf equipment, get a computer. Saving for college is the most positive.

17. Job share advantages: still collect an income, time off, less busy at work.

Job share disadvantages: less pay, lose seniority.

Exploration 9

Balancing A Budget

Notebook Assignment

1. Usual expenses:
   Clothes: $100.00 a month (need approximately $25.00 a week)
   Entertainment: $20.00 a week
   Bus fare: $15.00 a week
   Total usual expenses a week: $60.00

   Unexpected expenses might include: new hockey sticks, gifts, bike repairs. (Other answers are possible. The three rounds of the game have not been recorded as there are many possible answers.)

2. $50.00 a month can be spent on recreation.

3. $2000.00

Chapter Review

1. $97.80

2. $259.00

3. Lisa worked 7.5 hours (or 7 hours 30 minutes). She would earn $71.55

4. CPP $79.77
   EI $45.00
   Federal Tax $283.00
   Provincial Tax $112.10
   Net Pay $1480.13

5. $8.82

6. The 10% bonus is a better offer. Assuming a 40-hour work week, the difference in net pay is $5.20 a week.

7. Weekly gross pay: $437.50
   Assuming Sharon works each of the 52 weeks of the year, she can save $2275.00.

8. Gross earnings: $650.00
   Assuming she works each of the 52 weeks of the year, she earns $33,800.00.

9. He works 18.50 hours and receives a gross pay of $177.60.

Time Card

Employee Number: **83837**

Name: **WILLIAM WHITAKER**   Signature *William Whitaker*

Week Ending: **JUNE 24**

Date	Morning		Afternoon		Overtime		Hours		Total
	In	Out	In	Out	In	Out	Reg	OT	Hours
M	7:59	12:01					4.0		4.0
T	8:02	12:00					3.75		3.75
W	7:55	11:55					3.75		3.75
TH	8:27	12:03					3.5		3.5
F	8:00	11:32					3.5		3.5
S									
SU									
Total							___	___	___

	HOURS	RATE	AMOUNT	POSITION
REGULAR	18.5	$9.60	$177.60	Cook
OVERTIME				

10. She worked 17.75 h (regular) for $266.25 and she worked
    3 h 27 m for $77.63. Her total is $343.88.

Time Card

Employee Number: **7896**

Name: **MEGAN METCALFE**

Signature   *Megan Metcalfe*

Week Ending: **NOVEMBER 2**

Date	Afternoon In	Afternoon Out	Evening In	Evening Out	Overtime In	Overtime Out	Hours Reg	Hours OT	Total Hours
M	12:58	5:02					4.0		4.0
T			5:59	8:31			2.5		2.5
W	2:27	5:00	5:59	8:46			5.25		5.25
TH			6:18	9:04			2.5		2.5
F	1:09	4:48					3.5		3.5
S					8:35	12:02		3.45	3.45
SU									
Total							——	——	——

	HOURS	RATE	AMOUNT	POSITION
REGULAR	17.75	$15.00	$266.25	Instructor
OVERTIME	3.45	$22.50	$77.63	

11. Romeo earns $648.34 regular time and
$69.93 in overtime. His gross pay is $718.27.

Time Card

Employee Number: **4747**

Name: **ROMEO LOMBARDO** Signature *Romeo Lombardo*

Week Ending: **OCTOBER 12**

Date	Morning		Afternoon		Overtime		Hours		Total
	In	Out	In	Out	In	Out	Reg	OT	Hours
M	8:00	12:02	12:57	5:05			8.0		8.0
T	7:57	11:34	12:58	5:01			7.5		7.5
W	7:59	12:03	1:18	5:00			7.5		7.5
TH	8:06	12:00	12:59	4:50			7.5		7.5
F	7:55	11:58	1:00	5:03			7.75		7.75
S					9:15	12:00		2.75	2.75
SU									
Total							___	___	___

	HOURS	RATE	AMOUNT	POSITION
REGULAR	38.25	$16.95	$648.34	Corrections Officer
OVERTIME	2.75	$25.43	$69.93	

12. Juan works 38 h regular time and earns $302.10. He works 3 h 35 m overtime and earns $56.92. His total gross pay is $359.02.

Time Card

Employee Number: **9494**

Name: **JUAN VALDEZ**

Week Ending: **OCTOBER 12**

Signature *Juan Valdez*

Date	Afternoon		Evening		Overtime		Hours		Total
	In	Out	In	Out	In	Out	Reg	OT	Hours
M	13:00	17:01	18:00	22:02			8.0		8.0
T	12:57	17:02	17:55	21:31			7.5		7.5
W	12:59	17:03	18:07	22:03			7.75		7.75
TH	13:08	17:00	17:59	21:56			7.5		7.5
F	13:19	17:00	17:56	21:59			7.5		7.5
S					12:58	16:33		3.58	3.58
SU									
Total							____	____	____

	HOURS	RATE	AMOUNT	POSITION
REGULAR	38.00	$7.95	$302.10	Server
OVERTIME	3.58	$15.90	$56.92	

13. Hugh works 38.5 h and earns $404.25. He works 2 h 39 m
    overtime and earns $41.74. His gross income is $445.99.
    Deductions will vary.

Time Card

Employee Number: **686899**

Name: **HUGH JENNINGS**

Week Ending: **SEPTEMBER 21**

Signature *Hugh Jennings*

Date	Morning In	Morning Out	Afternoon In	Afternoon Out	Overtime In	Overtime Out	Hours Reg	Hours OT	Total Hours
M	7:56	12:01	1:14	5:00			7.75		7.75
T	8:00	12:02	12:55	5:04			8.0		8.0
W	7:56	11:50	1:30	5:02			7.25		7.25
TH	7:55	12:03	12:55	5:04	5:57	8:36	8.0	2.65	10.65
F	8:00	12:02	12:58	4:32			7.5		7.5
S									
SU									
Total							___	___	___

	HOURS	RATE	AMOUNT	POSITION
REGULAR	38.50	$10.50	$404.25	Barber
OVERTIME	2.65	$15.75	$41.74	

Gross Pay	$445.99
Federal IT	$26.80
Provincial IT	$9.05
CPP	$16.28
EI	$10.03
Med/Den. Ins.	$4.50
NET PAY	$379.33

14. Gabriel worked 37.25 h regular time and 3 h
    3 m overtime. His gross pay is $499.83.
    Deductions will vary.

Time Card

Employee Number: **14647**

Name: **GABRIEL GAGNON**

Signature *Gabriel Gagnon*

Week Ending: **JUNE 15**

Date	Afternoon		Evening		Overtime		Hours		Total
	In	Out	In	Out	In	Out	Reg	OT	Hours
M	13:00	17:00	18:03	21:02			6.75		6.75
T	12:56	16:35	18:25	22:04			7.0		7.0
W	12:58	17:02	17:58	22:02			8.0		8.0
TH	12:59	17:01	17:55	21:58			7.75		7.75
F	12:57	17:01	17:55	21:58			7.75		7.75
S					09:00	12:03		3.05	
SU									
Total							____	____	____

	HOURS	RATE	AMOUNT	POSITION
REGULAR	37.25	$11.95	$445.14	Car Salesman
OVERTIME	3.05	$17.93	$54.69	

Gross Pay	$499.83
Federal IT	$52.40
Provincial IT	$16.40
CPP	$18.60
EI	$11.25
Group Insurance	$3.23
Donation	$5.50
NET PAY	$392.45

15. Tyrone works 36.25 h regular time and 6.04 h
    overtime. His gross pay is $675.12.
    Deductions will vary.

Time Card

Employee Number: **111315**

Name: **TYRONE DESROCHERS**

Signature   *Tyrone DesRochers*

Week Ending: **FEBRUARY 17**

Date	Morning		Afternoon		Overtime		Hours		Total
	In	Out	In	Out	In	Out	Reg	OT	Hours
M	8:00	12:06	12:56	4:42			7.5		7.5
T	7:59	12:02	12:55	5:02	5:57	8:49	8.0	2.87	10.87
W	7:58	11:03	12:57	4:30	6:03	9:13	6.5	3.17	9.67
TH	8:00	11:47	12:59	5:00			7.75		7.75
F	8:02	12:00	1:14	4:05			6.5		6.5
S									
SU									
Total							____	____	____

	HOURS	RATE	AMOUNT	POSITION
REGULAR	36.25	$14.90	$540.13	Dept. Manager
OVERTIME	6.04	$22.35	$134.99	

Gross Pay	$675.12
Taxable Income	$642.37
Federal IT	$53.70
Provincial IT	$20.05
CPP	$26.14
EI	$15.19
Med/Dental Ins.	$4.50
Pension Fund	$32.75
NET PAY	$522.79

Case Study

1. John earns $825/week and $42,900/year at
    $22.00 for a 37.5 h week. He will save
    $4,290.00 after one year for college. His
    earnings for the first 6 months are $21,450.00
    with a savings of $2,145.00.

    With the salary increase, John makes
    $23.00/h at 37.5 h/week. His gross pay is
    $862.50, with a yearly income of $44, 850.00.
    For the six-month period, he would save
    $2242.50. John's total savings for college will
    be $4,387.50

2. Assuming Code 4:

Gross Bi-weekly salary	$1650.00
Federal Income Tax	$ 206.55
Provincial Income Tax	$ 79.95
CPP	$ 65.08
EI	$ 37.13
Net Pay	$1261.29

    Deduction answers will vary.

3. John's Monthly Budget = $2522.58

Rent	$400.00
Utilities	$180.00
Clothing	$125.00
Personal Care	$50.00
Telephone	$50.00
Recreation/Hobbies	$150.00
Food	$400.00
Transportation	$560.00
Savings (general)	$50.00
College Savings	$357.50
Vet	$100.00
Pet Supplies	$80.00

Assumptions:

1. John has bought a van. His transportation
    costs include loan payments, maintenance,
    repairs, and gas. This is for his personal use.
2. The net monthly take-home pay equals 4
    weeks, so figures in question 2 can be used.
3. The item "Recreation and Hobbies" includes
    books, magazines, and CDs.

Chapter 2

• • • • • • • • • • • • •

PERSONAL BANKING

In this chapter, the solutions or documents used must be accurate, complete, and neatly laid out. Pay close attention to detail and take care to fill in the forms so that others can understand what has been written.

Exploration 1

Using Bank Accounts

Notebook Assignment

1.

BANK OF EVERMORE
BLUE HARBOUR, B.C.

WITHDRAWAL

Date	Your Home Branch Location
Today's Date	

Received from Bank of Evermore

Twenty-five ———————————— ^{xx} /100 Dollars $ *25.00*

Your Account Number	Signature (Please sign in the presence of bank employee.)
2 4 6 – 9 1 9 – 3 4	*Henri Charles*

2.

DEPOSIT

BANK OF EVERMORE
BLUE HARBOUR, B.C.

Personal Account

Date	*Today's Date*
Account Number	*538-610-7*
Name	*Morris Stein*

INITIALS	
Depositor *M.S.*	Bank Employee *N.G.*

Signature for cash withdrawal. (Please sign in the presence of bank employee.)

Morris Stein

CHEQUES			CASH	
285	*00*		X5	
127	*83*		X10	
98	*97*		X20	
85	*00*		X50	
			X100	
			Coins/Other Cash	
			Total Cash	
596	*80*		Total Cheques	*596.80*
		Subtotal	$	*596.80*
		Withdrawal	$	*100.00*
		TOTAL	$	*496.80*

3.

DEPOSIT

BANK OF EVERMORE
BLUE HARBOUR, B.C.

Personal Account

Date	Today's Date
Account Number	3-785-11
Name	Your Name

INITIALS

Depositor	Bank Employee
Y.N.	C.G.

Signature for cash withdrawal. (Please sign in the presence of bank employee.)

Signature

CHEQUES		
	64	95
	64	95

CASH		
4	X5	20.00
2	X10	20.00
1	X20	20.00
	X50	
	X100	
	Coins/Other Cash	9.75
	Total Cash	69.75
	Total Cheques	64.95
Subtotal	$	134.70
Withdrawal	$	
TOTAL	$	134.70

4.

DEPOSIT

BANK OF EVERMORE
BLUE HARBOUR, B.C.

Personal Account

Date	Today's Date
Account Number	2892146
Name	Chad Allen

INITIALS

Depositor	Bank Employee
C.A.	R.H.

Signature for cash withdrawal. (Please sign in the presence of bank employee.)

Chad Allen

CHEQUES		
	64	20
	64	20

CASH		
	X5	
	X10	
4	X20	80.00
	X50	
	X100	
	Coins/Other Cash	18.20
	Total Cash	98.20
	Total Cheques	64.20
Subtotal	$	162.40
Withdrawal	$	100.00
TOTAL	$	62.40

5.

DEPOSIT

BANK OF EVERMORE
BLUE HARBOUR, B.C.

Personal Account

Date	Today's Date
Account Number	8649843
Name	Inga van Damme

INITIALS

| Depositor | Bank Employee |
| I.V.D. | A.H. |

Signature for cash withdrawal. (Please sign in the presence of bank employee.)

Inga van Damme

CHEQUES	
136	50
64	20
29	98
230	68

CASH	
X5	
X10	
X20	
X50	
X100	
Coins/Other Cash	
Total Cash	
Total Cheques	230.68
Subtotal $	230.68
Withdrawal $	125.00
TOTAL $	105.68

6.

DEPOSIT

BANK OF EVERMORE
BLUE HARBOUR, B.C.

Personal Account

Date	Today's Date
Account Number	1411-613-08
Name	Ranj Panikkar

INITIALS

| Depositor | Bank Employee |
| R.P. | L.H. |

Signature for cash withdrawal. (Please sign in the presence of bank employee.)

Ranj Panikkar

CHEQUES	
192	80
78	00
46	94
317	74

CASH	
X5	
X10	
X20	
X50	
X100	
Coins/Other Cash	14.50
Total Cash	14.50
Total Cheques	317.74
Subtotal $	332.24
Withdrawal $	150.00
TOTAL $	182.24

7a)

John Graham
ANY STREET
CITY, PROVINCE POSTAL CODE

Today's Date 20 *02*

Pay to the order of
Mike's Bike Shop

$ *70.00*

Seventy ——————————————— *xx* /100 DOLLARS

BANK OF EVERMORE
BLUE HARBOUR, B.C.

PER

John Graham
Signature

Account # *4567*

b)

John Graham
ANY STREET
CITY, PROVINCE POSTAL CODE

Today's Date 20 *02*

Pay to the order of
Northern Stores

$ *125.78*

One Hundred Twenty-five ——————— *78* /100 DOLLARS

BANK OF EVERMORE
BLUE HARBOUR, B.C.

PER

John Graham
Signature

Account # *4567*

c)

John Graham
ANY STREET
CITY, PROVINCE POSTAL CODE

Today's Date 20 *02*

Pay to the order of
Jeans & Tops

$ *7.50*

Seven ——————————————— *50* /100 DOLLARS

BANK OF EVERMORE
BLUE HARBOUR, B.C.

PER

John Graham
Signature

Account # *4567*

8a)

NAME
ANY STREET
CITY, PROVINCE POSTAL CODE

February 4　　20 *01*

Pay to the order of

J & M Department Store　　　$ *48.72*

Forty-eight ———————————————— *72* /100　DOLLARS

BANK OF EVERMORE
BLUE HARBOUR, B.C.

PER

Signature
Signature

Account #

b)

NAME
ANY STREET
CITY, PROVINCE POSTAL CODE

August 27　°20 *01*

Pay to the order of

State-of-the-Art Electronics　　　$ *158.95*

One hundred fifty-eight ———————— *95* /100　DOLLARS

BANK OF EVERMORE
BLUE HARBOUR, B.C.

PER

Signature
Signature

Account #

c)

NAME
ANY STREET
CITY, PROVINCE POSTAL CODE

June 1　　20 *01*

Pay to the order of

Manitoba Humane Society　　　$ *105.42*

One hundred five ————————————— *42* /100　DOLLARS

BANK OF EVERMORE
BLUE HARBOUR, B.C.

PER

Signature
Signature

Account #

8d)

NAME
ANY STREET
CITY, PROVINCE POSTAL CODE

April 30   20 *01*

Pay to the order of

Minister of Finance $ *1573.60*

One thousand five hundred, seventy-three ———— *60*/100 DOLLARS

BANK OF EVERMORE
BLUE HARBOUR, B.C.

PER

Signature
Signature

Account #

9.   Cheque #1: there should be a line after
"twelve"; needs "xx" in cents
Cheque #2: dollar amounts do not match; .79
is inverted on second line
Cheque #3: date should be January 2, 2002;
cheques are written in a two-week period

10.

DEPOSIT

BANK OF EVERMORE
BLUE HARBOUR, B.C.

Personal Account

Date	*Today's Date*
Account Number	*Your Account #*
Name	*Your Name*

INITIALS	
Depositor *Y.N.*	Bank Employee *K.G.*

Signature for cash withdrawal. (Please sign in the presence of bank employee.)

Signature

CHEQUES		
	149	76
	149	76

CASH	
X5	
X10	
X20	
X50	
X100	
Coins/Other Cash	
Total Cash	
Total Cheques	*149.76*
Subtotal $	*149.76*
Withdrawal $	*50.00*
TOTAL $	*99.76*

10. (continued)

NAME
ANY STREET
CITY, PROVINCE POSTAL CODE

Today's Date 20 *02*

Pay to the order of

The Leather Store $ *122.76*

One hundred twenty-two ——————— *76* /100 DOLLARS

BANK OF EVERMORE
BLUE HARBOUR, B.C.

PER

lay-away payment

Signature
Signature

Account #

11. Two drawbacks to carrying cash include the risk of robbery and losing cash, which is not traceable. Drawbacks of using cheques or debit cards are that they sometimes cost money to use and may be inconvenient for small amounts. Also, some businesses will not accept cheques and if you return merchandise purchased with a cheque you may need to wait a few weeks to get your money refunded.

Extension

12. There is not enough money to buy all the items. You need $306.82 to buy all items. The bicycle parts could be a high priority because you might need your bike for transportation.

Exploration 2
Keeping Records

Notebook Assignment

1. Monique's closing balance is $242.11:
   $112.36 − 25.99 − 45.59 + 254.32 − 52.99 =$
   $242.11

2.

Transaction Record

Cheque #	Date	Description	Payment/ Debit	√	Deposit/ Credit	Balance
						2397.50
	May 3	Deposit			625.00	3022.50
45	May 7	Auto Oil	76.00			2946.50
46	May 8	Hydro	67.40			2879.10
47	May 8	Telephone	24.90			2854.20
48	May 15	Car Lease	217.00			2637.20

3.

Transaction Record

Cheque #	Date	Description	Payment/ Debit	√	Deposit/ Credit	Balance
						998.43
243	Sept. 9	The Bay	48.00			950.43
244	Sept. 13	Esso	43.87			906.56
245	Sept. 20	Hydro	66.98			839.58
	Sept. 25	Deposit			200.00	1039.58
246	Sept. 30	Dale's Rental Agency	475.00			564.58

4.

Transaction Record

Cheque #	Date	Description	Payment/ Debit	√	Deposit/ Credit	Balance
						837.92
162	Feb. 10	Hydro	58.74			779.18
163	Feb. 10	Telephone	38.52			740.66
164	Feb. 14	VISA	194.71			545.95
	Feb. 17	Deposit			185.92	731.87
165	Feb. 18	Sam's Sports Hut	89.66			642.21
	Feb. 20	Deposit			300.00	942.21

5.

Transaction Record

Cheque #	Date	Description	Payment/ Debit	√	Deposit/ Credit	Balance
						78.72
72	Oct. 26	Wayne's Gas Bar	67.25			11.47
	Oct. 28	Deposit			402.96	414.43
73	Oct. 31	C & B Rental Agencies	400.00			14.43
74	Nov. 4	Baron's Dept. Store	12.75			1.68
	Nov. 6	Deposit			90.82	92.50
75	Nov. 7	Medical Ethics Assoc.	75.00			17.50
	Nov. 10	Deposit			153.72	171.22

6

Transaction Record

Cheque #	Date	Description	Payment/ Debit	√	Deposit/ Credit	Balance 426.97
	Dec. 2	Deposit			49.63	476.60
208	Dec. 4	J & M Dept. Store	67.25			409.35
	Dec. 6	Deposit			250.00	659.35
209	Dec. 7	I Computer Store	398.88			260.47
210	Dec. 10	Fast Gas Bar	32.75			227.72
	Dec. 11	Deposit			48.50	276.22
211	Dec. 14	Value Foods	86.12			190.10
	Dec. 15	Withdrawal	100.00			90.10

7.

Transaction Record

Cheque #	Date	Description	Payment/ Debit	√	Deposit/ Credit	Balance 592.84
98	May 29	Harrod's	57.00			535.84
99	June 1	Minister of Finance	407.82			128.02
	June 2	Deposit			629.50	757.52
100	June 4	World Wide Cable	32.75			724.77
	June 5	Withdrawal	400.00			324.77
	June 7	Deposit			80.00	404.77
101	June 8	Telus	86.12			318.65

Extension

8. Your final balance is $182.64:
   $345.78 − $20.51 − $56.99 - $10.00 − $75.64 = $182.64

   This assumes a tax rate of 7% PST and 7% GST.

Exploration 3
Using a Bank Card

Notebook Assignment

1. The withdrawal is $50.00 and the account balance is $275.39. The withdrawal was made from a chequing account on July 30, 2002.

2.

```
BANK OF EVERMORE
CARD NUMBER: 4518******5582
DATE:        TIME:        ATM:

06/01/02     12:15        1234567
Savings Account
Bill Payment $ 35.50
Withdrawal $ 20.00
Account Balance $ 140.25

Transaction Record VA41-9040
```

3. James might experience a robbery if he stops and uses an ATM late at night in a dimly lit location. An alternative is to drive to an ATM that is well lit and has lots of people around it, like those located in convenience stores.

4.

```
BANK OF EVERMORE
CARD NUMBER: 4518******5582
DATE:        TIME:        ATM:

16/11/01     12:21        1234567
Chequing Account
Deposit $ 1200.00
Account Balance $ 2100.00

Transaction Record VA41-9044
```

```
BANK OF EVERMORE
CARD NUMBER: 4518******5582
DATE:        TIME:        ATM:

16/11/01     12:23        1234567
Chequing Account
Withdrawal $ 250.00
Account Balance $ 1850.00

Transaction Record VA41-9045
```

```
BANK OF EVERMORE
CARD NUMBER: 4518******5582
DATE:        TIME:        ATM:

16/11/01     12:25        1234567
Chequing Account
Bill Payment $ 234.00
Bill Payment $ 150.00
Account Balance $ 1466.00

Transaction Record VA41-9046
```

5. Using an ATM accomplishes the same thing as using a teller in most cases. An ATM machine is often more convenient and less time-consuming than going to a bank. A bank teller, on the other hand, can answer questions and do other types of transactions such as converting money to American dollars.

6. Three advantages of a bank card: convenient, safe, fast. Three disadvantages: costly, may lose card or forget PIN, and cannot be used everywhere.

Extension 7.

7. $1.00 Cdn = $0.66 US
   $50.00 US + $1.00 US = $51.00 US

   $51.00 ÷ 0.66 = $77.27
   The total deducted is $77.27.

Exploration 4

Reconciling a Bank Statement

Notebook Assignment

1. Cheque #186 should be $126.50 in the Transaction Record

2. Cheque #164 is missing from the Transaction Record.

3.

BANK OF EVERMORE
BLUE HARBOUR, B.C.

STATEMENT OF RECONCILIATION

Bank Statement	Transaction Record
FINAL BALANCE shown on this statement	FINAL BALANCE shown in transaction record
$ 1153.41	$ 1815.70
ADD DEPOSITS made after the statement date	SUBTRACT WITHDRAWALS which are not shown in transaction record
$730.00	Service Charge $11.60
SUBTOTAL $ 1883.41	
SUBTRACT WITHDRAWALS made after the statement date	
$35.00	
$27.95	
$16.36	
FINAL BALANCE $ 1804.10	FINAL BALANCE $ 1804.10

4.

STATEMENT OF RECONCILIATION

BLUE HARBOUR, B.C.

Bank Statement	Transaction Record
FINAL BALANCE shown on this statement	FINAL BALANCE shown in transaction record
$ 199.53	$ 204.52
ADD DEPOSITS made after the statement date	SUBTRACT WITHDRAWALS which are not shown in transaction record
$45.00	Service Charge $14.75
SUBTOTAL $ 244.53	
SUBTRACT WITHDRAWALS made after the statement date	
$54.76	
FINAL BALANCE $ 189.77	FINAL BALANCE $ 189.77

5.

STATEMENT OF RECONCILIATION

BLUE HARBOUR, B.C.

Bank Statement	Transaction Record
FINAL BALANCE shown on this statement	FINAL BALANCE shown in transaction record
$ 837.71	$ 1577.67
ADD DEPOSITS made after the statement date	SUBTRACT WITHDRAWALS which are not shown in transaction record
$2000.00	Service Charge 8.75
SUBTOTAL $ 2837.71	
SUBTRACT WITHDRAWALS made after the statement date	
$854.00	
$57.10	
$146.58	
$211.11	
FINAL BALANCE $ 1568.92	FINAL BALANCE $ 1568.92

6.

BANK OF EVERMORE
BLUE HARBOUR, B.C.

STATEMENT OF RECONCILIATION

Bank Statement	Transaction Record
FINAL BALANCE shown on this statement	FINAL BALANCE shown in transaction record
$ 726.38	$ 1033.42
ADD DEPOSITS made after the statement date	SUBTRACT WITHDRAWALS which are not shown in transaction record
$724.32	Service Charge $5.50
SUBTOTAL $ 1450.70	
SUBTRACT WITHDRAWALS made after the statement date	
$37.32	
$385.46	
FINAL BALANCE $ 1027.92	FINAL BALANCE $ 1027.92

7.

BANK OF EVERMORE
BLUE HARBOUR, B.C.

STATEMENT OF RECONCILIATION

Bank Statement	Transaction Record
FINAL BALANCE shown on this statement	FINAL BALANCE shown in transaction record
$ 914.96	$ 407.47
ADD DEPOSITS made after the statement date	SUBTRACT WITHDRAWALS which are not shown in transaction record
$	Service Charge $ 5.00
SUBTOTAL $ 914.96	
SUBTRACT WITHDRAWALS made after the statement date	
$80.00	
$37.24	
$395.25	
FINAL BALANCE $ 402.47	FINAL BALANCE $ 402.47

8.

STATEMENT OF RECONCILIATION

BANK OF EVERMORE
BLUE HARBOUR, B.C.

Bank Statement	Transaction Record
FINAL BALANCE shown on this statement	FINAL BALANCE shown in transaction record
$ 680.37	$ 1214.44
ADD DEPOSITS made after the statement date	SUBTRACT WITHDRAWALS which are not shown in transaction record
$ 697.21	
SUBTOTAL $ 1377.58	
SUBTRACT WITHDRAWALS made after the statement date	
$56.00	
$61.16	
$45.98	
FINAL BALANCE $ 1214.44	FINAL BALANCE $ 1214.44

9.

STATEMENT OF RECONCILIATION

BANK OF EVERMORE
BLUE HARBOUR, B.C.

Bank Statement	Transaction Record
FINAL BALANCE shown on this statement	FINAL BALANCE shown in transaction record
$ 1546.44	$ 1892.74
ADD DEPOSITS made after the statement date	SUBTRACT WITHDRAWALS which are not shown in transaction record
$482.53	Service Charge $5.00
SUBTOTAL $ 2028.97	
SUBTRACT WITHDRAWALS made after the statement date	
$25.00	
$28.00	
$88.23	
FINAL BALANCE $ 1887.74	FINAL BALANCE $ 1887.74

Extension

10. A debit could be recorded twice if a clerk ran the debit card through the scanning machine twice, or a mistake could have occurred in the bank. A visit to the bank with the receipt for the goods and the bankcard receipt should solve the problem. A photocopy could be good to have in case the bank wanted the records and needed yours. The police should not be involved if the error was a simple mistake.

Exploration 5
Choosing the Best Account

Notebook Assignment

1. Since Gerard keeps a monthly balance of no less than $5000.00, no account will charge monthly fees.

Account type	# extra transactions	Cost
Value	30 – 10 = 20	20 x .50 = $10.00
Self-Serve	30 – 20 = 10	10 x .50 = $5.00
Full-Serve	30 – 25 = 5	5 x .50 = $2.50

The Full-service Account is best for Gerald.

2. Since Billy makes 60 transactions a month, the full-serve account is the cheapest. She should keep at least $2000 in the account to save the monthly fees, an amount which is much greater than the interest she would earn in a savings account.

Most students would make the following kinds of transactions:
- cash withdrawal
- deposit of paycheque or other monies
- Interac purchase
- bill payment
- transfer funds from one account to another

3. When comparing bank accounts, find ways to compare accounts using a standard situation. For example, which account is best if a person has less than $1000 and uses self-serve transactions twice a week?

4. Brochures should highlight the benefits of the account chosen, but must clearly state all the costs. The amounts should be realistic and competitive with local banking services.

Extension

5. Trial and error can be used to solve this problem. At 20 transactions the costs are equal. After 20 transactions the unlimited, no-cost transaction account is less expensive.

Exploration 6

Internet and Telephone Banking

Notebook Assignment

1. Steven could record the transaction using the same code his bank uses. Some banks use "TB" to indicate a transaction completed using telephone banking.

2.

Transaction Record CHEQUING ACCOUNT 1234						
Cheque #	Date	Description	Payment/ Debit	√	Deposit/ Credit	Balance
WWW	23/10	transfer to savings(#5678)	50.00			

Transaction Record SAVINGS ACCOUNT 5678						
Cheque #	Date	Description	Payment/ Debit	√	Deposit/ Credit	Balance
WWW	23/10	trf. from chequing (#1234)			50.00	

3. Three reasons for recording internet and
    telephone transactions are to keep the account
    balance current, to be able to check for errors,
    and to be able to complete reconciliation
    statements.

4. Confirmation numbers allow banks to check
    for errors easily, and quickly.

5.

Transaction Record

Cheque #	Date	Description	Payment/ Debit	√	Deposit/ Credit	Balance 210.00
DEP	Dec. 11	Cheque Deposit			450.00	660.00
WWW	Dec. 11	Locker	50.00			610.00
WWW	Dec. 11	Cable	40.00			570.00
IDP	Dec. 12	Shorts	23.00			547.00
354	Dec. 12	CD World	56.78			490.22

Extension

6. Sample Transaction Record

Transaction Record

Cheque #	Date	Description	Payment/ Debit	√	Deposit/ Credit	Balance 1000.00
WWW	Oct 1	Transfer (confirm WD 40)	50.00			1050.00
TB	Oct 2	Cable TV (confirm XY23)	25.00			1025.00
ATM	Oct 4	Paycheque			75.00	1100.00
123	Oct 5	A1 Deals (sports equipment)	200.00			900.00
IA	Oct 7	Lunch (Cocoa's)	11.00			889.00

Chapter Review

1. 1) g   8) a
    2) e   9) h
    3) m   10) l
    4) j   11) f
    5) d   12) k
    6) b   13) c
    7) i

2. shield the screen with your body while entering information; don't count money in front of others; allow other patrons their privacy; focus on counting accurately; pay attention to what is going on around you; don't allow yourself to become distracted; do only one thing at a time.

3.

DEPOSIT

BANK OF EVERMORE
BLUE HARBOUR, B.C.

Personal Account

Date	Today's Date
Account Number	22-763-4
Name	Terry Lynn

INITIALS

| Depositor | Bank Employee |
| T.L. | N.G. |

Signature for cash withdrawal. (Please sign in the presence of bank employee.)

Terry Lynn

CHEQUES		
	14	67
	53	26
	5	64
	73	57

	CASH	
	X5	
5	X10	50.00
	X20	
	X50	
	X100	
	Coins/Other Cash	45.46
	Total Cash	95.46
	Total Cheques	73.57
Subtotal	$	169.03
Withdrawal	$	
TOTAL	$	169.03

4.

DEPOSIT

BANK OF EVERMORE
BLUE HARBOUR, B.C.

Date	Today's Date
Account Number	211-843-521
Name	Ida Chow

INITIALS

Depositor	Bank Employee
I.C.	S.T.

Signature for cash withdrawal. (Please sign in the presence of bank employee.)

Ida Chow

Personal Account

CHEQUES		
	24	20
	100	00
	29	50
	153	70

CASH			
3	X5		15.00
	X10		
	X20		
	X50		
	X100		
Coins/Other Cash			6.00
Total Cash			21.00
Total Cheques			153.70
Subtotal	$		174.70
Withdrawal	$		50.00
TOTAL	$		124.70

5a)

NAME
ANY STREET
CITY, PROVINCE POSTAL CODE

February 14 20 02

Pay to the order of

Flowers for All Occasions $ 39.90

Thirty-nine ————————————— 90 /100 DOLLARS

BANK OF EVERMORE
BLUE HARBOUR, B.C.

PER

Account #

Signature
Signature

5b)

NAME
ANY STREET
CITY, PROVINCE POSTAL CODE

June 27   20 *03*

Pay to the order of

Folk on the Rocks $ *88.00*

Eighty-eight ————————————————————— *xx* /100   DOLLARS

**BANK OF
EVERMORE**
BLUE HARBOUR, B.C.

PER
————————————

Signature
Signature

Account #

6.

Transaction Record

Cheque #	Date	Description	Payment/ Debit	√	Deposit/ Credit	Balance
						898.43
43	Sept. 9	The Bay	47.00			851.43
	Sept. 10	Deposit			110.50	961.93
44	Sept. 13	Beaver Lumber	124.50			837.43
	Sept. 14	Deposit			75.00	912.43
	Sept. 20	Deposit			41.80	954.23

7.

Transaction Record

Cheque #	Date	Description	Payment/ Debit	√	Deposit/ Credit	Balance
						822.34
26	Sept. 4	Sports Wear	54.90			767.44
27	Sept. 4	Value Foods	64.95			702.49
	Sept. 5	Deposit			535.00	1237.49
28	Sept. 10	K. Tetley	200.00			1037.49
29	Sept. 21	Holme's Rental Agency	535.00			502.49
30	Sept. 23	CD Music	26.92			475.57
	Oct. 2	Deposit			250.00	725.57
31	Oct. 2	Fit Physiotherapy	31.00			694.57

8.

BANK OF EVERMORE
BLUE HARBOUR, B.C.

STATEMENT OF RECONCILIATION

Bank Statement	Transaction Record
FINAL BALANCE shown on this statement	FINAL BALANCE shown in transaction record
$ 398.09	$ 383.22
ADD DEPOSITS made after the statement date	SUBTRACT WITHDRAWALS which are not shown in transaction record
$203.14	Service Charge $14.75
SUBTOTAL $ 601.23	
SUBTRACT WITHDRAWALS made after the statement date	
$109.20	
$123.56	
FINAL BALANCE $ 368.47	FINAL BALANCE $ 368.47

Wendy's Transaction Record agrees with her Bank Statement of the service charges of $14.75 are included. The actual amount in her chequing account is $368.47.

9. Errors:
    deposit = $863.91
    cheque #130 = $64.20
    corrected Transaction Record = $498.13
    (Balance)

BANK OF EVERMORE
BLUE HARBOUR, B.C.

STATEMENT OF RECONCILIATION

Bank Statement	Transaction Record
FINAL BALANCE shown on this statement	FINAL BALANCE shown in transaction record
$ 532.98	$ 498.13
ADD DEPOSITS made after the statement date	SUBTRACT WITHDRAWALS which are not shown in transaction record
$200.00	Service Charge $4.50
SUBTOTAL $ 732.98	
SUBTRACT WITHDRAWALS made after the statement date	
$112.95	
$82.28	
$44.12	
FINAL BALANCE $ 493.63	FINAL BALANCE $ 493.63

10.

NAME
ANY STREET
CITY, PROVINCE POSTAL CODE

Today's Date 20 02

Pay to the order of

Frankie's CD House $ 27.49

Twenty-seven 49/100 DOLLARS

BANK OF EVERMORE
BLUE HARBOUR, B.C.

PER

Signature
Signature

Account #

11. Raquel's account costs $4.95 + 25 ($0.50) = $17.45 per month. Wilfred would have to make 18 transactions at $1.00 each for his account to be more expensive than Raquel's.

12. Yanu's new bank balance is $107.85.

Chapter 3

• • • • • • • • • • • • • •

SPREADSHEETS

Exploration 1
The Basics of Spreadsheets

Notebook Assignment

1. a) 4 columns, 8 rows, and 32 cells used (48 cells shown)
   b) cell D6
   c) A9: label
      B4: value
      C5: value
      D3: formula
      D9: formula
   d) The label GROSS PAY is on the left side of column D and all the numbers underneath it are on the right side of column D because labels are left justified and values are right justified.

Extension

2. =D2+D3+D4+D5+D6+D7

Exploration 2
The Style File

Notebook Assignment

1. **Possible answers:**

   move Bank of Yukon label

   change Column A width

   insert picture

   labels left, values right

   add colour

   align numbers

   numbers as currency where appropriate

2. Check with a partner.

Extension

3. Explore formatting options and describe two of the best.

Exploration 3
Smart Spreadsheets

Notebook Assignment

1. a) =G5+H5
   b) =C6/2
   c) =B7-B6
   d) =G7*H7*J7
   e) =SUM(E5:E9)
   f) =B4*0.07
   g) =C5/D5
   h) =AVERAGE(D3:D10)
   i) =(F5+F6)-8
   j) =(B2*B3)/2

2. SUM(B4:B8); $133.85

3. Using the square root function results in a positive square root. Put the number you want the square root of in brackets after SQRT. e.g., SQRT(16) equals 4

4. a) The formula in cell B6 adds all the values from B1 to B4.
   b) 116
   c) =B1+B2+B3+B4

5. a) The formula in cell B4 subtracts the value in cell B3 from cell B2.
   b) $8000

6. a) The formula in cell B3 multiplies cell B1 by cell B2.
   b) The formula in cell B4 multiplies cell B3 by 0.14.
   c) The formula in cell B5 adds cell B3 to cell B4.
   d) Cell B3: $23.50
      Cell B4: $3.29
      Cell B5: $26.79

7. E5: =B5+C5-D5
   E9: =B9+C9-D9
   B12: =SUM(B5:B10) or
         B5+B6+B7+B8+B9+B10
   C12: =SUM(C5:C10) or
         C5+C6+C7+C8+C9+C10
   D12: =SUM(D5:D10) or
         D5+D6+D7+D8+D9+D10
   E12: =B12+C12-D12 or
         E5+E6+E7+E8+E9+E10

Extension

8. See the Insert menu for other spreadsheet functions. Choose one and explain it to the class.

9. **Possible answers:**

   often faster than tables

   are always correct

   can change date without redoing formulas

Exploration 4
Starting from Scratch

Notebook Assignment

1. Answers will vary, depending on Rounding.

2. Detroit is in first place.

Extension

3. The rankings would stay the same.

4. **Possible answers:**

   calculations only have to be done once

   spreadsheets can remember formulas

   less chance of error

   spreadsheets can be saved

Exploration 5
What if . . . ?

Notebook Assignment

1. $17.54

2. Spreadsheets will vary. Minimum mark is 74%.

3. Answers will vary.

Extension

4. Spreadsheets will vary. Employee needs a minimum of $2000 in sales to match the straight hourly wage.

Exploration 6
Saving Precious Time

Notebook Assignment

1. a) =30*A2+25*B2
   b) =1.5*A2+0.75*B2
   c) Answers will vary
   d) Use the fill/down command to copy the formulas in cells C2 and D2.
   e) Answers will vary.

Extension

2. The phone plan offered by DASH is cheaper based on the information given. Individual choices will vary.

Exploration 7
Handy Uses and Applications

Notebook Assignment

1. Spreadsheets, predictions, and results will vary.

Extension

2. Combinations and recommendations will vary.

Chapter Review

1. a) 6 columns, 8 rows, and 48 cells
    b) cell E2
    c) label
    d) =(B2:E2)/4 or =AVERAGE(B2:E2)

2. **Possible answers:**

    set cost/price to currency

    bold and enlarge spreadsheet title

    justify labels left

    add colour to top row and two bottom rows

    add clip art as decoration

    add extra row beneath main header

3. a) =B2*C2
    b) =D2*0.14
    c) =D2+E2
    d) highlight and then choose Edit, Fill, Down
    e) =F2+F3+F4+F5+F6 or =SUM(F2:F6)

4. Answers will vary

5. Students must refer to deduction tables. Other answers include:

    D5=B5*C5

    I5=D5-SUM(E5:H5)

    D11=SUM (D5:D9)

6. Answers will vary based on preferences.

Note that in many cases the solution presented here represents only one possible way to solve a problem. There may be other solutions that are correct and appropriate. These solutions are intended as a guide to assist student understanding of the exercises.

Chapter 4

CONSUMER DECISIONS

Exploration 1
Smart Shopping

Notebook Assignment

1. Butter package #2 looks larger. This is because you notice its height more than its depth. Potato chip package #2 looks like it contains more potato chips because the package is larger. There is more space between the potato chips in this package than in the other one.

2. a) The ingredient that weighs the most in cereal #1 is whole wheat. The ingredient that weighs the most in cereal #2 is flaked milled corn.
   b) The serving size of cereal #1 is 30 g. The serving size of cereal #2 is 30 g.
   c) The energy per serving of cereal #1 is 110 cal or 460 kJ. The energy per serving of cereal #2 is 112 cal or 470 kJ. Cereal #2 contains more energy per serving.
   d) 29% of your recommended daily intake of iron is supplied by one serving of cereal #1.
   e) You have to eat 10 servings of cereal #2 to meet your recommended daily intake of Vitamin B6.
   f) You would place cereal in the grain products group of the Canada Food Guide. You would place cereal with milk in both the grain and milk products groups.

3. a) Tuna contains more protein than fat or carbohydrate.
   b) You would place tuna in the meat and alternatives group of the Canada Food Guide.
   c) The serving size listed on the can is 50 g.
   d) One weight is the net weight of 170 g. The other is the drained weight of 120 g.
   e) There are 2.4 servings of tuna in this can.
   f) The drained weight was used.

4. a) You would place peanut butter in the meat and alternatives group of the Canada Food Guide.
   b) Peanut butter contains more fat than protein or carbohydrate.
   c) According to the Canada Food Guide, 2 tablespoons of peanut butter make up one serving.
   d) You could get 46.9 servings from 1.5 kg of peanut butter.
   e) 2 tablespoons contain 8.4 g of protein.

Extension

5. Answers will vary.

Exploration 2
The Cost of One

Notebook Assignment

1. The unit price per box = $3.50 ÷ 2 = $1.75

2. The price of one apple = $2.50 ÷ 12 = $0.21

3. The unit price of 1 kg at fruit stand #1
   = $2.20 ÷ 1.4 = $1.57
   The unit price of 1 kg at fruit stand #2
   = $3.00 ÷ 2.4 = $1.25
   The unit price of 1 kg at fruit stand #3
   = $5.50 ÷ 4.5 = $1.22
   Fruit stand #3 has the lowest unit price.

4. The unit price per can in store #1
   = $2.00 ÷ 3 = $0.67
   The unit price per can in store #2
   = $2.50 ÷ 5 = $0.50

The unit price per can in store #3
= $3.25 ÷ 8 = $0.41
Store #3 has the lowest unit price.

5. The unit price per cola at store A
= $4.75 ÷ 4 = $1.19
The unit price per cola at store B
= $8.95 ÷ 12= $0.75
The cola is less costly at store B.

6. Answers may vary.
Possible answers:
The cost of 1 can of apple juice at the local supermarket
= $1.09 ÷ 3 = $0.36
or
The cost of 3 cans of apple juice at the corner store
= 37¢ x 3 = $1.11
The juice is less expensive at the supermarket.

7. The unit price per kilogram in store #1
= $0.89 ÷ 0.5 = $1.78
The unit price per kilogram in store #2
= $1.79 ÷ 1.5 = $1.19
The unit price per kilogram in store #3
= $2.98 ÷ 2.2 = $1.35
Store #2 has the lowest unit price.

8. The unit price per kilogram in package #1
= $0.79 ÷ 0.25 = $3.16
The unit price per kilogram in package #2
= $1.57 ÷ 0.5 = $3.14
The unit price per kilogram in package #3
= $3.09 ÷ 1.5 = $2.06
The third package has the lowest unit price.
These prices are higher than those in question 7.

Extension

9. a) The unit price when T-shirts are sold in a package of 2 = $5.49 ÷ 2 = $2.75
    b) The unit price when T-shirts are sold in a package of 3 = $7.89 ÷ 3 = $2.63
    c) The package of 3 offers the best unit price.
    d) 2 packages of 3 plus one individual shirt has the lowest price:
        $7.89 x 2 + $2.98 = $18.76

Exploration 3
Sales Tax: GST and PST

Notebook Assignment

1. a) 3 kg apples, no GST, no PST
    b) haircut, GST, no PST
    c) portable compact disk player, GST, possible PST
    d) box of chocolates, GST, possible PST
    e) restaurant meal, GST, possible PST
    f) pair of jeans, GST, possible PST
    g) jar of peanut butter, no GST, no PST
    h) electrical repair, GST, possible PST
    i) book, GST, possible PST
    j) package of paper towels, GST, possible PST

2. GST = 7% of $68.88 = 0.07 x $68.88 = $4.82
    PST = 7% of $68.88 = 0.07 x $68.88 = $4.82
    Total cost = $68.88 + $4.82 + $4.82 = $78.52

3. GST = 7% of $285 = 0.07 x $285 = $19.95
    PST = 8% of $285 = 0.08 x $285 = $22.80
    Total cost = $285 + $19.95 + $22.80
    = $327.75

4. GST = 7% of $12,675 = 0.07 x $12,675
    = $887.25
    PST = 7.5% of $12,675 = 0.075 x $12,675
    = $950.63
    Total cost = $12,675 + $887.25 + $950.63
    = $14,512.88

5. Total cost excluding tax = $450 + $235 + $189
    = $874
    HST = 15% of $874 = 0.15 x $874 = $131.10
    Total cost = $874 + $131.10 = $1005.10

6. Total cost excluding tax = $165 + $45 = $210
    GST = 7% of $210 = 0.07 x $210 = $14.70
    Total cost = $210 + $14.70 = $224.70

7. a) The unit price per pair bought as four
        pairs = $7.16 ÷ 4 = $1.79. The unit price
        per pair bought as three pairs
        = $5.19 ÷ 3 = $1.73.

    b) Buying three pairs is a better buy.
    c) The cost of 12 pairs of socks excluding
        tax is $20.76.
        GST = 7% of $20.76 = 0.07 x $20.76
        = $1.45
        PST = 7% of $20.76 = 0.07 x $20.76
        = $1.45
        Total cost = $20.76 + $1.45 + $1.45
        = $23.66

8. a) Total cost to the customer in Victoria:
        GST = 7% of $329.00 = 0.07 x $329.00
        = $23.03
        PST = 7.5% of $329.00 = 0.07 x $329.00
        = $24.68
        Total cost = $329.00 + $23.03 + $24.68
        = $376.71

    b) Total cost to the customer in Kugluktuk:
        = $329.00 + $23.03 = $352.03.
    c) The difference in these prices is
        $375.06 - $352.03 = $23.03.
    d) You can calculate this price difference by
        finding 7% of $329.00.

Extension

9. a) $1299.00 x 1.14 = $1480.86.
    b) GST = 7% of $1299.00
        = 0.07 x $1299.00 = $90.93
        PST = 7% of $1299.00
        = 0.07 x $1299.00 = $90.93
        Total cost = $1299.00 + $90.93 + $90.93
        = $1480.86

c) The totals are the same. Finding the total
    by multiplying by 1.14 gives the same
    total as first finding the GST and PST and
    adding these taxes.

10. a) $1224.95 x 1.14 = $1396.44.

Exploration 4
Sales Promotions

Notebook Assignment

1. a) The regular price of the groceries
        = $2.40 + $1.80 + $1.99 + $1.09 + $4.59
        = $11.87
    b) The amount Shauna saves using coupons
        = 0.35 + 0.25 + 0.75 = $1.35
    c) Shauna saves more than 10% by using
        coupons.
        10% of $11.87 = $1.19 and $1.35 is
        greater than $1.19.

2. a) He will pay $3.89 - $0.90 = $2.99.
    b) Using his coupon Claude saves
        approximately 25%.
        25% of $4.00 = $1.00 and .90 is close to
        $1.00.

3. a) The unit price of 1 coupon = $29.95 ÷ 10
        = $3.00.
    b) The regular price of 10 newly released
        videos = $3.49 x 10 = $34.90.
        The amount saved = $34.90 − $29.95 =
        $4.95.
        14% tax on $34.90 is $4.88.
        14% tax on $29.95 is $4.20.
        $4.88 − $4.20 = $0.68.

    c) Video Village sells the coupons to
        encourage people to rent videos from
        them.

4. a) The savings of the tennis racket on sale at
        15% off
        = 15% of $55.95 = 0.15 x $55.95 =
        $8.39
        The price of the tennis racket on sale at
        15% off
        = $55.95 - $8.39 = $47.56

b) The tennis racket on sale at 15% off is the better buy.

5. a) $149.95 x 1.145 = $171.69

b) The second store offers a better buy. Note that at the second store, GST and PST are still paid on the skateboard. The store reduces the price so that the final price the customer pays is the total of the reduced price plus the GST and PST.

Extension

6. a) The more expensive sweatshirt cost $35.95.
The second sweatshirt cost 50% of $29.95 = $14.98.
The cost of the two sweatshirts before tax = $35.95 + $14.98 = $50.93
GST = 7% of $50.93 = 0.07 x $50.93 = $3.57
The final cost of the two sweaters = $50.93 + $3.57 = $54.50

b) The store offers this type of promotion to encourage customers to buy more merchandise.

Exploration 5

Rate

Notebook Assignment

1. a) $7.75 per hour
   b) 1.5 doughnuts per person
   c) 12 cans per case
   d) $0.50 per bagel
   e) 250 paper clips per box
   f) $1.75 per bus ticket
   g) 80 km/h

2. a) His average speed, excluding his stop for lunch = 350 km ÷ 3.75 h = 93.3 km/h
   b) His average speed, including his stop for lunch, = 350 km ÷ 4.25h = 82.4 km/h
   c) Answers will vary.

3. a) Her average speed is 1150 km ÷ 2 = 575 km/h

b) To reach her destination, she must travel 1750 km ÷ 575 km/h = 3.04 hours

4. a) Robert's hourly rate of pay is $51.00 ÷ 6 h = $8.50/h
   b) Robert's net hourly rate of pay is 90% x $8.50/h = $7.65/h
   c) GST = 7% of $149.50 = 0.07 x $149.50 = $10.47
   Total cost for the skates = $149.50 + $10.47 = $159.97
   d) $159.97 ÷ $7.65 = 21 (rounded to the nearest next hour). Robert will have to work 21 hours to be able to afford the skates.

5. a) March has 31 days. Anna will use the bus 62 times in March.
   b) Paying cash will cost Anna $1.65 x 62 = $102.30
   c) Anna will need 62 ÷ 10 = 6.2 books of bus tickets.
   If she uses bus tickets each time she takes the bus in March, it will cost her $16.00 x 6.2 = $99.20.
   d) Anna saves $99.20 − $62.00 = $37.20
   e) She would save less for the month of February because February has fewer days than March.

6. a) The distance her boat will travel on 1 tank of gasoline = 115 ÷ 3 = 38.3 km.
   b) Marie can expect to go 38.3 km x 2 = 76.6 km/h.
   c) Answers will vary.

Extension

7. a) Answers will vary.
   b) Students should choose an amount so that Damien's hourly rate of pay is reasonable.
   c) Answers will vary.

Exploration 6
Ratio

Notebook Assignment

1. b and c are equivalent ratios. Since 4/20
    reduces to 1/5, the ratios are equivalent. Since
    64/16 reduces to 4/1 the ratios are equivalent.

2. a)   Answers will vary.
    b)   Answers will vary.
    c)   The terms in the ratios a and b are
         reversed.

3. a)   Answers will vary.
    b)   Answers will vary.
    c)   Answers will vary.
    d)   Answers will vary.
    e)   Answers will vary.

4. a)   1:3
    b)   1:4

5. a)   Three times as many loaves of white
         bread are sold as loaves of whole wheat
         bread. For every loaf of whole wheat
         bread sold, there are three loaves of white
         bread sold.
    b)   The supermarket would expect to sell
         300 loaves of white bread.

6. a)   12:8 or 3:2
    b)   Dan's gross hourly rate of pay is
         $79.20 ÷ 12 = $6.60
    c)   Cecelia's gross hourly rate of pay
         = $70.40 ÷ 8 = $8.80
    d)   The ratio of Dan's gross hourly rate of pay
         to Cecelia's gross hourly rate of pay
         = $6.60:$8.80 = 3:4

7. a)   The ingredients for 12 waffles are the
         following:

         3.5   cups flour
         6   teaspoons baking powder
         1   teaspoon salt
         2   tbsp sugar
         6   eggs
         8   tbsp melted butter
         3   cups milk

    b)   The ingredients for 3 waffles are the
         following:

         $7/8$ cup flour
         $1\frac{1}{2}$ teaspoons baking powder
         $1/4$ teaspoon salt
         $1/2$ tbsp sugar
         1-2 eggs
         2 tbsp melted butter
         $3/4$ cups milk

8. a)   The ratio of the length of the scale
         drawing to the length of the actual room
         = 6:300 or 1:50.
    b)   Area of the scale drawing = 6 cm x 7 cm
         = 42 cm^2.
         Area of the room = 300 cm x 350 cm =
         105,000 cm^2.
         The ratio of the area of the scale drawing
         to the area of the actual room = 42
         cm^2:105,000 cm^2 or 1:2500.

Extension

9. a)   If Sandeep uses a scale of 1:200 to build
         his model, the model will be 275 ÷ 200 =
         1.38 m high. It will be less than 1.5 high.
    b)   If Sandeep uses a scale of 1:150 to build
         his model, the model will be 275 ÷ 150 =
         1.83 m high. It will be more than 1.5 m
         high.
    c)   If Sandeep wants his model to be exactly
         1.5 m high, he should use a scale of
         1.5:275 or 1:183.

Chapter Review

1. a) $2.60 ÷ 12 = $0.22 per pencil
    b) $3.69 ÷ 3 kg = $1.23 per kg
    c) $5.00 ÷ 12 = $0.42 per bagel
    d) $7.88 ÷ 10 = $0.79 per disk
    e) $3.49 ÷ 225 g = 1.6 cents per g

2. a)   250 g for $0.89 or 0.36 cents per g
         500 g for $1.59 or 0.32 cents per g
         2.5 g for $2.99 or 0.12 cents per g
         or
         250 g for $0.89 or $3.56 per kg
         500 g for $1.59 or $3.18 per kg
         2.5 g for $2.99 or $1.20 per kg
    b)   2.5 g of salt has the lowest unit price.

3. a)   5 lb. bag of potatoes for $1.49 or 29.8¢

per lb.
20 lb. bag of potatoes for $3.99 or 20¢ per lb.

b) The 20 lb of potatoes has the lowest unit price.

c) Answers can include the following: the amount of potatoes you need; the amount of storage you have; the freshness of the potatoes.

4. a) GST stands for goods and services tax.
   b) The percent rate of the GST is 7%.
   c) Answers will vary.
   d) PST stands for provincial sales tax.
   e) Answers will vary.

5. a) Cartridges at 3 for $28.99 or 1 at $9.66
      Cartridges at 4 for $34.99 or 1 at $8.75
   b) The cost of 12 cartridges at the first store is $28.99 x 4 = $115.96
      GST = 7% of $115.96 = 0.07 x $115.96 = $8.12
      PST = 7.5% of $115.96 = 0.075 x $115.96 = $8.70
      Total cost is $115.96 + $8.12 + $8.70 = $132.78
      The cost of 12 cartridges at the second store is $34.99 x 3 = $104.97
      GST = 7% of $104.97 = 0.07 x $104.97 = $7.35
      PST = 7.5% of $104.97 = 0.075 x $104.97 = $7.87
      Total cost is $104.97 + $7.35 + $7.87 = $120.19

6. a) The amount of discount is 25% x $29.95 = $7.49
   b) The sale price = $29.95 – $7.49 = $22.46
   c) GST = 7% of $22.46 = 0.07 x $22.46 = $1.57
      PST = 7% of $22.46 = 0.07 x $22.46 = $1.57
      Total cost is $22.46 + $1.57 + $1.57 = $25.60

7. a) 7.5 m/s
   b) $8.00/hr
   c) $0.15/egg

d) 25 students/bus
e) $2.50/pair of socks
f) 50 km/h

8. a) Karl's hourly rate of pay is $225.20 ÷ 30 = $7.51.
   b) Dominique's hourly rate of pay is $280.75 ÷ 35 = $8.02.
   c) Karl will have to work $1400 ÷ $7.51 = 187 hours (rounded to the next nearest hour).
      Dominique will have to work $1400 ÷ $8.02 = 175 hours (rounded to the next nearest hour).

9. a) The numbers of cups of flour = $2^2/_3$ x 2 = $5^1/_3$.
   b) $5^1/_3$ cups flour to 1 cup sugar
      1 cup of flour to 3/16 cup sugar
      $3^1/_2$ cups of flour to $^{21}/_{32}$ or about $^2/_3$ cup of sugar.

10. The amount of discount is $22.98 - $19.95 = $3.03.

11. GST is 7% of $32.98 = 0.07 x $32.98 = $2.31
    The total cost of the watch = $32.98 + $2.31 = $35.29

12. a) The regular price of the two sweatshirts excluding tax = $29.98 + $24.95 = $54.93.
       GST = 7% of $54.93 = 0.07 x $54.93 = $3.85
       PST = 7.5% of $54.93 = 0.075 x $54.93 = $4.12
       Total regular price is $54.93 + $3.85 + $4.12 = $62.90
    b) The sale price of the two sweatshirts excluding tax = $29.98.
       GST = 7% of $29.98 = 0.07 x $29.98 = $2.10
       PST = 7.5% of $29.98 = 0.075 x $29.98 = $2.25
       Total sale price of the sweatshirts is $29.98 + $2.10 + $2.25= $34.33

Case Study

1. A & B Sportswear
    Answers calculated with a GST and a PST of
    7%.

Number of T-shirts	Cost of T-shirts	Cost of Printing per T-shirt	Cost per Printed T-shirt	Total of GST and PST	Final Cost of Printed T-shirt
1-24	$6.75	$1.95	$8.70	$1.22	$9.92
25-49	$6.50	$1.60	$8.10	$1.13	$9.23
50-120	$6.25	$1.35	$7.60	$1.06	$8.66
21-180	$6.00	$1.15	$7.15	$1.00	$8.15
181-240	$5.75	$1.00	$6.75	$0.94	$7.70
241-300	$5.50	$0.85	$6.35	$0.89	$7.24

2. The Specialty T-shirt Company
    Answers calculated with a GST and a PST of
    7%.

Number of T-shirts	Cost per Printed T-shirt	Total of GST and PST	Final Cost of Printed T-shirt
1-24	$8.40	$1.18	$9.58
25-49	$7.98	$1.12	$9.10
50-120	$7.58	$1.06	$8.64
121-180	$7.20	$1.01	$8.21
181-240	$6.84	$0.96	$7.80
241-300	$6.50	$0.91	$7.41

3.

Grade	Number of Students	Estimated Sales Ratio	Estimated T-Shirt Sales
9	135	1:6	23
10	142	1:4	36
11	138	2:5	55
12	127	2:3	85

4. a) Estimated sales are:
        23 + 36 + 55 + 85 = 199
        The A & B Sportswear Company has the
        better price for this number of T-shirts.
        Note that the price between the two
        companies for this quantity of T-shirt
        differs only by 11¢ per T-shirt.
    b) Other things the student council might
        consider are the reputations of the
        companies, any guarantees they would
        offer, the time it would take them to
        make the T-shirts, the locations of the
        companies and when they would require
        payment for the T-shirts.

5. a.) The profit per T-shirt is $12.00 – $7.70
        = $4.30.
        The student council would raise $4.30 x
        199 = $855.70
    b) It would not raise $1000.00.

6. a) The student council estimates it will sell
        80% x 199 = 159 T-shirts.
    b) The profit per T-shirt is $15.00 – $8.15
        = $6.85.
        The student council would raise $6.85 x
        159 = $1089.15.
    c.) It would raise $1000.

7. a) The student council estimates it will sell
        120% x 199 = 239 T-shirts (rounded).
    b) The profit per T-shirt = $10.00 – $7.70
        = $2.30.
        The student council would raise
        $2.30 x 239 = $549.70.

8. Answers will vary.

Chapter 5

. . . .

GEOMETRY PROJECT
Exploration 2
Measurement in the Metric System

Notebook Assignment

1. Screw: 6.5 cm or 65 mm
   Pencil: 14.2 cm or 142 mm
   Key: 5.3 cm or 53 mm

2. a) cm
   b) km
   c) mm
   d) m

3. a) 257 cm
   b) 0.45 m
   c) 517 m
   d) 500 mm
   e) 31.5 cm
   f) 60.27 m
   g) 2.5 km
   h) 630 cm
   i) 246 cm
   j) 0.016 km

4. Answers will vary.

5. Answers will vary.

6. Figure A: 14 cm
   Figure B: 9.5 cm
   Figure C: 9.5 cm

7. Figure A: 41 m^2
   Figure B: 15 mm^2
   Figure C: 226.98 cm^2

8. Figure A: 664 cm^2
   Figure B: 314.2 mm^2
   Figure C: 177.5 m^2

9. Figure A: 125 m^3
   Figure B: 84.8 cm^3

10. 110.5 m^2

11. 3562.6 cm^2

12. 12.3 m^3

13. 506.7 cm^2

Extension

14. The volume of a basketball whose radius is 12 cm is 7238 cm^3 or 7.238 litres. The volume of softball whose radius is 5 cm is 524 cm^3 or 0.524 litres.

Exploration 3
Imperial Measurement

Notebook Assignment

1. a) $^1/_4$ inch
   b) $4\ ^1/_4$ inches

2. Answers will vary. Possible answers:
   a) $8\ ^1/_2$" x 11"
   b) 24" x 18"
   c) 3' x 4'

3. a) $^3/_4$"
   b) $1^1/_2$"
   c) $2^3/_4$"
   d) $4^1/_2$"
   e) 5"

4. $^9/_{16}$"

5. $3\ ^{13}/_{16}$"

6. Answers will vary.

7. 8' = 96"
   Surface Area of 2" x 4" x 8' (unfinished)
   = 1168 in^2
   Surface Area of $1^1/_2$" x $3\ ^1/_2$" x 8' (finished) = 970.5^2

8. Answers will vary.

9. a) 150 in^2

b) 96 in^2
There is only one dimension given because all dimensions of a cube are equal.

10. a) Answers will vary.
    b) A. Volume = 64 cm^3
       Surface Area = 96 cm^2
       B. Volume = 60 cm^3
       Surface Area = 128 cm^2

11. a) 1552 in^2
    b) 5376 in^3

12. a) P: 31.25 inches
       A: 50.9 in^2
    b) P: 38 inches
       A: 58 in^2

13. 120 in^2

14. a) 13.2 yd^2
    b) $197.74 if exactly 13.2 yd^2 is purchased.

15. 4608 in^2

16. a) 120 ft^2 or 13.3 yd^2
    b) $454.55 in BC/MB and $426.64 for the northern territories, if exactly 13.3 yd^2 is purchased.

17. Answers will vary.

Exploration 4

Metric and Imperial Estimation

Notebook Assignment

1.

Item	Metric	Imperial
Length of a school bus	metres	feet
Length of a $10.00 bill	cm	inches
Volume of a garbage can	cm^2	in^2
Height of a 1-storey school	metres	feet
Area of a hockey rink	square metres	square feet

2. Answers will vary. Possible estimates:

Item	Metric	Imperial
Diameter of a soccer ball	20 cm	9 in
Volume of a bath tub	1 m^3	33 ft^3
Height of a flagpole	10 metres	30 feet
Area of a soccer field	6000 m	6000 yd

3. Answers will vary. 200 lb would be 91 kg. To check the estimate, you could visit www.nhl.com.

4. Small suitcase: 17820 cm^3
   Large suitcase: 30400 cm^3
   By volume, you could fit 178 bricks in the small suitcase. However, dimensions will limit the number of bricks that can be fitted into the suitcase. The actual number should be close to 171 whole bricks.

5. Cylinder: V: 37.7 in^3
             SA: 62.8 in^2
   Rectangular Prism: V: 27 in^3
                      SA: 54 in^3

6. A snowmobile track is about 15 feet long.

7. Answers will vary (Example: Our house is 30 x 50 feet which results in a perimeter of 160 feet.)

Extension

8. Answers will vary. One possible answer is
    4 ft x 5 ft x 8 ft or 160 ft^3 and
    1.22 m x 1.53 m x 2.44 m or 4.6 m^3.

Exploration 5
Working to Scale

Notebook Assignment

1. The actual distance is 60 inches.

2. Answers will vary. Possible answer: 1 cm:40 km. This will give a line on the map that is 6 cm long. This is small enough to fit on a map but large enough to show some detail.

3. Answers will vary. Possible answers:
    a) 1 cm = 10 m
    b) 0.4 cm
    c) If the width is the 30 m side, there would be 8 bushes, assuming the first bush is planted at the edge of the yard and the bush is not very wide.

4. | Drawing | Actual |
    |---------|--------|
    | 5 cm | 1500 cm |
    | 3 cm | 900 cm |
    | 8 cm | 2400 cm |
    | .4 m | 120 m |

5. The wheel is 4 x 0.5 or 2 cm.

6. If the width is doubled, the area is also doubled, making it twice as big.

7. V = 128 cubic inches
    SA = 160 square inches

    2"

    2"

    2"

8. 96000 cm^3

9. a)

Width	Length	Height	Outside SA	Volume
2	2	2	24 in^2	8 in^3
4	4	4	96 in^2	64 in^3
5	5	4	130 in^2	100 in^3
2	10	3	112 in^2	60 in^3

    b) Doubling the width, length, and height makes the volume eight times as large. The volume is not doubled because all three dimensions are doubled.

10. a)

Width	Length	Height	Volume
1	1	1	1 cm^3
1	1	2	2 cm^3
1	2	2	4 cm^3
2	2	2	8 cm^3

    b) If you change one dimension, the volume changes by that factor.

11. Bedroom: 14.4 cm x 14 cm
    Bed: 7.8 cm x 5.6 cm
    Night Table: 2.4 cm x 1.6 cm

12. a) 15:1
    b) 0.33 mm
    c) 7.5 mm

13. a) Bedroom A: 6 m x 3.75 m
        Bedroom B: 5 m x 3.75 m
        Bathroom: 2.5 m x 3.5 m
        Hall: 2.5 m x 7.5 m
        Dining Room: 3.75 m x 3.75 m
        Living Room: 6 m x 3.75 m
        Kitchen: 3.75 m x 5 m
    b) 49.5 m

Extension

14. If you double the dimensions, the perimeter doubles and the area is four times as big.

Exploration 6
Representing Three-Dimensional Objects

Notebook Assignment

1. A - i
   B - iii
   C - ii

2. A - iii
   B - i
   C - iv
   D - ii

3. a)

Top	Front	Side

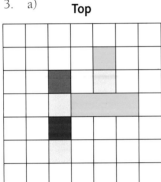 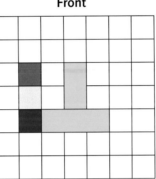 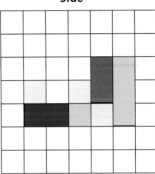

Top	Front	Side

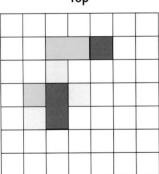 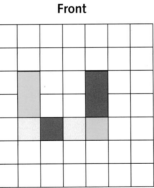 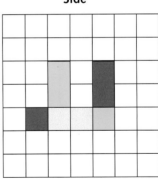

Top	Front	Side

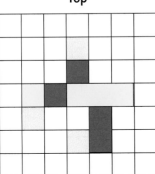 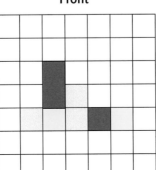 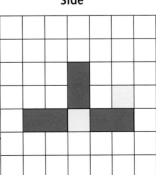

4.

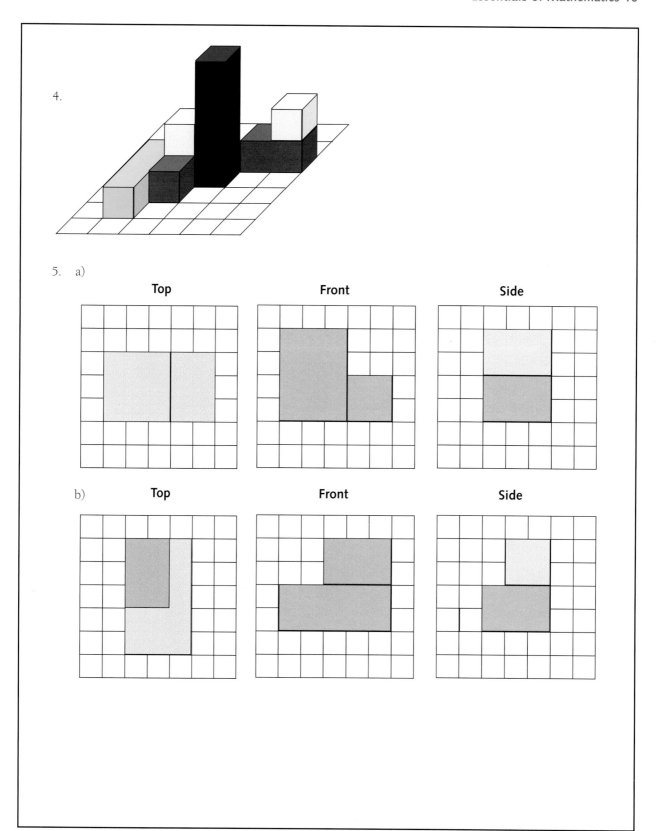

5. a)

Top   Front   Side

b)

Top   Front   Side

6. Answers will vary.

7. Answers will vary.

8. Answers will vary.

9. Answers will vary.

Extension

10. Answers will vary.

Exploration 7
Isometric Dot Paper

Notebook Assignment

1.

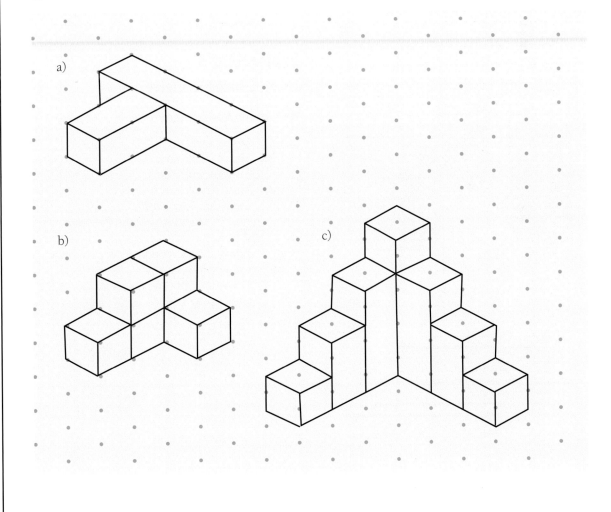

2.

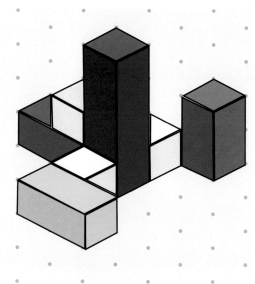

5. Answers will vary.

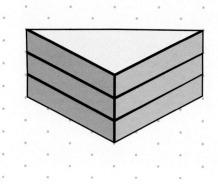

Extension

6. Answers will vary.

7. Answers will vary.

3. Answers will vary. Possible example shown.

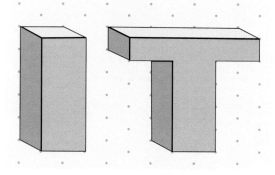

Exploration 8
Using Similar Triangles

Notebook Assignment

1. a) Answers will vary.
    b) Answers will vary.
    c) Answers will vary.
    d) Answers will vary.
    e) All the ratios equal 1.
    f) $\frac{a}{d} = \frac{b}{e} = \frac{c}{f}$ and $\frac{a}{b} = \frac{d}{e}$ and $\frac{a}{c} = \frac{d}{f}$ and $\frac{b}{c} = \frac{e}{f}$.
        Ratios of corresponding sides are equal.
    g) Answers will vary.
        The ratio of the areas is the square of the ratios of the sides.

4. Answers will vary. Possible example shown.

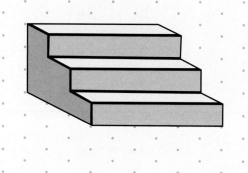

2. a) d = 26 cm
        b = 16 cm
    b) q = 13.3 cm
        n = 24 cm
    c) h = 19 m
        v = 5 m
    d) t = 6.6 cm
        a = 2.2 cm

3. a) UV = 35.3
    b) EF = 0.9 m
    c) VW = 158.6

4. The tree is 4.2 m tall.

5. x = 21.3 cm

6. EF = 9.8 cm

7. The pole is 9.9 m.

8. The building is 84 m tall.

Exploration 9
Using Trigonometry

Notebook Assignment

1. a) sine
    b) cosine
    c) tangent
    d) cosine
    e) sine
    f) tangent

2. The guy wire must be 1110 cm.

3. The cable must be 248 cm.

4. The ramp is 8.7 m long.

5. The kite is 23.5 m above the ground.

6. The rope meets the tree at an angle of 64.2°.

7. The horizontal part of the brace is 34.3 cm.

8. The staircase is 6.9 m high.

Exploration 10
Indirect Measurement

Notebook Assignment

1. a) 160 km
    b) 174.5 km
    c) 3750 km
    d) 3535.5 km

2. a) 2.5 m
    b) 5.4 m
    c) Yes, the person on the top of the ladder will see over the wall. The ladder reaches 5.4 m on the wall, and the person is 2 m tall. This makes 7.4 m, which is taller than 7 m.

3. a) 12.2 km
    b) 7.0 km
    c) The measurements are not exact because of possible errors in measurement.

4. 56 m

5. 11.2 m

6. a) 52.3 m
    b) 52.1 m
    c) The answers are close. The difference could be a slight error in measurement.

7. 573.22 m

8. 73.1 m

9. 296.5 m

Extension

10. a) A possible sketch might be:

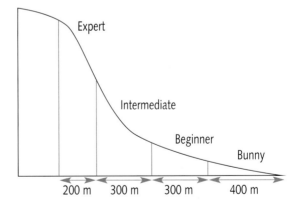

    b) Bunny: 400.5 m
        Beginner: 302.3 m
        Intermediate: 333.8 m
        Expert: 261.1 m

Chapter Review

1. Answers will vary.

2. Estimates and answers will vary.

3. a) 100
   b) 1.5
   c) 274.3
   d) 6512
   e) 44.4

4. a) 1 13/16"
   b) 11.9 cm
   c) 1 5/16"
   d) 36.4 cm

5. small:large
   1:2.25

6. 24 cm

7. Answers may vary. Shown is one possibility.

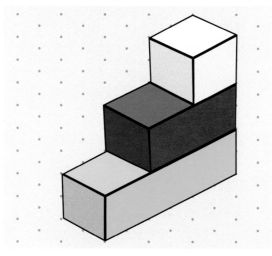

8. Find the volume of the cone with diameter 7.5 m. Subtract the volume of the cone with diameter 5.5 cm.

9.

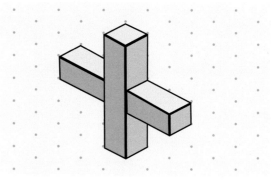

Assuming the cross is laying flat on a table, the three views are:

Top

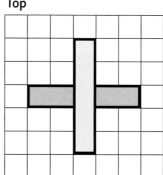

Front

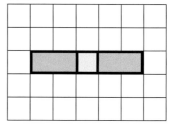

Side

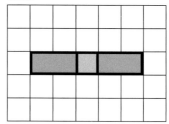

10. Answers will vary. One possibility is:

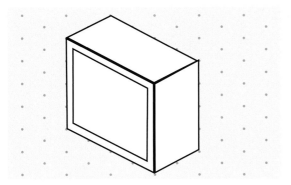

11. a) The volume of the new box would be twice as large since only one dimension is changed.

b)

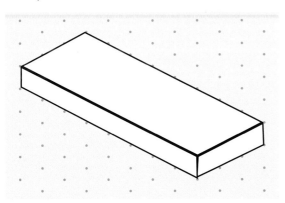

12.

| Top | Front | Side |

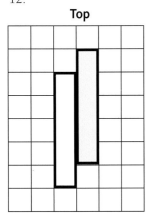
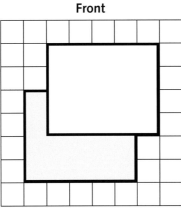
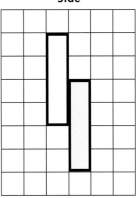

13.

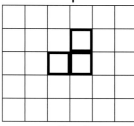

Top

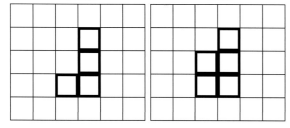

Front   **Side**

14. a) 1323.75 kg
    b) You would save 1.58 kg.

15. a) Answers will vary depending on the dimensions of the doghouse.
    b) Models will vary.

16. 40.7 cm^2

17. 34.1 m^3

18. Including the bottom: 210600 cm^2
    Excluding the bottom: 143000 cm^2

19.

Ratio of Side Length	Ratio of Surface Areas	Ratio of Volumes
1:5	1:25	1:125
1:8.5	1:72.25	1:614125
1:6	1:36	1:216
1:12	1:144	1:1728
1:10	1:100	1:1000
1:15	1:225	1:3375

20. 328 cm^2

21. 561.6 cm^3

22. 1:1.8

23. 1:1.4

24. a) 1:39.6
    b) 1:1.3

25. a) 36.555
    b) 0.151
    c) 7.512
    d) 6.538

26. a) 27.925
    b) 50.214
    c) 21.422
    d) 32.222

27. The tree is 10.1 m tall.

28. The distance across the marsh is 666.8 m.

29. Each wire is 5.8 m long.

30. The flagpole is 28.5 m long.

31. The lake is 533.1 m wide.

Chapter 6
● ● ● ● ● ● ● ● ● ● ● ● ●

SAMPLING AND PROBABILITY SOLUTIONS

The following solutions are to be used as a guide. In many cases there are different, but equally correct approaches and answers. Estimates have been rounded.

Exploration 1
Determining Total Population

Notebook Assignment

1. Answers will vary.

2. $\frac{46}{T} = \frac{7}{90}$
   $7T = 4140$
   $T = 591$ (rounded)
   591 is an estimate.

3. $\frac{43}{T} = \frac{17}{115}$
   $17T = 4945$
   $T = 291$ (rounded)
   291 is an estimate of the number of marmots on the mountain. This is not necessarily the exact number.

4. 1st 4 years: $(22 + 23 + 20 + 15) \div 4 = 20$
   2nd 4 years: $(25 + 13 + 11 + 14) \div 4 = 15.75$
   Overall, the number seems to be decreasing. The rancher's count may not be representative. The elk may have changed migration routes, or the rancher may not be watching at a consistent time.

5. Overall, the advertising seems to have helped, all other things being equal. The mean number (rounded) with internet advertising is 159, so that could be an estimate for next year. Visits may have decreased in 2001 due to bad weather, exciting tourist events elsewhere, or world events reducing travel overall. Without the advertising, tourist visits might have been even fewer.

6. $\frac{35}{112} = \frac{T}{200}$
   $112T = 7000$
   $T = 63$ prairie dogs (rounded)
   An estimate would be 63 prairie dogs in the larger town.

Extension

7. Average in $100 \text{ m}^2 =$
   $(8 + 12 + 11 + 7 + 4 + 5 + 13 + 11 + 10) \div 9$
   $= 9$
   $\frac{.09}{1 \text{m}^2} = \frac{x}{80,000,000}$
   $x = 7,200,000$ trees
   An estimate of the total number of trees is 7,200,000.

Exploration 2
What Type of Sample?

Notebook Assignment

Answers may vary. Possible answers:

1. a) draw ticket numbers at random
   b) test every 100th chocolate
   c) survey all the people on one street
   d) each province is assigned a number to survey based on the number of curlers in the province.

2. For a restaurant survey, a random sample would work. The class is too small for other methods.

3. Survey every tenth person on a school list. That way all areas would be fairly represented.

4. Since each grade has different numbers, select 8 grade 8's, 10 grade 9's and 11 grade 10's to fairly represent each grade.

5. Answers will vary.
6. Answers will vary.
7. Answers will vary.

Extension

8.   Answers will vary.

Exploration 3
Random Numbers

Notebook Assignment

1.   The spinner is divided into sections equal to the number of groups. Whichever group it lands on has batting practice first.

2.   The number seven has a greater chance of being rolled, so the results are not random.

3.   Answers will vary. It is important to note that in a random list, numbers may be repeated.

4.   Answers will vary.

5.   The company can randomly select names from the phone book. A possible problem is that people with unlisted numbers do not have a chance to be picked.

Extension

6.   This would not be a random list because the process is biased. Unintentionally, a person may not think of certain numbers and then they are less likely to be picked. The list then is not random because not every number has an equal chance of being picked.

Exploration 4
Representative Samples

Notebook Assignment

Answers will vary. Possible answers:

1.   Edward could number all students' names and then use a random number feature on a spreadsheet or calculator to pick numbers between 0 and 90. Such features ensure random selection.

2.   Jean could survey every fifth person entering the school cafeteria.

3.   Susie could pick one grade 8, one grade 9, and one grade 10 homeroom class at random to do her survey.

4.   This is not a fair survey. Michelle should not ask only her friends. They have not been randomly selected and so would not be a representative sample.

5.   This is not a fair survey. Richard should not just ask his hockey team. They have not been randomly selected and so would not be a representative sample.

6.   For grade 10 students in Canada, one could assign each province and territory a number of students to survey based on their population of grade 10 students. Each province could then pick students at random from a complete list of all the grade 10 students in their province.

Exploration 5
Collecting Data: Surveys and Experiments

Notebook Assignment

Answers will vary. Possible answers:

1.   People in a mall could be asked to sample a small amount of several soft drinks and asked which one they prefer.

2.   Telephone numbers are usually randomly allotted and so using them to select participants would be random. A random number spreadsheet could be used to generate lists of telephone numbers.

3.   Every fifth household by street could be surveyed. Names would be withheld to protect privacy.

4.   A tally count could be made of students leaving the school who are wearing black tops.

5. The scientist could put an ad in the university paper for students to participate in the study. One problem with this method is that the participants would not represent the whole population because they would usually be grouped by age.

6. The participants could create several copies of each nose cone shape. They could use the same types of engines and do the tests under the same conditions as much as possible. They could find the height the rockets went to and could find the mean for the same shaped rockets. The mean of the greatest would be the best shape for maximum height.

Extension

7. Answers will vary. What is important is that the questions are clear and easy to answer.

Exploration 6
Survey Results

Notebook Assignment

Answers will vary. Possible answers:

1. a) An example is a favourite sport to play. A list of the sports played at your school could be made and each sport could have a rating of 1 to 3. Students could select if they didn't like the sport (1), thought it was okay (2), or really liked the sport (3).
    b) Groups complete their own surveys.
    c) Five members of the class were asked about basketball. The mean score was 2.5, so basketball is liked by the class.
    d) Answers will vary.
    e) Answers will vary.

2. **Answers will vary. Possible answers:**

    Do you have a computer in your home?
    Do you have access to the internet?
    Do you do homework on the computer?

3. a) What was the question asked of the dentists? Were they asked, "Do you prefer sugarless or sugared gum for your patients?"
    b) Who was asked? Parents? Students? Young students?
    c) Which adults were studied?
    d) Who was asked? Adults or sixteen year olds?

Extension

4. Answers will vary. An advantage of using the internet to do a survey is that people worldwide could participate. A disadvantage is that there might not be a way to control the survey or find out who is participating.

5. Answers and points of view will vary. The survey method should be discussed in the letter, and the conclusion should match the known information or question what is unknown.

Exploration 7
Presenting Data

Notebook Assignment

1. The greatest cause of forest fires is human activities.

2. Draw a pie graph.

3. It is possible that the fires caused by human activities are noticed and fought more quickly than those fires started by lightning. The result would be that the fires started by human activity burn less land than those started by lightning, which may happen in very remote areas.

4. Answers will vary. Possible answer: Since Nova Scotia is a relatively small province the number of fires started by lightning would be expected to be small. Quebec is a huge province and so would be expected to have many more lightning strikes and more fires, especially in isolated areas.

5. Answers will vary. A letter to the editor should explain that perhaps there are very few fires at all in PEI and so the fact that a large number of those that occur are started by humans does not necessarily mean that people are at fault. Since the data for PEI is unavailable, no one can compare PEI with similar provinces to see if there are similar problems elsewhere. It could be that PEI has the same rate of human-caused fires as anywhere, but the number of lightning fires is very low.

6. The bar graph should show the measurements on the horizontal axis and the number of students on the vertical axis. The vertical range should be from 0 to 5 students.

    The circle graph should be developed using a table similar to the following:

Measurement (cm)	Frequency	Per Cent	Degrees
53	3	20.0	72
54	2	13.3	48
55	5	33.3	120
56	1	6.7	24
57	2	13.3	48
58	2	13.3	48
Total	15	100	360

7. This data is best displayed using a bar graph because the regions are discrete and the bar graphs show the values clearly.

8.

Sport	Number	Per Cent	Degrees
Hockey	450	45.0	162
Football	240	24.0	86.4
Baseball	120	12.0	43.2
Soccer	58	5.8	20.9
Volleyball	24	2.4	8.6
Other	108	10.8	38.9
Total	1000	100	360

Extension

9. To support the idea that computers be made mandatory in school, find data that shows some schools don't have computers while others do. Data showing that students will need computer skills in the future would also be valuable. An imaginary example graph could show computer use compared with grades on provincial exams, for example, and could show that the higher the number of computers a school has, the better the students do on final exams. While this wouldn't prove that using computers alone increases grades, it would be good information to support the idea of computers in school.

Exploration 8
Probability Statements

Notebook Assignment

1. $P(\text{same}) = \frac{1}{2}$. Students should note that the greater number of coin flips made, the closer the data will get to $P(\text{same}) = \frac{1}{2}$.

2. Students should note that the greater the number of kernels counted (the larger the sample size), the greater the accuracy of the estimate of how many are marked.

3. The probability statements will vary depending on how many kernels were marked. If 20 were marked, the probability statement would be $P(M) = {}^{20}/100$ or $^1/5$. In this case, if 20 kernels were selected, you would expect 4 to be marked.

Extension

4. Removing kernels from the bag would change the probability statement because the total number of possibilities would decrease.

5. A magazine might have a no photocopy rule because of a fairness problem. Someone might photocopy vast numbers of coupons and therefore increase their chances of winning unfairly. The denominator of the probability statement would increase if photocopies were allowed and so the chances of someone else winning with just one coupon would be much less.

Chapter Review

Answers will vary. Possible answers include:

1. Wildlife officials could use banding to track birds and to estimate the total population of birds using capture-mark-recapture methods.

2. Officials could select a train at random and check everyone's ticket on the train.

3. The store could select every fiftieth person through the checkout to participate in the draw. This method is a systematic sample.

4. Students in the prairie provinces are probably not representative of the rest of the country. A stratified random sample that surveys each province according to its population would be fairer.

5. The coyotes trapped near Vancouver are not likely to be representative of the rest of the province because Vancouver is very urbanized. The scientist could discover the eating habits of coyotes raised in an urban environment and then compare them to those of rural coyotes.

6. The committee could use class lists and a list of random numbers to select those to participate. They would have to get permission from the students and their parents. A sample survey question might be, "Have you ever felt afraid to report a bullying incident?"

7. Graphs will vary. A graph of this data could be a bar graph where the vertical axis is beyond 80 and Number of Sweatshirts and Sizes make up the horizontal components.

8. $P(7) = \frac{6}{36}$ or $\frac{1}{6}$

9. a) Mean = 73.56 (rounded)
Median = 75
Mode = 75
   b) Mean = 33.33
Median = 25
Mode = 20

10. Answers will vary.

11. New Mean = 66; New Median = 67
Money Mean = \$82.50; Money Median = \$83.75

12. Answers will vary.

Glossary

adjacent: means beside; in geometry, it means the side adjacent to the angle is beside the angle

automated teller machine (ATM): a self-service banking machine that lets you conduct routine banking transactions

bank card: a plastic card with a magnetic strip that allows you access to bank services or to make a direct payment

benefits: money or allowances such as life insurance, clothing allowance, dental coverage, or extended health care

bias: inaccurate representation; if a sample is biased, it is an inaccurate representation of the population

budget: an estimate of the amount of money to be spent on a specific project or over a given time frame

clinometer: a device used to determine the measure of an angle from the horizontal

data: information gathered from a study

floor plan: a top-down view of a floor area that shows the placement of furniture or other structural features superimposed on the floor area

full-serve transaction: when a teller performs a bank transaction

gross pay: the total amount of money earned; also called gross earnings

GST: Goods and Services Tax; a federal tax calculated on goods and services

HST: Harmonized Sales Tax; combined federal and provincial tax applied in some provinces

income: money or other assets received

Interac™: a computer network that gives people access to their money through banking machines and direct payment

isometric dot paper: used for technical and architectural drawings to illustrate three-dimensional perspectives where all distances between the dots are the same

job-share: to split a job with another person; each person does part of the work and receives part of the salary

mean: measure of central tendency sometimes referred to as the average or arithmetic mean; it is found by adding the numbers in the list and dividing by the number of entries

median: middle number when a series of numbers is arranged in either ascending or descending order

mode: most frequently occurring number in a list of numbers

overdraw: to take out more money than is in your account

overtime: 1. hours worked beyond the regular hours; 2. payment for this time

population: the total collection of items or individuals being studied

probability: the likelihood of an event happening expressed on a scale from 0 to 1

PST: Provincial Sales Tax; a provincial sales tax calculated on goods and services sold—different provinces or territories impose PST at different rates and on different items

rate: one quantity measured in relation to another quantity, for example, km/h

reconcile: to make one account record consistent with another

salary: a fixed regular payment, usually calculated on an annual basis and paid monthly

scale drawing: a drawing in which the dimensions are proportional to the actual object

sample: 1. to sample means to select a number of items or individuals from a total population 2. a sample is the group selected to represent a total population

self-serve transaction: when you perform a bank transaction at an ATM, by telephone, or on the web

seasonal employment: work that occurs at specific times of the year, for example, fishing guide

semi-monthly: twice a month; twenty-four times a year

service charge: a fee that the bank charges to your account for its services

similar triangles: triangles that have the same size of angles but whose sides are not necessarily the same size

take-home pay: often called net pay; refers to the money paid to an employee after deductions

taxable income: the amount of income on which you pay tax

unit price: the cost of one unit of a product expressed as cost per unit

wage: payment made by an employer in exchange for work or services provided

waive: in certain circumstances, a bank will not collect a service fee; in that case, the bank is said to waive the fee

Index

Credits

Credits and Acknowledgements

The publisher wishes to thank the following sources for photographs, illustrations, and other material in this book. Every effort has been made to determine and locate ownership sources of copyrighted material (text and photographs) used in the text. We will gladly receive information enabling us to rectify any errors or omissions in these credits.

Photos/Illustrations

Cover
Winnipeg Mint: Dave Reede, Dave Reede Photography; St. Boniface Cathedral: Dave Reede, Dave Reede Photography; Churchill polar bear: Dennis Fast

Chapter One: p. 10 Luke Macmillan/ www.whistlerphotography.com; p. 14 Gerry Kahrmann/Province; p. 17 Lauchlin McKenzie, Vancouver Community College; p. 19 Mark Van Manen/Vancouver Sun; p. 25 Jon Murray/Province; p. 30 Lauchlin McKenzie, Vancouver Community College; p. 35 Stuart Davis/Vancouver Sun; p. 36 Fredette's Family Food, Nancy Gajdosik, photographer; p. 66 Education Nunavut, Eric Anoee Junior, photographer; p. 68 Fred Cattroll, Cattroll Photo Associates; p. 71 Lauchlin McKenzie, Vancouver Community College; p. 80 Bill Keay/Vancouver Sun; p. 88 Michael J. Taylor, David Conway, photographer.
Chapter Two: p. 91 David Edwards; p. 96 Gerry Kahrmann/Province; p. 102 Fred Cattroll, Cattroll Photo Associates; p. 105 Wahl, photographer; p. 116 Luke Macmillan/ www.whistlerphotography.com; p. 131 The Yukon Government; p. 138 Tony Heron, reprinted with permission of the Canadian Bankers Association; p. 143 Gerry Kahrmann/Province.
Chapter Three: p. 146 Ric Ernst/Province; p. 150 Bill Keay/Vancouver Sun; p. 152 Ward Perrin/Vancouver Sun; p. 161 Lauchlin McKenzie, Vancouver Community College; p. 166 Faculty of Forestry, University of British Columbia; p. 170 Dave Reede, Dave Reede Photography; p. 171 Jon Murray/Province; p. 179 Debbie Gajdosik; p. 181 The Developmental Disabilities Association; p. 186 Warren Clark; p. 192 Death by Chocolate, Debbie Gajdosik, photographer.
Chapter Four: p. 196 The Yukon Government; p.197 Ross Taylor; p. 201 Lauchlin McKenzie, Vancouver Community College; p. 207 The Girl Guides of Canada; p. 222 Fred Cattroll, Cattroll Photo Associates; p. 223 Peter Battistoni/Vancouver Sun; p. 226 Jon Campbell, Jordan Lilwall, photographer; p. 233 David Edwards; p. 237 The British Columbia Soccer Association, Evan Seal, photographer, www.sporting-images.com.
Chapter Five: pp. 248 and 249 Wahl, photographer; p. 250 and 251 Nick Milkovich Architects, Inc.; p. 252 Luke Macmillan/ www.whistlerphotography.com; p. 253 The Boeing Company; p. 267 Steven Daniel; p. 268 Dave Reede, Dave Reede photography; p. 276 Mark van Manen/Vancouver Sun; p. 287 Wahl, photographer; p. 298 Science World

British Columbia; p. 317 Dave Reede, Dave Reede Photography; p. 333 Luke Macmillan/www.whistlerphotography.com.
Chapter Six: p. 336 Lauchlin McKenzie, Vancouver Community College; p. 337 The Government of British Columbia, Bill Westover, photographer; p. 338 (top) Fred Cattroll, Cattroll Photo Associates; p. 338 (bottom) Fisheries and Oceans Canada; p. 339 Mike Eckersley, Mike's Mini Lab; p. 340 Fisheries and Oceans Canada; pp. 359 and 369 Dave Reede, Dave Reede Photography; p. 372 Glenn Baglo/Vancouver Sun; p. 375 Krista Mullally; p. 376 Education Nunavut, Eric Anoee Junior, photographer; p. 379 Ric Ernst/Province; p. 380 Krista Mullally; p. 385 Ward Perrin/Vancouver Sun; p. 388 Gerry Kahrmann/Province

Text Credits

Tax Tables reproduced with permission of the Minister of Public Works and Government Services Canada, 2001. pp. 57, 59, and 61

"The Ferry Ride," p. 186, is reproduced with permission from *A Sourcebook of Applications of School Mathematics*, 1980, National Council of Teachers of Mathematics. All rights reserved.

"Quilting," p. 208, is reproduced with permission from *A Sourcebook of Applications of School Mathematics*, 1980, National Council of Teachers of Mathematics. All rights reserved.

"Black Holes," p. 209, is reproduced with permission from *NCTM Student Math Notes*, 1993, National Council of Teachers of Mathematics. All rights reserved.

"Group Activity," pp. 352–357, and question 7, p. 344, are reprinted with permission from *Dealing with Data: Probability and Sampling*, 1st ed., by R. Montesanto and D. Zimmer, 1995, Nelson Thomson Learning, a division of Thomson Learning, fax 1 (800) 730-2215.

Forest fire data, pp. 377 and 378, reproduced with the permission of the Minister of Public Works and Government Services Canada, 2001, and courtesy of the Canadian Forest Service.

Forms

• • • • • • • • •

CHAPTER 1 Time Card

Time Card

Employee Number: _____

Name: _____

Week Ending: _____

Signature

Date	Morning		Afternoon		Overtime		Hours		Total
	In	Out	In	Out	In	Out	Reg	OT	Hours
M									
T									
W									
TH									
F									
S									
SU									
Total							____	____	____

	HOURS	RATE	AMOUNT
REGULAR			
OVERTIME			

Statement of Earnings & Deductions

STATEMENT OF EARNINGS AND DEDUCTIONS
SALARY PAYROLL

PERIOD ENDING: _____   CLAIM CODE _____

BANK ACCOUNT: _____

BANK: _____

SUMMARY OF EARNINGS		DEDUCTIONS	
HOURS	_____		
RATE	$_____		
REGULAR	$_____	CPP	_____
OVERTIME	$_____	EI	_____
		FEDERAL TAX	_____
		BC TAX	_____
		OTHER DEDUCTIONS	_____
			_____
			_____
			_____

| GROSS PAY | $_____ | TOTAL DEDUCTIONS | $_____ |
| NET PAY | $_____ | | |

CHAPTER 2 Deposit Slip

DEPOSIT

BANK OF EVERMORE
BLUE HARBOUR, B.C.

Personal Account

Date			CHEQUES		CASH	
Account Number					X5	
Name					X10	
					X20	
INITIALS					X50	
Depositor	Bank Employee				X100	
					Coins/Other Cash	
					Total Cash	
					Total Cheques	

Signature for cash withdrawal. (Please sign in the presence of bank employee.)

Subtotal	$
Withdrawal	$
TOTAL	$

Withdrawal Form

BANK OF EVERMORE
BLUE HARBOUR, B.C.

WITHDRAWAL

Date

Your Home Branch Location

Received from Bank of Evermore

/100 Dollars $

Your Account Number

| | | — | | | — | |

Signature (Please sign in the presence of bank employee.)

Cheque Blank

JOHN DOE
20 ANY STREET
CITY, PROVINCE POSTAL CODE

_____ 2001

Pay to the order of

_____ $ [   ]

/100   DOLLARS

BANK OF EVERMORE
BLUE HARBOUR, B.C.

FOR

_____

Signature

26167 001 1234 567

Transaction Record

Cheque #	Date	Description	Payment/ Debit	√	Deposit/ Credit	Balance $

Bank Statement

B$ BANK OF EVERMORE
BLUE HARBOUR, B.C.

STATEMENT OF ACCOUNT		Branch No.		Account Number
STATEMENT DATE				Account Type:
Description	Withdrawals	Deposits	Date	Balance
Balance Forward				

Statement of Reconciliation

B$ BANK OF EVERMORE
BLUE HARBOUR, B.C.

STATEMENT OF RECONCILIATION

Bank Statement	Transaction Record
FINAL BALANCE shown on this statement	FINAL BALANCE shown in transaction record
ADD DEPOSITS made after the statement date	SUBTRACT WITHDRAWALS which are not shown in transaction record
SUBTOTAL $	
SUBTRACT WITHDRAWALS made after the statement date	
FINAL BALANCE $	FINAL BALANCE $